PLOTS and CHARACTERS

A Screenwriter on Screenwriting

PLOTS and CHARACTERS

A Screenwriter on Screenwriting

by

MILLARD KAUFMAN

Photo and excerpt credits on page 263.

Really Great Books, P.O. Box 292000, Los Angeles, CA 90029
Visit our Web site at www.reallygreatbooks.com

First Printing: May, 1999

10 9 8 7 6 5 4 3 2 1

Library of Congress Cataloging-in-Publication Data
Kaufman, Millard
Plots and Characters: A Screenwriter on Screenwriting
288 p.   15.24×22.86 cm.
ISBN 1-893329-03-8
1. Screenwriting   2. Hollywood   3. Film Industry
I. Title   II. Kaufman, Millard
CIP 98-89055

Cover design: Amy Inouye
Cover photograph: Larry Underhill

To my wife,
Lorraine Paley Kaufman,
with love and gratitude,
for sharing and caring and pointing the way.

ACKNOWLEDGMENTS

To Arthur Laurents, for all the talk and explorations past midnight, spanning more than fifty years.

To Dorris Halsey, my agent, whose discernment was always tempered with kindness.

To Nina Wiener, my editor, whose flights of logic and guidance were always on the wings of excitement.

To my daughters Mary and Amy, and their respective husbands, Scott and Bern, and to my son Frederick and his wife Lizzie, and to my grandchildren David, Kevin, Anschel, Jared, Ariela, and Phoebe, for all the fun I would have missed without them.

For the students of the Writing Seminars at the Johns Hopkins University and at the Sundance Institute, who gave as good as they got.

For the membership of the Writers Guilds of America, East and West, for questioning everything as writers should.

And in memory of the men of the Third and Sixth Marine Divisions in WWII, without whose expertise and sacrifice I'd never have made it this far.

TABLE of CONTENTS

FOREWORD

In the last half-century—give or take a few years—everything report-ed in the following pages took place. It should be noted that with only the slightest variations, it is still going on.

In chronological time this book deals with Hollywood people and their relationships, their affinities and their contrarieties, when the great monolithic studio system crested to the meridian of its health and wealth, and then with cataclysmic suddenness, declined and dis-appeared back into the primordial gumbo from which, like the dinosaurs themselves, it had emerged.

They could rise up again, modified to some degree, in the future. In cyclic Hollywood the vibrant present is always prologue to the past. The citizens who make up this earth-circling community today might have been cloned from their archetypes, so alike they are in their rea-soning, their attitudes, and their actions, since this scorched and dusty village between the desert and the sea coagulated into the entertainment capital of the world. Alfonse Karr's delphic epigram—the more things change the more they remain the same—certainly applies to Hollywood.

The focus of this book is three-fold. It examines what it's like to be a working writer in the picture business. It explores aspects of the business itself, and the people in it. And, primarily, it concentrates on the requisites of a viable screenplay.

Throughout the text, examples have been drawn and emphasis has been placed on classic, keystone films regardless of their age. Trendiness and immediacy have been sacrificed; in most cases they are better ignored than extolled.

As regards the art (or craft) of screenwriting, both theory and technique flow down the ages from the works of playwrights anterior to ours. Their dramaturgic values still derive from and conform to ele-ments that go back as far as the tragedies of Aeschylus and the analy-sis of Aristotle about 2,300 years ago. Style, stance, and technology change, but the elements of drama do not. They are as valid and as applicable in twenty-first-century Hollywood as they were in Athens more than three centuries before the birth of Christianity.

Like the Greek dramatists, we are constantly revamping our cherished myths, reinterpreting our historic archives to reexamine man and his humanity or lack of it. Drama, in whatever form, is as necessary to our survival as food, clothing, shelter, as irresistible as the songs and games children invent.

I hope critical readers will find that my advisories on storytelling are sound, prudent, and helpful.

I

The Business of Writing

1

PITFALLS and PRATFALLS
You Know Who Did the Hair?

It is a conviction generally embraced by people who work in Hollywood that everybody, regardless of qualification, wants to be in show business.

I had been in Malibu at a party made memorable only because of what happened the following day. The phone rang and "Hi," a strained voice said, "It's Jack."

No need to tell me. I recognized the bourbon baritone of a good friend, a movie star, a Homeric boozer.

"You have any idea," he went on, "when we were talking last night?"

"When? Must have been about eleven o'clock. Why?"

"What happened then?"

"I hung around for maybe another hour, and split."

"I mean what happened to me?"

"How the hell should I know?"

"Well, shit, I don't know either, and that's the point. Next thing I know, I open my eyes and I'm in the Santa Monica drunk tank with a buzz saw in my head. There's a clock on the wall, it's ten after six and this large lump of gristle is sitting on a cot about four feet away, staring balefully at me. You still there?"

"I'm not going anyplace."

"The lump gets to his feet—he's bigger than a linebacker for the Raiders—and he moves in on me. I know the type, so do you, one of those muscle-bellied bastards who loves to hit an actor. So I stagger to my feet, fixing to belt him in the balls, which is about as high as I can reach. Hell, I couldn't have reached his jaw on stilts.

"He pulls up, his chest in my face. He looks down and says, 'I know you.'"

" 'I don't think I've had the pleasure,' I tell him."

" 'Not like personally,' he says. 'What I mean, I seen you in pictures.' And then he says, 'You're pretty good.' "

" 'Why, thanks.' I'm relieved but not out of the woods yet because he's still looming over me.

"He says, 'You know Peggy Ann Garner?' "

"I tell him I've met her a couple of times, I don't really know her.

"He grins at me like a buddy. He swaggers standing there, no longer a menace. He hitches up his pants and says proudly, 'I fucked her maid.'"

A moment of silence. A sigh. Then, "Jesus, you're no help," Jack said accusingly. "Good-bye."

"Wait a minute. What happened with the lump of gristle?"

"Nothing. It wasn't the beginning of a beautiful friendship, if that's what you mean."

"I mean, why would he tell you that story? Just bragging about a conquest?"

"It had nothing to do with conquest," Jack said tiredly. "It was his way of telling me that his little act of love, if only by extension, put him in show business."

Now, Jack's confessional might be dismissed as just another show-biz anecdote, but some years later George C. Scott claimed, in a piece reported by columnist Liz Smith in the *Los Angeles Times*, that he had found himself under the same circumstances in the same distressing bind in the same Santa Monica poky. And once again Peggy Ann Garner's anonymous maid plays a significant off-stage role in the proceedings.

Perhaps the tale is no more than a joke of minimal social significance told in the first person by two talented raconteurs having a bit of fun in the telling. But all jokes, according to no less an authority than Sigmund Freud, are meaningful. This one, following the reductive pattern of jokes, conjures up that same enduring theme—the irresistible attractions of show business among a broad swath of civilians.

What is remarkable: If indeed involvement with pictures and plays appeals to most everybody, nobody seems to think that it involves hard work and brutal competition, the unawareness of which must be a large part of the allure.

I've always found pictures enthralling, although it wasn't until I became involved in them that I learned what the business was about, which I suppose can be said about any business. As for writing, I can't remember a time when I couldn't or didn't get high on words. Back in the sixth grade of grammar school, I recorded my oddball drive to be a screenwriter whenever the subject of careers arose in what was then called "vocational guidance."

The decision was sealed with apocalyptic fervor on a summer night in 1934. I was sixteen, a newly minted high school graduate with a job aboard an intercoastal freighter. In Portland, Oregon, the crew without warning was kicked off the ship for twelve hours while the old rust bucket was being fumigated. I was given an advance of three dollars to cover a room in a waterfront fleabag. I chose instead to spend the money on an all-night movie, a large Coke, and enough popcorn to lodge between my teeth for a month.

I saw *The Informer*, screenplay by Dudley Nichols from the novel by Liam O'Flaherty, over and over again until daybreak. I left that theater overwhelmed, the experience imprinted in my mind's eye. If I couldn't spend my life doing the kind of work Dudley Nichols did, I thought I would perish.

About eighteen years later, amid the din and bustle of the M-G-M commissary, I told Nichols about that revelatory night in Portland. A shy and sensitive man, he didn't consider screenwriting high on the list of distinguished callings. My story seemed to embarrass him, as if he were being accused of contributing to the delinquency of a minor.

I assume that you, too, want to be in show business or you wouldn't be reading these pages. Perhaps you seek more direct access to the Profession, along a road less circuitous than that taken by Jack's or George's accidental and possibly apocryphal companion in the slam.

But entry level is always difficult. If you want to be a producer, you'll have to raise a monumental concentration of green to get your project off the ground. Aspiring directors and actors must be hired by executives who have faith in their ability, a doubtful procedure when that ability has yet to be demonstrated. Unlike St. Paul, executives don't have much faith in the evidence of things unseen. But to gain access as a screenwriter, all you need is a pad and a pencil. Plus a mysterious element called talent, a modicum of craftsmanship, and an ability to string words together without hitting too many clinkers. Sounds easy? Just remember that for the great majority of us, skill and judgment come slowly, if at all. Mediocrity reigns, talent is rare. In the end, even your talent may be overlooked without a connection to get your foot in the door somewhere—anywhere—and a hell of a lot of persistence to keep that door open.

Let's take a look at some of the pitfalls and pratfalls of the craft. Writers have little power in the physical making of a movie, hence they can be hoist on a petard not of their own making. They are seldom consulted, once they hand in the script. Their suggestions are ignored in such vital elements as casting, budgets, and the confabulations of summitry. Successful writers may be therefore motivated to become directors and producers or both, by broadening their ambit in order to safeguard what they put on paper. Many become disenchanted when they are discouraged, subtly or otherwise, from contributing anything but words to the total picture.

Christopher McQuarrie, who wrote the superbly sinuous *The Usual Suspects,* has this to say on the subject along with some wise and sundry insights about his calling:

I have a dream. A dream that one day, for every successful director with a final cut, there will be a successful writer with script approval. I have been told this is a silly dream, a wasted dream. But I live for the day when all writers can shout to the heavens: Free at last. Free at last. Thank God there is finally a reward for writing.

Alas, it is still a dream. To that end, I have constructed a rough code by which I live in an effort to maintain my sanity and keep myself alive until the ghost of Paddy Chayefsky can lead us to the promised land.

1) Nobody knows anything. Except the audience. They are smarter, meaner, and more critical than you can ever be of yourself. And they have seen more films than you have, too. Treat them with respect. You never fool an audience without their consent.

2a) No one will ever make your movie. They will only make their movie. If all you want is for one word on page forty-one to be left untouched for you to be satisfied, you'd better direct the whole goddamn film yourself to make sure it gets there. No, they didn't make the movie you wrote. They didn't spend the money you made either.

2b) Direct because you want to direct, not because you want to be a director.

3) It is amazing what can be accomplished when no one cares who gets the credit. The happier you are in knowing what you did when most of the world will never know, the happier you'll be. From my observation it has almost always been that the really important people know anyway.

4) Talent, passion, conviction. The holy trinity. If you knowingly lack one or more, I'll have fries with that.

5) Never read scripts. Watch how they turned out instead. The script is a means, not an end. And nothing is more tedious than reading a script. Especially your own. Thus:

6) If your script is perfect, it probably stinks. A script is never finished, it is abandoned.

7) Ditto for films.

8) There is nothing wrong with development. Unless you care one iota how the movie turns out. Want more money? Want more control? Want a say in who makes your film? Don't quit your day job. The writer is the only person in the film business who is capable of working for free. Everyone hates when they do that. Thus:

9) If anyone says, "You can't do that," it is most likely because doing it serves you. Keep doing it.

10) Everyone is a writer. Except the slob who sits for ten hours at the keys and writes. This person is known as "that pain in the ass."

11) "We reserve the right to fail." Embrace the inevitable. You will write many bad scripts. The greatest career is 50% failure—and I am being kind. If you have been hustling the same script for ten years, it is time to write a new script. In fact, it is nine and a half years over-due. The greatest part of being a writer is that most of your dreadful work will never see light. No director in history can make such a claim. And finally:

12) Just about everything Ernest Hemingway ever said about writing was correct. For him.

Producers and directors invariably credit themselves for the success of a project, which they characterize in a highly personal manner as "my picture." If it fails, they blame the writer. Although it should be pointed out that producers never find anything they're involved with less than magnificent; to admit the slightest deficiency is an unpardonable sin that might adversely affect box office receipts.

Producer Samuel Goldwyn, in a conference one morning with writer Daniel Fuchs, deviated for a moment from the script under discussion to introduce a somewhat irrelevant footnote of self-congratulation.

"Danny, my boy," he began, flinging modesty to the winds, "I've enjoyed many a triumph in my life, but nothing," he paused for emphasis, "nothing can touch what happened last night." A smile gentled the corners of his mouth.

"Last night," he went on, "we sneaked *Roseanna McCoy* in Pasadena," and he shook his head in wonderment. "The audience laughed and cried and cheered—at one point, for four minutes and fifty-eight seconds by my stopwatch, you couldn't hear the dialogue for the applause—it was fabulous. Brilliant."

"I know, Mr. Goldwyn," Danny said, "I was there."

Without hesitation Goldwyn said, "We can fix it."

Certainly writers are not alone in their vexation with executives, producers, and the like. On the back lot one day, Robert Mitchum was walking off his anger at the brass when a friend, a renowned star, known equally for her piety and her compassion, picked up on his mood. He told her about the perpetration of some outrage or another, and she was properly incensed. "Fuck him! Fuck 'em all!" she cried. "Be one with Jesus!"

Anyone who has ever glanced through the entertainment section of his local blat is familiar with Goldwyn's barbarisms, yet a few of his most tortured lollapaloozas have escaped the attention of those outside the picture business.

He liked to introduce a weighty decision with the clause, "I've got just two words for you . . ." The two words, when he rejected an idea presented by a youthful Norman Mailer, were "Balls." To another writer they were "Im possible." And, according to the film historian Lee Harris, he always called *Wuthering Heights* "Withering Heights," and Lillian Hellman's *The Little Foxes* he called *"The Three Little Foxes."*

It might be mentioned that Goldwyn held no monopoly on haywire constructs. Agents are brilliant at it. One once said to me, "I have been building a tent in Darryl Zanuck's pancreas, and that is where I will be until you go on his payroll."

Another liked to employ a euphemism for stealing clients rather than developing his own. "I don't want to plant a seed," he said. "All I want is to transplant a tree."

And of a client, "He will give you something grandiose—larger than life."

Although many producers and directors pay lip service to the concept of parity for writers, they often manage to convey the impression that they'd knock off the script themselves if they weren't so pressed for time or so deeply immersed in more important matters.

A reluctant corollary: Unless your relationship with your producer/director is atypical, it's not a bad notion to steer clear of him socially while you're working with him professionally. There's no wisdom that I've ever found in chumming about or hanging out with someone who is critical and judgmental of your work just as you are of his. Of course there are exceptions, and while everyone on a picture strives, it is hoped, for harmony, concord remains a state of affairs exceedingly hard to achieve.

To the typical producer, a writer is an upstart imp or ogre whose primary duty is to do his bidding, and who fouls up the proceedings when he does not. In all fairness, however, it should be pointed out that producers are not alone in assuming this godlike posture, for pixbiz is heavily populated by know-it-alls. Actors, directors, writers themselves—just about everybody laboring in the Hollywood vineyards—sees his co-workers as foes driven to destroy the brilliance of artistry or the competence of craftsmanship other than his own. The attitude possibly derives from a paranoid approach to survival, or a need for heightened self-esteem. Whatever its genesis, it carries a possessory codicil: Everybody involved in a shoot sees it indisputably as his own.

James Mitchell signed to play a principal part in a biblical nose-bleed. Immediately the producer decided that Jim's talent as a dancer could best be exploited if he were a mute, expressing himself in mime-like movement. Further inspired, the man inexplicably decided to dye Jim's hair red.

Jim soon found himself in a barber's chair on the lot where he overheard the following dialogue:

1st Hairdresser: You catch the sneak last night?
2nd Hairdresser: No. How was it?
1st Hairdresser: Bomb. Sank without bubbles.
2nd Hairdresser: I could have told you that. You know who did the hair?

* * *

How does a screenwriter deal with directors, producers, executives? Certainly interpersonal chemistry has a lot to do with it. Humility will get you nowhere and, on the other end of the spectrum, neither will arrogance. Above all, never make a joke at their expense.

Harry Cohn: Guess where I was last night.

Norman Krasna (writer): Night school.

Cohn fired him.

Harry Cohn has become, to many critics of the studio system, the ultimate monster of absolute autonomy. He was personally and deeply involved in all the workings of Columbia Pictures, which he owned. He was dangerous when provoked; anything could piss him off and sweep him up in a towering rage. When a colleague suggested tentatively—everyone was tentative around Harry Cohn—that he make some attempt to temper his transports or run the risk of coming down with ulcers, "I don't get ulcers," Cohn told him, "I give them."

He could be rude and crude, but only by design. Once, to a writer he fancied briefly, he said, "Anybody you want to fuck around here? Take Stage Six and I'll watch the door for you."

About a week later he withdrew his support. "You were doing all right until page fifty-six," he told him, "which is where you trip over your own prick."

He admired novelist-screenwriter Michael Blankfort who, working at Columbia, couldn't ignore him. It was Christmas Eve, and Harry Cohn had responded, perhaps uncharacteristically, to the milk of seasonal kindness. He sent a gofer to find Mike and invite him up for a drink. Mike was already drinking, and shooting craps with a pack of grips in the corner of a sound stage. His response to Harry's invitation was uncharacteristically brusque. "Tell him," he directed the messenger, "I'm busy."

Conscientiously, the young man delivered the message. Cohn called the police and had Blankfort arrested for gambling on his property.

One quiet evening at home, Cohn confided to his wife that he was thinking about retiring.

"If that's what you want, fine," she told him. "But if you do, consider that we'll probably never be invited out to dinner, or to a party again."

9

He decided to keep on working.

When he died, a surprisingly large number of people showed up for the funeral, which confused many of his employees, all of whom at one time or another had been victims of his nastiness, but not a certain writer who knew him well. "It's just another example of the old show-biz adage," he said. "Give 'em what they want and they'll flock to it."

Producers like Cohn and Goldwyn and Louis B. Mayer had a tendency to consider their work not as a contribution to the finished product but as a one-man show, with the input of all others as nugatory if not downright malicious. They couldn't get along with writers, and they couldn't get along without them. Not unlike directors. As William Wyler was once reported to have said, a bit peevishly, "I know exactly what I want. I just need a writer to tell me."

But much of the time directors and producers adamantly refused to be told. They shunned compromise which in politics and in many other endeavors is usually the best solution in combating discord. "Every human benefit and enjoyment," said the great parliamentarian Edmund Burke, ". . . Every virtue and every prudent act . . . is founded on compromise."

Not in pictures, particularly when each warring party, righteous in his belief that God is on his side, is totally intractable.

Mayer and writer-director Jules Dassin were at odds over a story point. Neither would budge an inch, although rebellion on the part of the hired help is rare. When it does happen, all it takes most of the time is a threat, direct or oblique, from the production entity to restore order. When threats come they can be ugly and untidy.

In the case of Mayer versus Dassin, the deadlock was absolute until L.B. said, "Once I had a stallion, reminds me of you. He was stubborn, unresponsive, unreasonable. Damned animal was what you call oppositional. But I finally got him to see things my way."

"What did you do?" Dassin wanted to know.

Mayer said, "I cut his balls off."

What do you do, short of surgery, when you're at loggerheads with a director, when you can't break the deadlock? There's no bible on the subject, and many writers flounder into denial, refusing to admit that a problem *exists*. But it does, inevitably, if only on a sub-liminal level. Perhaps the best advice comes from T.E. Lawrence (of Arabia). He touched on the subject indirectly but brilliantly in *The Seven Pillars of Wisdom,* his manual for British political agents on how to deal with the leaders of the Saharan Arabs: ". . . keep the confidence of your leader. . . . Never refuse or squash schemes he may put forward; but ensure that they are put forward in the first instance privately to you. Always approve them, and after praise, modify them, insensibly causing the suggestions to come from him until they are in accord with your own opinion. When you attain this point, hold him to it, keep a tight grip of his ideas and push him as firmly as possible but secretly so that no one but himself (and not too clearly) is aware of your pressure." There is no assurance that the technique, despite its virtuosity, will work in Hollywood.

Actors, directors, and producers do not pursue their chosen crafts simply to drive writers up the wall. They are assailed by more demonic forces.

Actors, particularly stars with flat stomachs, lead lives adored, idealized and unrealistic; their objective is to solicit attention which more often than not is accorded them with a kind of talismanic knee-jerk spontaneity. They are afforded the unique opportunity of leading multiple lives, each of them more adventurous, more spectacular, more gratifying than their own, with a fresh persona for every picture. "I always wanted to be someone else," an aspiring actress once told me.

Actors are double-gaited. They enjoy their work, and they enjoy equally seeing themselves at work on the screen, a colossal moving mirror two-and-a-half times larger than life, which by its very size has a tendency to reduce the triviality of any enterprise.

Actors are ordinary-extraordinary people. While many of them seem repellently self-confident, brimming with narcissistic entitlement, egregiously pleased with themselves, it should be remembered that they don't all lead lovely lives of quiet contentment any more than the rest of us. Read all about 'em in your hometown paper. Remember too that they didn't get where they are by being quiet and contented.

Actors more often than not are a paradoxical composite—half aggressive, half shy, as though they are under some shameless compulsion to prove to themselves that they can get up there before millions of global villagers and strut their stuff. Writers in their own self-absorption seem quick to assign the frowns and bafflements of actors to the inadequacy of a screenplay. This is seldom the case. Usually, the sighing and groaning derive from the inadequacies, real or imagined, of the actor himself. "What am I, Shirley Shrift from Brooklyn," Shelley Winters asked herself, "playing the female lead in a picture with James Stewart?" What she didn't know: Ten minutes earlier James Stewart of Indiana, Pa. asked rhetorically, "How did I ever get here, in a picture with Shelley Winters?"

Actors respond to scripts in mysterious ways ranging from love to hate. Whatever the response, it usually has more to do with whim or quirkiness than with the caliber of the screenplay.

Goldwyn sent a script to Gary Cooper, asking for a quick commitment if he were interested in it. Weeks went by without an answer, the nervous writer in turmoil. Sam called the star. "Aren't you interested?" he asked. "Yes!" Coop replied emphatically. "Then why the delay?" Goldwyn asked. "Because I am interested," the cowboy told him, "I'm so interested I'm reading it word for word."

In contrast, writers were quick to applaud Alan Ladd who read screenplays with alacrity. But it turned out his promptitude had little to do with dramatic values. Once, when the subject of his swift response came up, "How else," he asked, "can I find out what kind of wardrobe to wear?"

Once a star (i.e., an actor in great demand) agrees for whatever reason to do a film, strange and confusing predicaments can rear up unexpectedly when the camera rolls.

We were shooting a two-scene with Elizabeth Taylor and Montgomery Clift in *Raintree County*. It was an uncomplicated sketch, rather static, an exchange of a few words of dialogue. Yet for two hours Monty, a fine actor, kept blowing his lines.

I went off in a corner of the sound stage and examined the script. Were the words I had given him unutterable? I didn't think so, but yet . . . and then I realized what caused the impasse.

Elizabeth had bounced in that morning with an excessively large rock on her finger. An engagement ring, she told everybody, from

Mike Todd. She was so winsomely eager to make it part of her that she had worn it to work even before it had been insured.

Monty didn't consider the annunciation of her betrothal as glad tidings. Many of his friends, I among them, thought that he wanted most fondly to make Elizabeth his wife.

By a curious coincidence the two-scene on the morning's schedule took place in the cabin of a Mississippi river boat directly after the marriage of the principals. The only prop required was a wedding band for the bride. Elizabeth decided to wear Mike's ring in the scene, with the diamond cradled in her palm, and with only the gold band showing. That's when Monty began flubbing his lines.

Could it be possible that Monty was hurt and angered by her choosing Mike, and that, further, he was expressing his hurt and anger unconsciously by messing up himself and his figment of a wife in the scene? It was time for a bit of conspiracy.

I improvised a three-scene with her, Monty, and, of all people, myself. This is how it played out: I moseyed over to Clift, began some dopey, totally irrelevant conversation. Elizabeth joined us, twisting Mike's ring on her finger. As I paused in my prattle, Elizabeth called the prop woman, told her that she wanted the prop wedding band, that Mike's ring was uncomfortable. The woman gave her the prop. Elizabeth slipped it on, said something like, "That's better." She handed me Mike's ring. "I'll get it later," she said.

The scene was completed in one take. Before we wrapped for the day, Elizabeth said, "Mike's picking me up. Like to have a drink with us?" I did, and then we went our separate ways.

At almost three o'clock the next morning, I jackknifed into total wakefulness so vehemently that I scared my wife. "What's the matter?" she asked.

· "The ring!" I told her. Of course she had no idea what I was yelling about. I staggered to the dirty clothes bin, fished out the khakis I had worn on the set, and found the ring. I handed it over to Elizabeth the moment I saw her the next morning.

"Oh, thanks," she said mildly, and put it back on her finger.

Unflappable was the word for Elizabeth. Whatever the crisis onstage or off, she was as imperturbable as a monument. She was,

13

moreover, the quickest study in the picture business. She'd glance at three or four pages of dialogue, take her chicken marks before the camera and deliver her lines faultlessly. Other than scripts, however, she didn't devote herself to much reading.

Some actors are omnivorous readers whose literary forays venture far beyond screenplays. One of them was Farley Granger; another, Burt Lancaster; and a third, Tallulah Bankhead, who was happy to meet the young Norman Mailer shortly after he wrote *The Naked and the Dead*.

In the book, you might recall, the author confounded and confused censors who were unsuccessful in their attempts to bowdlerize his text. He simply, brilliantly substituted "fug" for the most popular word in the picturesque vocabulary of our fighting men.

Shortly after the publication of his enormously successful book, Bankhead greeted him warmly at a party in New York. "You're the bright young man," she said, "who doesn't know how to spell fuck."

If actors, as many sociologists have noted, are America's royalty, then directors and producers can be said to be the kingmakers. They want to be in charge of everything—every shot, every nuance, every gesture, every line of dialogue—one from his office, the other on the set. So how can both be in charge? The operative point is that each thinks he's sovereign, and thinking makes it so.

Most producers and directors get themselves in a cross-purposeful bind in dealing with writers. They want an original and spectacularly brilliant approach to the work in progress, which postulates what could lead to a rebellious clash, for at the same time they want compliance—a dutiful submission to their every wish and comfort.

Many producers and directors see writers as assistants cranking out a conveyor belt of ideas to be refined and finalized by the master. But there are others who appreciate individuality. Jerry Wald was one of them. He wanted a picture based on Clifford Odets' play *Rocket to the Moon*. I discussed it with him in a meeting that consumed hours. With every point I made he'd say, "I agree" or "Exactly as I see it." Finally I said, "Well, Jerry, do I get the job?" "What do I need you for?" he asked. "You think the way I do." Obviously, he wanted somebody who thought better.

At that time many successful—ambitious and aggressive—people

14

in Hollywood were, like Jerry, depression kids who grew up in urban poverty. He couldn't land a job in New York City, but he tried hard. Not hard enough, however, to please his father.

Jerry tried to be a writer, an inactive form of striving his father was quick to criticize. Jerry would stretch out on his bed with a pad and a pencil while his sire would storm at him for his limp unproductivity. Until one halcyon day when a tabloid bought a piece he wrote. His father read it, strode into Jerry's room. "Would you like another pillow?" he asked.

Jerry had a favorite writer, Julius Epstein. Julie asked for a raise and was duly fired. Jerry was aware that Julie had a twin brother, Phil. Believing firmly that genes are destiny, Jerry sent him a Greyhound ticket west from Pennsylvania. Having been alerted by Julie, Phil refused to work for less than his brother, so Jerry—what the hell— hired them both.

Perhaps Wald was right about genetics. The Epsteins, not much later and with Howard Koch, wrote *Casablanca* (based on the play by Murray Burnett and Joan Alison).

In reality producers, uncontaminated by their own fantasies, do know how to finance and budget a picture. Some of them manage to keep the full equation of a film's physical production in their minds— no insignificant feat. But once the money man or woman invades the mysterious realm of story aesthetics—construction, progression, dramatic conflict and all the rest of it—he or she is, with few exceptions, like the concierge of the one-star hotel in W. Somerset Maugham's *Up at the Villa*, who "speaks half a dozen languages fluently but understands none."

Producers can be wrong but they are infrequently confronted with doubts, bringing to mind Marshal Henri Philippe Omar Pétain's characterization of a rather arrogant officer in his command. "The man knows everything," Pétain said, "but he knows nothing else."

A comprehension of one language even Maugham's concierge never attempted to mangle was presumably claimed by a producer, according to the writer of a sci-fi epic.

The dialogue, the producer told him, was lousy. "Why?" the writer wanted to know.

"Because," the producer explained, "they don't talk like that on Mars."

The story has all the attributes of apocrypha, but I've never met a writer who didn't believe it.

Producers, directors, and many others involved in the filmmaking process have ideas for improving the script, there being no one way to tell a story. Everyone sees it differently and strives mightily to stamp it with his own imprint. It also happens with remakes. Anyone in any way associated with the twice-told tale tries to put his/her spin on it, no matter how riveting or venerable or successful the original. It cannot be otherwise, I suppose, for human beings are so constructed; our chemistry seems to be coded that way. We cannot leave things alone—compulsively we must change them even when the results fall short of the prototype. The Germans have a grand word for the process: *Schlimmbesserung*—improvements that make things worse. It can with relevance be applied to the inability of non-writers to keep their mitts off a script, a practice which is usually destructive.

There's another reason why this sort of interference prevails. Everyone connected with a script is paid to make a contribution to it. Therefore, everyone in the studio's upper echelons acts on the irresistible incentive to alter what's on the page; nobody picks up a fat check to rubber-stamp a script. Do so and your expendability will be seriously considered. You'll be challenged with a chilling question: What are you getting paid for?

No artist is immune to the ravages of outrageous meddling. Bessie Smith, the peerless jazz chanteuse, was exceedingly miffed by the intrusions of the manager of the Apollo in Harlem where she was working a gig.

"I don't have to take this shit," she told him. "I can go home, get drunk, and be a lady."

Majority opinion has it that many an impresario, with the tease to hire you, deems it his unassailable right, according to the credo of capitalism, to tell you what to do and how to do it. All of which leads to a kind of writer's remorse, because writers for the most part like nothing more than to be the determinant of what they write, and at times they get pissed off.

Perhaps justifiably, they do resent the domination of people who cannot write and who have been known at times to have trouble reading.

"I don't think I'm forbidding," wrote Dame Edith Sitwell, "except when I absolutely refuse to be taught my job by people who know nothing about it."

Contention persists. "I cannot write to cheap specifications," Scott Fitzgerald said, "particularly someone else's."

Most producers will give a little here and take a little there, compromising to the degree that no one gets hideously mauled, although a scuffed ego is not beyond possibility. Only twice over a period of (gulp! could it have been . . .) fifty years have I encountered a boss (in this case a boss man) who was egregiously insistent that every line of the screenplay should not deviate the breadth of a whisker from the way he envisioned it. And who, it turned out, had ties to some very unpleasant people.

When we disagreed, rather mildly I thought, over the working of a scene, he said, "Do it my way or I'll have Jack [his chauffeur and bodyguard] break your arm."

I was so young and so dumb and so taken at the time by such swashbucklers as Sam Spade and Philip Marlowe that I threw a typewriter at him. I wanted to miss and fortunately I succeeded. The racket, however, did bring Jack lumbering into the room. The boss dismissed him. He was apparently impressed by my gruesome, death-defying stupidity.

There was another time when I was aggrieved by unbudgable tenacity, in this case Harry Cohn's. In my nonage, when I jumped at any job I could get, I latched on to a little gem with the working title of *Cable From Arabia*. It was an action-adventure epic that was anemic in both categories. The producer was Buddy Adler, who later won an Academy Award for *From Here to Eternity*. For better or for worse, he was indentured to Old Harry, who laid down the ground rules.

I didn't know how to do it Cohn's way. I told Buddy. He agreed it was kind of unworkable but he reaffirmed that it was the way Old Harry wanted it. I said I had a better idea and outlined it. He agreed it might work my way. "Let's tell Cohn," I suggested.

"I don't know," Buddy said hopelessly. "Maybe I can tell Sylvan Simon." S. Sylvan Simon was Cohn's number-one man, certainly the most sibilant straw-boss in the history of cinema. Simon liked my idea, but he wasn't enthusiastic about acquainting Harry with it. Finally, with much trepidation, he agreed.

And so it came to pass that a few days later Buddy, S. Sylvan, and I were ushered before the storied head of Columbia, a generalissimo of ominous vitality and handsome enough to qualify as one of his own dynamically mature stars.

A long strangulated pause, then Sylvan said, "Buddy, tell him," and Buddy said, "Mill, you tell him." I started to. Immediately Cohn interrupted me. He said to Sylvan and Buddy, "You two agree with the kid?"

They nodded, unemphatically, but Sylvan added, "After all, Harry, the score is three to one."

Harry's handsome face contorted in a terrible rictus of a grin. He walked slowly to the open window overlooking Gower Street and spit. He said, "I'll tell you the score—it's one to nothing. Sylvan," he went on, "Gower Street is paved with the old bones of people like you. Now, the three of you get your asses out of here."

S. Sylvan Simon renewed his uneasy truce with Harry Cohn. Buddy Adler was reassigned to another project. That same day I was fired.

Of course I was on two levels ill-equipped for the assignment: I knew nothing about Arabia and less about the oil business, which served as the foundation of the piece. But ignorance of that sort had never to my knowledge disqualified a screenwriter from a job, regardless of his/her unfamiliarity with a subject.

I was reminded of the peculiarities involved in the pairing of writer and picture on my way up to see Harry Cohn. As the elevator doors ghosted together, an elderly writer scrambled into my ever-narrowing purview. I jammed my hands between the fusing panels and with a deep frictional rustling they reversed direction and opened wide.

The elderly gentleman joined me and said, "Thanks." "Glad to have you aboard," I said, World War II still fresh in my mind.

His eyes lit up. "You were in the Navy?" he asked.

"No, Marine Corps."

"You're doing the Marine picture?"

"I'm doing the thing about oil in Arabia."

Now his eyes went soft and mellow, "I spent ten of the happiest years of my life in Arabia," he said.

"What are you working on?" I asked.

"The Navy picture," he said.

With due respect to Harry Cohn, he wasn't in the same league with Jack Warner, the fastest and most volatile gun in the West when it came to sacking the help.

Warner dallied at the writers table on the lot one day until somebody asked politely, "How are you?" Warner said, "Terrible," and launched into a remarkable monologue.

"We're shooting this picture in Arizona," he said, "a goddam epic. Errol Flynn and a cast of thousands. Payroll twenty thousand a day and this morning Flynn doesn't show up. Disappears. Son of a bitch, I found him in Australia, a bum, a beachcomber, and I made a star out of him. And now this is what I get."

He looked around the table and his eyes settled on a handsome young man, a journeyman writer who had been an unsuccessful actor.

"You," Warner said, "I could make a star out of you. I'd make you rich, and then you'd go on location some damn place and disappear. That's appreciation," he said morosely, "that's what I'd get for making you a star." His eyes narrowed. He said to the guy, "You're fired." It took a meeting with the writers' shop representative to get him back his job.

This sort of invasion of the writers table, even by the head of a studio, was extremely rare. For writers, the table provided a lunchtime oasis of laughter and one-liners where you could relax from the morning's disorders. It provided lunch with your extended family of peers and partisans, a shared commonality that was sorely missed with the demise of the studio system.

19

2

TOP DOGS, BIG BRASS
Don't Show Up

Every writer, director and producer on a picture, striving to stamp it with his own individuality of expression, can make himself a colossal nuisance to those around him. However, the pursuit of uniqueness can pay handsome dividends even with an age-encrusted tale. The remake of a good picture can become a treasure the second (or third) time around. Certainly Mel Brooks put one hell of a delirious twist on *Frankenstein*. Although some transfigurations are degenerative, many another "haircut," as insiders employing pixspeak are prone to call them, is an enhancement of the source material: *Bonnie and Clyde, Beauty and the Beast, The Three Musketeers, Robin Hood, Tarzan of the Apes*. On and on it goes, to the degree that Hollywood, long known as the capital of Make-believe, might with equal accuracy be called the domain of re-Make-believe.

Francis Ford Coppola's signature is indelible on most pictures he makes or remakes. *The Godfather* saga is more vibrant and more moving than the works from which it derived, praise that cannot be assigned to his *Dracula*. Coppola apparently attempted to accentuate the oral eroticism of the book and the earlier films that followed, although the carryings-on in every case were exhaustively obvious.

Another sort of revisionism has appeared before in Coppola's vitae. *Apocalypse Now* swerves far from its origin, which the writer–director identified as Joseph Conrad's *Heart of Darkness*.

The film suffers from an inadequate third act, from a resolution that confounds plausibility and denies its audience the consolations of catharsis. It drifts off into a kind of improvisational inconclusion, awkward and unsatisfying, because the screenplay was never hammered out. An old gnome of dramatic construction applies here: If it ain't on the page, it ain't on the stage.

Nonetheless, the flaws of *Apocalypse* fade before the onslaught of spontaneity and strength of scene after memorable scene. Even kinks and crochets in the hands of a master achieve at times an energy and excitement lacking in the pale, mechanized rigidity of rules and craftsmanship.

Many other filmmakers besides Coppola get mired down in a climactic slough, whether in original screenplays or in adaptations, some of them outstanding practitioners. Robert Altman's improvisations may not adhere to a classical unity of action, but they hold a fine lunatic haphazardry that transcends logic.

In a not dissimilar manner, the wit of Paul Mazursky unfurls like a bright flag in a brisk wind for two-plus acts, but the resolution of his otherwise happy screenplays lapse into a facile and quite often shallow extemporaneity. *Bob & Carol & Ted & Alice, An Unmarried Woman,* and *Down and Out in Beverly Hills* rivet and delight an audience until, on a final note of vapidity, they trickle off like a leaking faucet.

Of course, you might say that most lives trickle off like a leaky faucet. It was Dumas *fils*, I believe, who pointed out that life, never as neat as a well-made play, doesn't have a third act. As regards the triumvirate of Altman, Mazursky, and Coppola, it bears repeating that the overarching excellence of their work transcends by far the few discomforting flawed scenes sometimes appended to them. It is, however, exceedingly difficult to copy their individual styles, and you don't want to emulate their blemishes. Such is their skill that the blemishes are integral to their artistry.

It'll probably be a year of Shrove Tuesdays plus a sharp deviation in your karmic alignment before you achieve the power and the glory of the dynamic trio noted above. Meanwhile, our concern, in the immediate here and now, is with screenplays turned out by writers at the starting gate, who neither direct nor produce.

Now is as good a time as any to express a deep and abiding prejudice (as some would call it) or an ineradicable truth (as many of my colleagues in the Writer's Guild of America would see it) about plays and pictures: Of all the manifold components that go into their making, the most important is the written word. Without it there's nothing.

A play is considered the creation of its author; the director interprets it. Yet in film it is the director who holds creative primacy, and who at the moment is the darling of critics and fans alike. Whatever the enterprise, the major contribution is deemed his; he is the undisputed master of the revels. The evaluation will, I think, shift in time, just as in the comparatively recent past the predominance of the producer in feature films was appropriated by the director (not so in TV because of the rigors of a shooting schedule dictated by economics, which the producer controls). As long as the director wields hegemony, it is essential for a writer to become a director in order to preserve and protect what he sees as the integrity of his work.

Nonetheless, and contrary to accepted opinion, there are writers, a minority to be sure, who consider directing tedious and a drag. As glamour jobs go, it can be a bore—all that waiting around a dreary sound stage while, for example, the cinematographer and his army light the set, a process that seems interminable. What if you prefer the blessings of aloneness while you work instead of being surrounded constantly by a gang of assistants, dialogue coaches, hairdressers, wardrobe and makeup specialists, set decorators and art directors, sound technicians, horticulturists, grips, and the gaffer and his best boy and the jasper who supplies the cast and crew with coffee and dough-

23

nuts, to name a few? If you cherish solitude you'll have to find another, more rewarding outlet for your energy. Or if you must write pictures, do it with the sobering awareness that your screenplay will be mangled much of the time to meet what the producer wants on TV or what the director demands in feature films.

I directed one picture, *Reprieve*, a.k.a. *Convicts 4*, from the autobiography of John Resko, with a superb cast of Ben Gazzara, Stuart Whitman, Rod Steiger, Sammy Davis, Jr., Broderick Crawford, and Ray Walston. As champagne jobs go, I found directing a drag, and gave it up.

It was a large mistake. My vaulting self-indulgence was hardly a boon to me and my family. Had I been more mature and less irresponsible and continued to direct, I would have husbanded a hell of a lot more money and gained greater control over the pictures I wrote. All of which proves that my hindsight is as keen as anyone's.

Writer and director Alex Cox made a more sensible choice:

24

I started writing feature screenplays in a class at UCLA in 1977. There wasn't much tuition—how can there be? The benefit of the class, for me, was the deadline it imposed. (Twenty years later when I taught production at UCLA Film School nothing had changed—the students loathed deadlines, but they seemed to be just about the only beneficial thing I could impose . . .)

Like a lot of writers, I got into directing films partially because I wasn't satisfied writing scripts which didn't go into production. I wrote the script of *Repo Man* for myself to direct. Over a period of two years (not much time, really—how lucky we all were!) I wrote and rewrote the script. In the end there were fourteen, at least fourteen, drafts. The story was based partially on a series of interviews I did with a car repossessor, Mark Lewis, while driving around with him in his car. As it went through its metamorphoses, this original documentary material became increasingly important. In the end it proved to be the spine of the film.

Since then nothing has changed. Original, documentary material has remained the essential element of almost all my films as a director. *Walker, Sid & Nancy, Highway Patrolman, Three Businessmen*—all have a documentary basis which gives them their reality, no matter how weird that might be (and most of these scripts were done by other writers, based on material we found together). There is something about original material that almost cannot be beat . . .

Other than that, I've learned a few brief "rules" which help me, as a director, to read other people's scripts. Keep them ninety pages or less. There is no excuse for 100-to-140 page screenplays. They are invariably boring and will not, in reality, be read. No scenes longer than three pages! You can break this rule (*Three Businessmen* has one nine-page scene, done in a single master) but it is still a good rule.

25

Perhaps most importantly—do your characters have individual voices? This is the most important rule of all. They may be called LARRY and BOB, but unless they speak with different voices, your characters are all really named BLOB. Each new name which appears on the page must speak—somehow, alchemically—in a different way, with a different voice.

And finally—don't waste your hard-earned cash buying "screenplay writing software." There is no need for it. All screenplay format involves is the setting of two tabulation points. This doesn't even require a computer. It can be done on a typewriter, and you can buy a used typewriter for around ten bucks. If you can't set two tabs and differentiate between upper and lower case, you shouldn't be a writer: Be a producer instead.

Generally, scripts by writers plowing through strange, unfamiliar fields all seem to benefit most when the producer or director maintains a policy of laissez-faire, when intervention is minimal, and instruction is limited to generalities rather than specifics. I worked with a producer who'd summon me to his lair about once a week, flip through the script, nod sagely and admonish me to "make it interesting, make it rich." Splendid. Writers are always eager to heed that sort of command.

Messing with a writer's work is not restricted to Hollywood directors and producers. When Elia Kazan wanted changes in a drama by Arthur Miller, the playwright countered with a good question, "Where were you," he asked, "when the page was blank?"

Many film directors are handicapped by another sort of burden: improving the script until it is thoroughly dead. They change the content or the thrust of a scene, alarmingly unaware that in a unified three-act form, such alterations require further changes in scenes that follow or the work becomes, to use a technical term, a mishmash. They seem to invoke a peculiar creed: If It Ain't Broke, Fix It.

We all have a pulsebeat that insists beyond a shadow of a doubt that each of us knows what's best for a picture. Changes in a script are not made out of malice; it's part of the creative process: Everybody sincerely believes he's making it better. This is not to be construed as criticism. It is a rather elementary observation on our organic chemistry.

Harry Rapf, who headed a unit of B-picture production at M-G-M, could never leave well enough alone. Like just about any executive, he had an imperious faith in his ability to determine the value, i.e., the potential profits of an unreleased pix. Yet, in a season when not much else on the slate promised even an approximation of a blockbuster, he released with some reluctance a picture he personally expected to thud at the box office.

Rapf was shocked to discover at a series of previews that the audience loved it. He figured that he could improve it, turn it into a smash hit. He recalled the picture from general circulation and personally re-edited it, took it out for a second time. The audience hated it. So once more Harry returned to the cutting room to restore its original truth or beauty or goodness or whatever the audience saw in it.

But it was a Humpty-Dumpty sort of flick. Harry couldn't put it together again. The picture was never released commercially.

Rapf was best remembered not as a high-octane apparatchik

but as a wolf with a knife and fork. He attacked a plate of food with the gusto of an Olympian going for the gold. On one occasion in the commissary, he bit into a piece of strawberry pie; his eyes sparkled in ecstasy as he announced, "This is the best piece of pie I ever had in my whole mouth." Watching him plunder a plate of pasta was unforgettable. "Harry doesn't eat spaghetti," a colleague once noted, "he goes down on it."

Another hands-on executive at M-G-M was Joe Cohn. In charge of physical production, Joe deplored the wastage he detected everywhere. He felt writers concocted too many scenes, directors shot too many takes, covering too many angles, using too much stock that ended up on the cutting room floor. His forceful arguments appealed to a number of his peers—everyone's always for filing the fat off pictures—and he was finally given a picture to direct and produce. He shot it in record time—no frills, no embellishments, not even a wrap party. He put it together, loving every exciting moment of it, and called in a group of friends to take a look.

It wasn't a long look. The picture ran thirty-nine minutes. It was shelved, never again to be shown, not even in a projection room.

Equally distressing to the writer is the script that is emphatically and inexplicably rejected upon submission, and thereby sentenced to death without further scrutiny.

At a time when Westerns were popular, a writer friend made an in-depth study of the genre. As a professional, and a highly competent one, he emulsified all the most workable ingredients, put them together and built a good story that was marketable—he thought.

It wasn't. Finally he told a smart producer what he had done—his analysis of a dozen successful Westerns, the inclusion in his work of what seemed to make them glow, etc., etc. He topped his pitch with a criticism of his own—He had seen in the past couple of years a number of Westerns much worse in the telling, the directing, the production, than his own rejected effort. "Why?" he asked, angrily and plaintively, "Why?"

"You've got to understand," the producer told him rather wistfully, "we don't buy 'em that way, we make 'em that way."

They make 'em that way by trial and error, for everyone associated with a picture, in her search for the elusive surefire smash, has no idea whatsoever if a picture will work, and so they intrude and improvise, at times recklessly, to improve the product.

There are other considerations that go into movie making. The best you can do is guess at them. You never know how long it will take to write the picture, and where the ideas will come from. I wrote *Bad Day at Black Rock* in three weeks, possibly because I was stimulated by its focus: racism in that bastion of egalitarianism, the American West. *Raintree County* with a pro tem committee running the studio after the production chief had been fired, took a year to complete. They tampered and monkeyed around, and while the film wasn't exactly for the dogcatcher, it did not sparkle. *Black Rock,* anyone including your six-year-old nephew would agree, is a better picture. Incidentally, it cost a fraction of *Raintree.*

True, Ross Lockridge, Jr.'s novel had epic proportions—1,060 pages, a magical, mythic evocation of heartland Americana that did not lend itself easily to film. Its volume was enough to instill a certain trepidation. I was lugging it home when in the parking lot I ran into producer Arthur Loew, Jr.

"Ever read this?" I asked.

"Read it?" he said, "I can't even lift it."

Attempts to predetermine if a picture will make money have included the use of demographics—neither more nor less revealing than the emotional response of a studio executive before the picture's release. At Columbia, *2001: A Space Odyssey* was expected to fail while *Fail-Safe* was anticipated as a smash. The opposite happened. *The Eddy Duchin Story* was deemed to bomb until it opened, and it took off. The crit on *The Great Caruso,* starring Mario Lanza at M-G-M, was so god-awful that the Keepers of the Roaring Lion let it escape without fanfare. It opened in a small Pennsylvania village in a life-threatening blizzard, sold out before eleven A.M. and went on to become a colossal hit.

The irreducible fact of the matter is disheartening, but experience proves conclusive: There's no way of predicting a picture's success or failure, a sobering thought best reduced perhaps in a succinct analysis of baseball formulated by Joaquin Andujar, former pitcher for the St. Louis Cards. "I can tell you about baseball," he said, "in one word: You never know."

While anybody can badmouth a movie, still it seems anomalous that it is often studio executives who, to save face among themselves, do it first, but only with their most intimate affiliates, off the record, and as privileged, confidential information.

Everybody—CEO to the gofer on the set—criticizes a picture. Everybody in America feels it's his inalienable right within the over-all calculus of free speech. And there is another psycho-dynamic involved in sounding off: Most everybody—there are few exceptions—labors under the self-delusion that he is gifted, an elegant arbiter of what is Good and True and Beautiful and Right and Tasteful. All he wants is that those less gifted listen to him and respond accordingly. This sort of atrocious subjectivity exists on every level of the food chain.

Criticism comes most easily from those who have nothing to do with making a picture; the writer or anyone involved in it exposes himself to the world and its censure. Sometimes it hurts. As conductor Leopold Stokowski told Bernard (Benny) Herrmann (1911–1975, the eminent film composer and arranger), "You must have a shell like a turtle to withstand the pummeling." 29

What hurts most is the agony of self-criticism, when those deeply involved can't turn back and can't pull the mess they've created out of the fire that consumes the whole ill-fated enterprise.

Outstanding writers and directors with impeccable credentials at times come up empty. "I was pregnant with a dead child," said Mike Nichols, realizing that Catch-22 was in trouble before it was in the can.

It has been mentioned in passing that there are times, rare but valuable, when a writer can benefit from the contributions of others. Not only from producers and directors, but from any source. Some years ago, during the shoot of Raintree County, a greensman suggested a deep cut which made a series of scenes infinitely sharper than I had envisioned them.

Producers, directors, and stars guard their prerogatives zealously. They are outraged by any writer who trespasses on their turf, and while some of them are prone to get ruthless about it, they never hesitate to intrude on writers. They see it as an act of entitlement. They can even talk about it with an air of impunity.

One evening, somewhere in Kentucky, after we wrapped the day's shoot on *Raintree*, Clift and I were invited to appear on a radio program. Our host, a pleasant young man, danced around us in the usual innocuous fashion until he mentioned Monty's well-known predilection for writing.

Monty was modest and gracious. "I'm only good," he said, "in cleaning up dirty pages."

I was possibly wrong, but I thought he was referring to my screenplay, and I was exceedingly pissed off. "Just make sure," I told him, "to keep your goddamn mitts off my dirty pages." In a matter of milliseconds we were off the air.

It is particularly galling for a writer to go up against the dictates of a star, moreso when the star is the owner or the partner in the company doing the picture. In writing *The War Lord* (from the play *The Lovers* by Leslie Stevens), I was constantly rewritten by Charlton Heston. Everyone involved was aware that he was rotten at it, but it was his vehicle and his company and there wasn't much to do about it. I yelled but to no avail.

Yelling affords little relief from the sickening feeling of frustration and outrage whenever that sort of thing happens. The gastric juices go sour, there's a compound sensation of pain and benumbment in the pit of the stomach, like a punch in the solar plexus. You find yourself hating whoever rewrites you.

Yet the nature of the work necessitates, at times, a complete reversal of fortune on those occasions when you're tapped to rewrite someone else, and the Sermon on the Mount and Kant's categorical imperative—both roughly translated as the Golden Rule of ethical conduct which prescribes that you "do unto others as you would have them do unto you"—go right the hell down the toilet. In the area of rewrite, what you do unto others is precisely and uncomfortably what they do unto you.

Only the bravest or the most secure or suicidal of writers would go up against the head of a studio. One of them was James Thurber. He decorated the walls of his office with priceless cartoons. A horrified janitor reported the offense to L.B. Mayer. "You clean up those walls by six o'clock or you're fired," L.B. told him.

Thurber decided on further decorations. He got to work on the part of a wall facing the door. At six, when Mayer stormed in on a personal inspection, he was confronted by a caricature pointing a colossal penis at him. Hovering above the urinating figure's head was a bubble enclosing the words, "L.B.—DUCK!"

Hemingway expressed his defiance in a way that was equally emphatic but less confrontational.

I was corralled to rewrite a Western, and only when I finished was a search launched to find a name for it. An executive, Benny Thaw, came up with a great title: *The Sun Also Rises*. I refused to accept it, the oater having nothing whatever to do with Hemingway's novel. Benny explained to me that while he was fully aware that Twentieth Century Fox owned the book, some bizarre and obscure agreement had been reached for us to use the title. Still I refused, so Benny took an immediate action that redefined and intensified the meaning of the term chutzpah. He put in a call to Hemingway in Idaho, managed to locate him, told him of the problem and asked him pointblank if he could come up with an appropriate title.

Hemingway hesitated. He said, "Wait a minute, let me think about it. Hold on."

Benny held on for more than four hours. Of course Hemingway never came back.

What seems to set executives apart from the rest of suffering humanity is their uncompromising seriousness. Benny Thaw again: Keenan Wynn told him a joke. "He opened his mouth to laugh," Keenan said, "and dust came out."

31

3

WRITING AND WRITHING
Growing Corns
on Your Ass

There are little, exclusionary prescripts in the governance of a studio that encourage friction between the populace and its chieftains.

A writer named Hopkins approached Bill Ludwig one afternoon in the Iron Lung, M-G-M's launching pad of hits, where executives, writers, directors, and producers were lodged. "Do you know," he began, "that there's a sauna on the top floor?" Bill said he was aware of it. "So let's go up and get a steam," Hoppy said. "It's not for us," Bill told him. "It's for executives only."

Hoppy heaved a great sigh, half in sadness, half in anger. "That's another thing I hate about this joint." he said. "They keep the wrong people in shape."

Just as a signed contract is the beginning of movie negotiations, so a completed script is the beginning of changes, few of which encourage vocational serenity. Everyone contributes, including agents. The result is a distortion of democracy and a debasement of craft. This kind of intrusion is scab labor, unskilled and imprecise, undercutting the writer's legitimate function. And they all believe they're making it better. If Mel Gibson so much as touched a camera, a prop, a lamp, or a Ritter fan, the whole backlot would strike, but he can cock up a script with immunity.

There are times when you think of your colleagues as bubble-headed dinosaurs, writer-bashing nutters with souls of clay, hell-bent on drawing you into a collaboration of sleaze. Camus' lapidary precept that "It is both impossible and immoral to judge an event from the outside" seems to be lost on producers. They tread heavily, but sometimes, and herein lies the paradox, they speak the truth.

No writer, as much as he'd like to, can claim inerrancy. To throw words together is an inalienable right, which includes the prerogative to throw them together badly.

And we do get carried away. We go overboard. We take license. We indulge ourselves, discarding the dictates of restraint. Remember Ben Jonson's observation on Shakespeare: "Players have often mentioned it as an honor . . . that . . . he never blotted out a line. . . . Would he had blotted a thousand."

That's when the ministrations of a good editor come in, whether she answers to that title or calls herself by another. There have been times when all of us have benefited from the counsel of a producer to muzzle our excesses, temper our transports, and pinpoint where we zigged when we should have zagged.

It is difficult to concede that an outside force might be a better arbiter of your writing than you are. But writers, as William Burroughs contended, "are notoriously bad judges of their own work." His declaration embraces an unqualified truth for it also applies when writers, for reasons best known to themselves, underestimate, even castigate, their own yield.

Avows Scott Frank, whose wild, funny screenplay of Elmore Leonard's novel *Get Shorty* was praised by critics and public alike:

I hate everything I write. To this day I can't bring myself to read my own screenplays once I've turned them in. In fact, I can't ever remember sitting around and thumbing through old drafts of my work just for fun.

Fun, nothing. It's torture.

If I can't read them, I certainly can't bear to watch my films either. Usually, if I have to be there, I just stare at a corner of the screen, waiting for my wife to pat my hand and tell me, "It's over, honey. You can let go of my arm."

And it's not because I hate the way my films have been realized. For the most part, they've been well made and I've been extremely well-treated. It's simply because: I hate everything I write.

I don't understand this, because I love my ideas. In fact, I am the happiest guy in the world when I first come up with an idea. That moment in the shower or in my car or operating heavy equipment when it comes to me. Sometimes it's just a title: *Dead Again*. I'll think about it for months, years, and then, magically, the rest will emerge whole cloth from my subconscious (usually when I'm supposed to be working on something else): Two people fall in love only to find out one of them killed the other one in a past life.

And then I do nothing. I just think about it.

I have to be passionate about an idea before I write it or I give up. That's why I have to ruminate for a long time before I can begin working. It's a test: If I still like this a few years from now, it must be good.

Even then, I don't simply start writing the script; I start writing *about* the script. Scenes I know have to be in the movie. Snippets of dialogue. Names of characters (Ray or Rae?). Lines or pieces of descriptions that I've stolen from books that I want to find places for.

Opening scenes.

I spend months on my opening scenes. To me, an opening scene is like the key of a song. Without the right opening, I can't hum the rest of it.

35

Then I do outlines. Lots of outlines. Dozens of outlines. Occasionally if I'm having trouble finding the right structure, I'll sketch each major character's story separately, and then meld those smaller outlines into one larger one.

Then, finally, when I can't take it anymore, I'll start to write. At this point, I agonize over everything. Words. Punctuation. Even sentence breaks, how the paragraphs look on the page.

Each day I sit down to write, I begin by rewriting the work I did the day before. My thinking is that this will give me a running start into the new material. Instead, I find, more often than not, that I get bogged down in fixing what I did yesterday instead of moving on to what needs to be done today.

I once read an interview with Francis Ford Coppola where he said—this was back when he was writing films like *Patton* and *The Conversation*—that he would write a script all the way through without going back. If he changed something that would affect the pages that came before, he just kept going forward, assuming (pretending) the earlier stuff had already been changed. Only when he had a completed draft would he then go back and rewrite.

That's not me.

There's just no way I can go on pretending everything's fine until I get a draft done. I have to go back. I have to know *everything's* perfect. At least for now.

Days go by. Months. Years.

Then one morning it happens: I wake up hating my script. Maybe it was a movie I saw the night before that was kind of similar only much better. Maybe it was a novel I read that I wish I was adapting instead of Steve Zaillian.

Or maybe I'm just tired.

Either way, on *every* script I've ever written, whether original or adapted, I've reached the point where I say to my wife something like, I can't believe I'm writing a movie about reincarnation . . . or a seven-year-old kid who misses his mom when he goes to college . . . or a loan shark who wants to make movies. I mean, who really gives a shit?

And she'll say something infuriating like, Well, at one point, you did.

Damn her.

Then she says, Why don't you tell me the story again?

I really hate her.

So I tell her my story. And every time, without fail, I catch it again. No longer bogged down by having to choose the right words or the right punctuation or whether I should call the character Chili or Palmer, I'm free to just tell the story.

And I like it.

Back when I was a bartender, still working on my twenty-seventh draft of *Little Man Tate*, a drunk agent once wrote down on a cocktail napkin what he claimed were the "four P's to success in Hollywood." They were: Persistence, Perseverence, Proximity and Perspiration.

To that list I'd have to add Perspective.

. . . which is always the first thing we lose, especially after we've spent a really long time working on something and suddenly we can no longer surprise ourselves with the material. When I feel this happening to me, I always tell my story to anyone who will listen. For me, there's something in the telling—like reading dialogue aloud—that, on the one hand, makes it fresh, while on the other brings into relief any problems there are structurally. I can tell when I gloss over something in the telling that I haven't worked that part out yet. You know . . . And then a bunch of stuff happens that shows they're in love, but aren't right for each other.

Perhaps that's why I can't read my own work: If it's in print or, worse yet, on-screen, it's permanent. There's nothing I can do about it. If I just tell the story, it's alive, but fluid, I don't have to commit to any of it. Watching my movies, all I can ever think about are the thousands of ways I could have done it differently had I had the time. And I guess that's what's so hard about writing movies: As screenwriters, our work isn't done when we think it is, it's done when someone else takes it away from us.

To which I say, Thank god.

If it were otherwise I'd never finish anything.

When William Burroughs pointed out that his compeers were not to be trusted in evaluating their own pages, his words were aimed, of course, at those storytellers who, unlike Scott Frank, are infatuated with their own writing and not in the least embarrassed to make a public display of love. Certainly it's true that admiration for one's own jewel-like skills can be perilous; we tend to lose touch with reality, and the niceties of perception take flight. It can happen to the best of us. "I went ten rounds with Tolstoy," Hemingway announced, "and got a draw."

Not quite. Which brings us to the heart of the matter: Before you dispute every push and pressure from the outside, before you insist on being the absolute be-all and end-all of your work out of adamancy or principle, you might consider addressing yourself to the world-famous question of that kid in the progressive nursery school. "Do I always have to do," he asked his teacher, "whatever I want to?"

If writers are so unique, so individual a subspecies, so hell-bent on a unilateral, noninterfering approach to their work, why do so many of them land in what Sir Pelham Grenville Wodehouse, in one of his more serious moments, called "Dottyville-on-the-Pacific," a workplace notorious for collaboration and compromise? Four-fifths of the answer is money; one-fifth is the scrumptious company you keep. Truman Capote had plenty of bread, but he couldn't resist the glamour of disporting with Ava Gardner, John Huston, Humphrey Bogart, and others of that celestial ilk.

His devotion was understandable. Most people in show business are fun and infinitely more interesting than any other species of professionals I've run into. As for the ogres and Calibans, they are at least sufficiently bizarre to radiate their own peculiar aura of fascination.

The hours at the studio were long and at times they could be difficult, but like the people surrounding you, they were for the most part fun and fascinating.

I've been a carpenter's helper, a plumber's apprentice, a seaman on a freighter, a newspaper reporter, a Marine Corps officer. For me, at any rate, show business is better. Another positive point: You travel all over the planet with the company picking up the tab. You meet the damnedest people—paragons of virtue and of villainy, earthshakers and shitheels, larger and more imposing than life. It's invigorating.

You start in the morning, banging it out painfully, if you're a slow bleeder, oblivious to everything but the blank page before you, filling it with words words words, the foot soldiers of your phantom army. You march them along, except for those terrifying interludes when the obstinate bastards won't budge, and after a long day's hike you are only aware of your surroundings when the voice of a spouse (if you're lucky enough to have one and if you're working at home) calls, "Aren't you ever coming in for dinner?"

You think, Jesus, the whole day's shot to shingles already? And you close down the shop, only to reopen it tomorrow at the crack of doom.

Some of the twentieth century's best writers rebelled at times against the incessant isolation their craft/art demanded. Dorothy Parker, who loved to socialize, suffered from the aloneness of her chosen profession, so on the door of her office at Warner Bros. studio she hung for those in need of physiological relief—one word, three letters—MEN.

The outside windows of the writers' building at Warner's were barred. On one occasion Parker glanced out, saw on the street a clutch of tourists being ushered around the lot by a guide. "Let me out of here!" she screamed down at them. "I'm as sane as you are."

Why would anyone choose to become a writer, to embrace an ink-stained trade in which most of your waking hours are spent in a deep coma, hermetically sealed, in parentheses, cut off from what most civilians conceive as the real world? Sitting at a desk in your uneasy chair, growing corns on your ass? Why? For a number of reasons, some of them good.

George Orwell suggests four great motives for writing:

"Sheer egoism. Desire to seem clever, to be talked about, to be remembered after death, to get your own back on grown-ups who snubbed you in childhood. . . .

"Aesthetic enthusiasm. . . .

"Historical impulse. Desire to see things as they are, to find out true facts and store them up for the use of posterity. . . .

"Political purpose. To push the world in a certain direction, to alter other people's ideas of the kind of society that they should strive after."

Still it is difficult to assign, with even a modest degree of certitude, one or more of Orwell's drives to an individual.

General Ezer Weizmann was a man of great and grave accomplishments. His courage bordered on the gruesome. The scion of a distinguished family, he was an outstanding fighter pilot in the British R.A.F. in WWII. He was the first commander of the Israeli Air Force. He served in the highest echelons of Zionist statesmanship and diplomacy.

On a quiet day in the garden of his home in Tel Aviv, he told me that what he'd really like to do was write a Western.

Orwell adds that "Every book is a failure . . . a horrible, exhausting struggle, like a long bout of some painful illness. One would never dare undertake such a thing if one were not driven on by some demon whom one can neither resist nor understand."

Some writers work from necessity. They are blessed or cursed with an obsession; the very process is food and drink, sleep and shelter. They have an incurable itch to write, every bit as strong as Magellan's to explore, Einstein's to discover, Barbarossa's to plunder, Bonnie and Clyde's to rob banks. They suffer from a disease that has no cure.

To others, writing is an act of catharsis, a purgative that expels the poisons from the blood. Sometimes it is an act of stabilization, clarifying our thoughts about ourselves and the world, telling ourselves what we believe, where we stand. "How can I tell what I think," said E.M. Forster, "till I see what I say." And to paraphrase Descartes, "I write, therefore I am."

It should be clear by now that writers don't lead lives of halcyon sparkle any more than actors, or, for that matter, directors or producers or anybody else on this imperfect planet. Which possibly sustains the hoariest cliché about why we write: the aspiration to play God. Dissatisfied with reality and our own lusterless, untidy lives, unable to write our own scripts of life, we remake the world to fit our fantasies.

Don't ignore your fantasies, no matter how untamed. A realist knows they're essential to movies, providing the spark that lights the fire, the kaleidoscope through which we launch our conceits, our self-sustaining myths, our sand castles on the airy screen.

All of us are the heroes of our own fantasies. Indeed, just about every romantic and prevaricating flick can be viewed as the wish-fulfilling projection of its writer.

Whatever the compulsion, just about everyone who ever wrote a postcard thinks he can write a novel, a phenomenon that astounded the usually unflappable Samuel Johnson, who saw it as an "epidemical conspiracy for the destruction of paper."

"When I was a kid," said Jackie Fields, welterweight champion of the world (1929–30), "I used to sleep on my nose so I would look like a fighter."

Some people have a great desire to look like a writer and talk like a writer and act like a writer, despite the fact that there is no stereotype for any of these classifications. The only requirement for membership in the group is the ability to write like a writer. And that in itself is no guarantee for financial success or literary acclaim. For most hopefuls, it's a rocky road, long and winding, just to reach the gates of the promised land.

Bryan Gordon is a young man from Dover, Delaware, who has just entered the gates. He wrote comedy TV, wrote and directed a twenty-one minute short, *Ray's Male Heterosexual Dance Hall*, in a week, for which he won an Academy Award. How he approaches his work, how he goes about executing it, tells a lot about the art/craft he practices:

I never really think I have a legitimate "writing process." Come to think of it, I never think I'm really a writer. My "process," I feel, does not have the order and refinement of those I know who sit down between nine and five and pound keys. My process looks more like some Rube Goldbergesque contraption. After all, I write in bed, in the shower, in the car, and even when my wife and friends, I hate to admit it, are talking to me. I use paper, the back of credit card stubs, used napkins, oh, yes, a computer—I use practically anything to write on. I've even once written on a stranger's hand. If I don't, I know it's lost forever in this absent-minded head of mine.

I'm more of a morning person. It's quieter and there are fewer distractions. My head isn't yet filled with such thoughts as "Do I still have a career?" My most productive writing seems to occur before lunch. I use food as an incentive. And why not? A "good thought" is usually worth a snack. A witty piece of long dialogue—why, I'm apt to reward myself with an early and long lunch. Therein lies a problem. If I'm productive, I tend to look bloated and overweight, and if I'm going through writer's block, I sure as hell look nice and trim.

When I begin a project, I try to experiment as much as I can. I write a lot of monologues . . . monologues that will never see the light of day in the script, but it may give me some insight as to who my characters are. Sometimes I'll write a script using numerous voice-overs from a dozen points of view. And again, I'll slowly whittle the voice-over out of the script and hopefully what will emerge is a story told through my scenes and characters. Experimenting helps me find and trust my own voice and way of telling a story.

Years ago, when I was in my early twenties, plenty arrogant and just beginning to jot things down, I showed my work to some big agent in New York City. Believe me, my total writing totaled no more than fifty pages. He read it and said . . . "What else you got?"

I said, "That's it, my complete work." I thought,

based on those pages, I would be discovered and life would be easy.

He looked at me and said, "These pages are OK, but what I think you should do is go out and live a life."

At that time, I deeply resented what he said. After all, I was twenty-three, what more of a life do I need? "Go live a life," he repeated. What the heck is he trying to tell me? He then said that James Michener and Isaac Singer were his clients and they weren't published until they were in their late thirties, early forties. They went out and lived a life.

It was years later that this story really hit me and I try to remember that what is important in the process of writing is to "live a life." When I practice that, I seem to go deeper and have more satisfaction with my work.

Well, I just reread what I wrote and I can't decide whether to head for the refrigerator or keep writing.

43

Once you're established in Hollywood you'll have your inevitable share of flops, just like all the rest of us. A few examples of my own should suffice; listing them is neither a thrilling nor a rewarding enterprise. Anyway:

Aladdin and His Lamp. The producer, a charming and talented man named Walter Wanger (he later did the Burton-Taylor rendition of *Cleopatra*), had just gotten out of prison for having shot an executive who was fooling around with Mrs. Wanger, the actress Joan Bennett. *Aladdin* was his first picture after his release from confinement.

It was pretty bad, but Walter and I were unaware of its grosser limitations. A preview audience in Pasadena was not unaware, and emphatically they let us know.

When the natives settled down and the house lights went up, Walter leaned toward me. "Maybe," he whispered in my ear, "I should have stayed in jail."

Valentino. After which forty-one relatively civilized members of the Writers Guild, myself included, fought like barbarians to keep their names off the credits.

Krakatoa, East of Java. The director and the producer refused to talk to each other. I was called in to prop up their ridiculous nosebleed and prod it onto the screen. It was a disaster from its most un-immaculate conception. Even the title was a violation of geographical accuracy: Krakatoa is *west* of Java. The people involved knew it but refused to change it because *east*, they insisted, sounded more romantic and exotic than *west*.

"A playwright," said Bernard Shaw, "must write three or four bad plays before he writes a good one."

But what do you do after you write eight or ten turkeys? Most critics of plays or probers of psyches might suggest you find a less resistant outlet for fulfillment.

If you don't enjoy writing, abandon it, for it is at best a hard hustle. Many people who claim they don't like it keep at it, possibly to avoid more strenuous labor, although the solitary, distillative process of getting words on paper seems to hold little joy for some of its best practitioners. When asked what he liked about his job, "Everything," said Peter De Vries, "except the paperwork."

Dorothy Parker, who was at best ambivalent about her profession, seized on the apposite oxymoron to describe it as "a miserable delight," adding, "I write five words and erase seven."

P.G. Wodehouse was rare indeed when he proclaimed, emphatically and unconditionally, that he enjoyed writing.

When a writer looks at her work, she never knows until she drops anchor whether the bruising voyage was worth it.

Inversely, however, most writers would agree that the most gratification that attends a script is the writing of it, the act of composition. The tripping and tramping from word to word to reach your destination justifies whatever that destination holds. The Greeks had a word for it, *poiesa*, which incorporates the splendid notion that the greatest enjoyment of art, whether it's composing, painting or writing, is in its creation, in the odyssey toward its completion.

Talkers don't necessarily make good writers; a silver tongue is not requisite. Off-the-cuff, most writers are pitifully tongue-tied; articulate speech has little to do with craft. Dr. Johnson, as fine an authority on composition as any man who ever lived, described one Tom Birch "as brisk as a bee in conversation; but no sooner does he take a pen in his hand than it becomes a torpedo to him, and benumbs all his faculties."

Johnson also perceived the obverse side of the coin. Of Oliver Goldsmith he said, "No man was more foolish when he had not a pen in his hand, or more wise when he had."

Goldsmith's death in 1774 prompted the great actor David Garrick to extemporize:

"Here lies Nolly Goldsmith, for shortness called Noll,
Who wrote like an angel, but talked like poor Poll."

45

It should be emphasized, and this is possibly as good a time as any to point out that it is no crime to try writing and give it up when it becomes irksome and unprofitable. It should be clear from the two contrary examples above that some extraordinarily intelligent people, like Tom Birch, endowed with the speech of angels, simply cannot write, while the literary Poll Goldsmith, who wrote with charm and wisdom, couldn't talk his way out of (or into) a net brassiere or even think without a pen in his hand.

If you share Mr. Birch's struggle with the written word, drop the whole misbegotten enterprise before you become a schlockmeister. It is interesting to note that Goldsmith qualified as such before he emerged as one of the most versatile of authors. He toyed with the idea of entering the Church, drifted into the study of law, gave it up to become a hack doctor until he finally found himself as a man of letters. Whatever his penchant for speaking without due thought, he had sense enough to switch professions until he latched on to something that worked for him.

It is hard to think of an occupation that prohibits artistry and creativity. You can be a creative doctor, lawyer, merchant, or thief; the arts hold no monopoly on originality and imagination. So don't allow yourself to become obsessed with any undertaking you're ill-suited for, or have difficulty coming to terms with. If it's not for you for whatever reason, don't let a favorite teacher or a how-to word-flogger lure you into it. The result, inevitably, is unhappiness.

In this vein, *Dead Poets Society* by Tom Schulman creeps disturbingly to mind. In the film, Robin Williams portrays the supposedly brilliant and lovable teacher John Keating, who stresses the ultra-importance of being "artistic" and "creative." Preaching a gospel of cloudy aesthetics, he plays brainwashing, mind-fucking games with a class of sophomoric, impressionable preppies, and the audience is supposed to applaud his intrusions. Happily, no good comes of this effrontery, but somehow Williams emerges as a martyr. For all the wrong reasons.

Yet something else emerges, a worthy notion that should not be dismissed or condemned because of its on-screen presentation. The writer is spreading the credo of "Seize the day" and its corollary: Never surrender to the mundanity of life. And that's a fine credo.

46

4

RUNNING THE BASES
You've Got To
Hit It First

Writers never relax. There are times when just about everybody, at the end of the day's disorders, lies in bed listening to their nerves jangle, but the case of the writer is more than marginally different. The writer never puts his work to bed. There's always a whirligig going lickety-split inside his skull. Deep in the horny hours of the night, you'll find that your mind will amaze you with its discomposure. You'll worry about story construction, plot points, the apposite word or phrase that escapes you—things that don't come to mind when you want them to, and things that come effortlessly when you don't.

Writers write everywhere except (I'm not even sure of this) underwater. Richard Brooks took a pen and a pad with him to the toilet. Otherwise, and God forbid, he might have lost a stylish sentence, or even a word.

James Thurber would go into a trance at the dinner table. The family around him would say, "He's writing again." They were exceptionally perceptive. Most of those nearest and dearest to us do not respond favorably to the odd but valid conceit, propounded by Victor Hugo, that "A man is not idle because he is absorbed in thought. There is a visible labor and there is an invisible labor." Try laying that on your wife while she's scrubbing the floor.

Where and when a writer writes is a highly individual and personal decision. Eric Roth, who wrote *Forrest Gump*, prefers an ocean view:

> I work upstairs. In a small room. A room without much room to pace. A room with a view of the sea. I love and hate that room. It is a place of great joy and terrible failure. A place I earned in both respects. Good writing does not come easily, except in those precious times, those fleeting moments when, unannounced, God enters the room. The search then, for me, in that little room with a view of the sea, is for one brief shining moment, to find God.
>
> Screenwriting is a bastardized art form at best. A screenwriter is one part novelist, one part playwright, one part salesman, one part liar. It is a craft. And there are many who are particularly artful at their craft. But it is a form that needs a stage and without a stage it is nothing but a good bookend. That said, I love what I do. I love the solitude. I love the adventure. I love the discovery. I love the play between what the words tell us, and the visuals say. I love the movie . . . the sound of the wind maybe, and the music, echoing the wind, maybe, and the quality of light that seems just right for the sound and the music, and that man I never met before, but know so well now, walking over the hill, across the next valley, trying to find "his" way home. I love the movie . . . until, many times, alas, I see the movie. How wrong I was.

Alone, in the room with a view of the sea, you are rarely wrong. There is the courage to fail. Each new screenplay another possibility. A world you've never been in before. Finding the glorious details. How a wall was built in 1916, how a gambler's mind works, how to ride a horse . . . and yet, something else is at work, the need to say something about yourself, that is so exhilarating or so frightening, it can only be on paper. Men in overcoats talking in dark rooms. Lovers meeting for a brief affair. Armies marching. The hope you can leave behind some part of yourself and find out why that man was walking over that hill, across that next valley, and why he was trying to find his way home.

I work upstairs. In a small room. I get to write movies.. . .

49

Some writers have no problem with time-place determinants for their work. "A man," said Samuel Johnson, "may write at any time if he will set himself doggedly to it." However, there are day writers and night writers, each of whom responds to the mysterious dictates of some internal clock. There are writers who bang away in a hotel room with all the curtains drawn. I know one writer who steers his van to the most spectacular vista he can find and, ignoring the immensity of the Earth spread out before him, sets up shop on the shoulder of the road. Then there are those whose anima pulls them to a specific topography: Günter Grass claimed he could only write in Berlin.

Laura Z. Hobson too had a favorite haunt for writing. A woman of vitality, grace, and outspokenness, she was seen by the more introverted among us as a bit daunting. She insisted she could only write in New York, a confidence she shared with me when she was writing, and writing well, in Hollywood. I found her baffling, not for her views on benevolent geography, but because she was beautiful despite what I in my twenties considered her advanced age. She was perhaps forty-five at the time.

A vendetta directed toward your workplace can in itself become the base for a blockage. Whatever the rationale, highly personal imperatives can mirror your distress and plaguey awareness that you're expendable wherever you are. Perhaps the producer/director doesn't appreciate your type of uniqueness and would prefer a uniqueness more compatible with his own.

You also know that in the eyes of a studio executive you're only as good as the last time you went to bat. Once in a while—it happens with blue-moon infrequency—a screenwriter gets big enough to allow himself a few indulgences, but no more than a threadbare few because if your last picture was less than a smash you think you'll never work again, although there are a few executives who will allow a writer three whiffs before he's relegated to the ranks of the superannuated or, as the Brits say, made redundant. One hit compensates for three subsequent flops—this is known as "catching a thermal"—riding out the K's until you connect with another dinger.

But you're expected to knock the ball out of the park each time. Hollywood courts a miracle worker, a savior rather than the garden-variety, run-of-the-mill hero. If you ever achieve that exalted station, whether as savior or hero, don't relax, not even for a minute. Another baseball axiom applies here: When you're hot, stay hungry. And another: Don't get high or you'll get humbled.

Producers generally are a tough sell, particularly if you're young and untried, because they are, for the most part, neophobic. A discouraged young writer once observed that the best way to break into pictures was to get your second job first. Producers also seem to favor propagation wood that comes from elsewhere, supplied by the playwright and the novelist. As a neophyte, your best chance for work will probably come from an entrepreneur who hasn't the bread to hire a heavy hitter with impressive credits. There are always exceptions. I got my first job at M-G-M writing a picture called *Take the High Ground* because producer Dore Schary wanted somebody with military experience and I was fresh out of the Marine Corps. It seemed that every other combat-weary veteran in the Writers Guild was signed up and heavily occupied.

On a dark, dank, summer day, the kind displaced Easterners relish because it provides a brief respite from the otherwise incessant sun-broil, there appeared at Metro's Iron Lung a distinguished novelist from a prairie state. He wrote an authentic brand of muscular prose; he was in Culver City to do a picture based on one of his books.

He was eager to get started. His secretary told him there was no need to hurry—he was on the studio payroll—but that Mr. Thalberg wanted to see him before he began, and would be contacting him directly.

This was one Midwesterner who looked the part—a strung-out series of leathery leannesses with hands and shoulders that belonged to a much larger man.

The first month at the studio he spent reading while chewing toothpicks, but that was too passive an outlet for a man of his brooding sensibilities. He couldn't work on a book—the possibility of an imminent phone call shot holes in his concentration. The second month he decided to learn Spanish.

Every week for the next two months a Berlitz man in a Basque beret reported to the Iron Lung. The Midwesterner finally grew tired of it; the Basque kept trying to sell him a dreary script about the hilarious adventures of a Spanish-language teacher in America, and Pedro Calderón's ceremonial dramas were as dull in his native language as they were in English. "I think I'll learn to play the guitar," the Plainsman said, and soon he was striking chords and lifting his lanky voice in a folk tune.

For five months he waited for a summons that never came. He began to doubt that Thalberg really existed. He thought of writing him a witty note, or phoning him, or storming the gates of the sanctum to beard the god-monster in his den. But each time he considered it, Thalberg grew in size and strength until he overran the boundaries of the mind, and the writer would banish the thought and reach for the guitar.

Then one day Irving Thalberg walked into his office, smiling cheerfully. He introduced himself. He said, "Can you be in my office in five minutes?"

But the Plainsman couldn't keep the appointment because when Thalberg introduced himself, the writer shit in his pants. He left town the next day.

Fear. That's what thins out the ranks.

* * *

Dore Schary was the key contributor to M-G-M's program of pictures when he served as vice-president in charge of production, that is, when he ran the studio. For a brief period he was the right man for the right job at the right time, possibly because of his enthusiastic endorsement of the reigning values of American culture.

A champion of middle-class morality, he was the Great Scoutmaster of the Movies. His novelist daughter Jill once described him as "the last man in America who believed in God, politicians, and movie stars."

Schary expected his assistants to share with him their ideas on any picture in progress. He didn't enjoy the allegiance of yes-men. But inevitably in any studio, in every hierarchy there is an army of ass-kissers, a veritable Greek chorus eager to maintain their residency, and to be counted on both sides of the fence.

Dore once asked a personal assistant if a certain story progression, somewhat obscure, needed an added scene or two for clarification.

"Well," the young man said frowning, stroking his jaw, narrowing an eye, lumping together all the external manifestations of deep thought, "well," he repeated, "yes and no."

"If there's anything worse than a yes-man," Schary told him, "it's a yes-and-no-man."

A curious observation, possibly self-destructive on an unconscious level. For it was Schary, the liberal, the feminist, the human and civil rights activist who, at the infamous Waldorf meeting with other film executives, endorsed the legitimacy of loyalty oaths, leading inevitably to the blacklist that began the panic of political persecution in Hollywood.

At times I too have suffered a tendency to self-destruct, not on a political level to be sure, but on two occasions that involved Schary. The first cropped up when I arrived at M-G-M to be interviewed by Dore for *Take the High Ground.* I got as far as the reception desk at the main entrance to the studio when I lost my voice, completely. Retreating in a near panic, I found a saloon around the corner. Behind the bar, most unexpectedly, was an old Marine buddy. He fueled me with steaming black coffee, my voice returned, I got the job.

Two weeks later I was leaving the Iron Lung at the end of the day when a voice called my name. It was Dore. He apologized for not having read the pages I had funneled to him. He had been busy, tied up on the phone and so forth. "Tell you what," he said, "I'll read them tonight, you come out to the house tomorrow morning, and we'll discuss them while I'm taking a shower."

All the rotten, gothic tales I had heard about the treatment of writers in Hollywood hit me at that moment.

"What'll we do then," I snarled, "play unnatural games?" and huffed off.

The enormity of my rebellion didn't register until that evening when I told Lorry, my wife, about it. "The hell with him," she said. And then the phone rang, as if it were a prop in a bad movie. It was Mrs. Schary's secretary inviting us to dinner. Dore, apparently, was embarrassed by what he had said, but why, I asked myself, had I, on the cusp of getting what I wanted, placed obstacles in my way to keep from achieving it? On some deep subliminal level, was I afraid that I'd fail at the job, get fired as a woeful incompetent? And therefore, to keep from getting ignominiously canned, I canned myself. Just as a crackpot, afraid of being disliked by his peers, acts nastily to give them an understandable reason to dislike him. 53

In any field where the entry level is difficult, you can land a job and still get humbled before you have a chance to celebrate. People in just about every branch of pixbiz have on occasion been subjected to some rite of passage.

Ed Morey, Jr. was hired in the production arm of an independent picture company owned and operated by the King brothers. One of them—I don't recall which—liked to break up the daily routine with one or more refreshing showers. Nothing wrong with that, but he liked to take them sitting down.

Ed spent his first month of employment searching for and finally finding a wooden stool that met King's specifications.

No work on a writer's preparations would be complete without touching on the value of cinema schools. "Anything worth teaching," observed Oscar Wilde, "can never be taught." Epigrammatic but untrue, although film schools can only provide the soil that nurtures growth. Growth, essentially, is up to you. But they can smooth the roughness and sweeten the acerbities by teaching how to deal with them as we stumble across the uneven cobblestones of adversity.

Film schools provide four years of devotion to the craft of picture-making: writing, directing, editing, cinematography. And other preliminary arcana you could have picked up in less time on a studio stage in an era before there were film schools.

The best way to become a screenwriter is to write a screenplay someone will buy. The best way to get a job in a studio is to know someone who can clinch it for you. The third best way is to go to film school. You'll not only learn some things of intrinsic value but you'll acquire a certain cachet en passant: Your credentials will appeal to those in a hiring position the same way a young person applying for a metropolitan newspaper job will get preference if he has graduated from a good journalism school—Columbia or the University of Missouri, for example. Shows you're serious, devoting all that time preparing, practicing what you hope some day to perform.

The benefits of cinema schooling are further enhanced, I feel, if you combine your major with great chewy gobs of English and American literature, plus a dishy chunk of creative writing not limited to pumping out movie or TV scripts.

Perhaps the best thing about film school is that it gives you precious time to learn your craft, and imposes a discipline in practicing it. The earliest college curriculum devoted to film was established at the University of Southern California in 1929. Since then, film schools have become gathering places for young and eager filmmakers to bang out their first five-finger exercises, a latter-day Mermaid Tavern or an Algonquin Round Table for novices of promise to exchange notions with their peers and professors. It is where they learn for themselves the three ingredients that Darryl Zanuck insisted were essential to a movie: "story, story, story."

With that determination Zanuck shared a belief with an authoritative predecessor. "The most important contribution to a picture is made by the writer," Irving Thalberg said. Then, in keeping with his corporate policy, he added, "And we must do everything we can to keep him from finding out." Certainly he was more charitable than Jack Warner, whose generic characterization of writers was "shmucks with Underwoods."

Thalberg was right about craft, but he wasn't infallible about technologies. Color and sound, he thought, were fads that would pass in the night, neither of them to hold any enduring place in pictures. Charlie Chaplin went further; he dismissed the entire industry early and in toto. "The cinema," he declared in 1916, "is little more than a fad."

Practice does not make perfect, but it can sharpen your skills, assuming you learn good habits that you'll use every day. Which in itself is a good habit. Even without schooling, try to work on a regular schedule at least five days a week. Or at the very least with as much regularity as your life can afford. To borrow a saying from track and field, "When you are not practicing, remember that somewhere someone is, and when you meet him he will win."

Which raises the issue of competition.

55

If further proof is needed to illustrate the difficulty of screenwriting at the entry level, consider:

More than 35,000 original scripts for theatrical or TV films were registered in 1997 at the Writers Guild of America West. Only a fraction of them was optioned and only a fraction of that fraction was produced. In 1998 just under 40,000 scripts were registered with it. Add to that the 8,000 to 10,000 scripts registered with the Writers Guild East (based in New York) on a yearly basis, and you're in for some competition.

As a screenwriter you will compete against skilled and established practitioners of the trade, as well as mediocrities, hacks, hustlers and the spiritual descendants of the man from South Carolina who wrote to John Meston, the producer of *Gunsmoke*.

"Dear Mr. Meston," the letter began in accordance with custom, "I heard you on the radio when you said CBS would pay $1,000 for a scripp. What is a scripp?"

II

Writing in Hollywood (or Anywhere Else)

5

GETTING GOING
Prejudice and the Script

Before you rewrite you have to write, and before you write you have to embrace an idea, a concept, a notion, a reverie, a tincture of a soupçon of a point of view, a grain of truth, a trace of prejudice.

William Faulkner showed up time and again at M-G-M to replenish his collection of U.S. coins. His closest friend on the lot was Jack Sher, a screenwriter and a former sports columnist with the *Detroit Free Press*. They were inseparable, lunching together, rambling around the back lot, sharing drinks in the evening.

And then one day, another companion of Jack's raised a discomforting issue. "How can you tolerate Faulkner?" he asked. "How can you accept his anti-Semitism—it's all over his books."

Next day Faulkner noticed Jack's unease and asked what was

wrong. "Bill," Jack asked, "is it true that you don't like Jews?" "That's right," Faulkner said. Jack's face mirrored his sadness and regret. Quickly Faulkner said, "You've got to understand, Jack—I don't like Gentiles either."

Their friendship continued to prosper. Jack himself wasn't all that enthusiastic about the human race.

Some writers sit down and immediately and unceremoniously put words to paper. Some writers have to think first about what they want to say and how they intend to say it. The depth of their cogitations is evident.

The first large question that pops up is: How to Begin. Nicholas Kazan, who wrote *Reversal of Fortune* says:

> I begin by writing notes. Character sketches, lines of dialogue, whole scenes I suddenly see or hear (often without knowing who is speaking or what is happening or where the scene fits into the story), the last line or image, a dozen different openings, sustained and often nasty arguments with myself, attempts to find the mythic underpinnings of the narrative, harsh analyses of pitfalls and how to avoid them, outlines, more outlines, detailed outlines, and so forth. Never cards.
>
> My notes are *always* longer than the finished script. And they're fun to do, because I never approach them in an organized fashion. I free-associate. If I hear dialogue, I write it down; if I wonder how a character will evolve, I analyze various possibilities. Then I get a peculiar idea for an underlying visual metaphor and explore it. The next day, it's forgotten. I'm always on the watch for clichés: I nourish them until they're in full flower, then turn them on their heads.
>
> When I finally write the script, I use the many outlines, but barely refer to other notes, except for certain moments when I suddenly remember something delicious and dig back to find it. Usually it has turned to dust.
>
> I don't begin writing the screenplay until I've

analyzed the thing to death and cannot *bear* to write notes any longer. I've reached critical mass and must explode.

At this point, I used to write a draft in ten days. I'd put it aside for two days, then rewrite—again in two days. Two more days off, another ten-day wonder, and at the end of 34 days I'd have a document suitable for scrutiny by my friends.

The great virtue of the method was the energy required to achieve it and the energy thereby communicated to the script. It was all done in white heat and the result sometimes burned.

Just as frequently, however, the burn victim was me. However thrilling that 34-day process was, however intimately it connected me with my own creative forces, however often I was visited by the muse, the improvisatory nature of the process often created structure problems. I'd find that scenes I loved, scenes with sparkle and wit and contradiction, led me in the wrong direction. And painfully so.

In my experience, cutting a great scene (or at least a scene which has great importance for *me)* is like amputating a limb: Even though it's not there anymore, I can't stop thinking about it and trying to use it.

What's worse: One powerful but misguided scene can propel me into a series of scenes with considerable entertainment value but no narrative purpose.

So, with considerable regret, I have changed my process.

I now move slowly through my first drafts. I go back. I cut, I polish. If I even *wonder* whether something is wrong, I change it. If a warning bell goes off, I wince and *listen* (instead of turning up the stereo). In making the necessary changes, I ignore the beauty of my scenes, the endearing character touches: I cut them quickly, before I become too attached.

As you gather, ugly decisions are made. The writing is not as much fun, not as sloppy and exuberant, but the results, I am sad to say, seem better. Instead of finishing a first draft in 34 days, it takes three times as long, but the draft seems to hold up. I am older, wiser, and no longer a victim of my own enthusiasm.

Some writers prepare by doing nothing that's detectable except stare with blank eyes into the nearest void, like ravaged victims of autohypnosis. "I have to do nothing," a writer friend tells me, "before I can do something."

Resorting to this sort of anodyne can be injurious to relationships. It's hard for a spouse, a roommate, a close companion to realize that you're actually working when you appear to be off the charts of apperceptive consciousness, for one of the most difficult activities in the world to explain is quiescent thinking.

Once you get beyond this point and begin the physical act of writing, ideas you had never anticipated present themselves like a cherished intruder.

"Until one is committed," Goethe observed, "there is hesitancy, the chance to draw back, always ineffectiveness, concerning all acts of initiative (and creation). There is one elementary truth the ignorance of which kills countless ideas and splendid plans: that the moment one definitely commits oneself . . . all sorts of things occur to help one that would never otherwise have occurred. A whole stream of events issues from the discussion . . . which no man would have dreamed would come his way. Whatever you can do or dream you can do, begin it. Boldness has . . . power and magic in it. Begin it now."

Power and magic. Both at times have taken a peculiar turn as a subject of movies: the power to vanquish death, and its corollary, the magic of a desacralized creed. *Ghost* deals with paranormalcy, *Dead Again* with reincarnation. *Field of Dreams* is possibly the best, certainly the best crafted in the postmodern supernatural genre. Both are popular desiderata of our times, promising eternal rewards without striving for them through faith or good works. Angels walk the Earth, while on the dark and bloody side of the moon the inheritors of Bela Lugosi explore the oral gratification of vampirism, much of it served up with the legerdemain of special effects.

Ideas can come from anywhere—an experience, a fantasy, a journey down an imaginary road. Somerset Maugham was prone to develop urbane and witty short stories from Yiddish jokes; Thomas Hardy wrote great books from a few paragraphs of newspaper reportage. You can write about anything, anybody. One man's heavy is another's hero. Nathan Hale was a despicable spy to the British in the Revolutionary War, but enough of a patriot and a hero to merit a statue at Yale, his alma mater. Such are the blinkers of nationalism. Sean O'Casey's protagonist in *The Plow and the Stars* is a terrorist. To those who react with understandable squeamishness to his activities and those of his confreres, he says, "A few hundhred scrawls o' chaps with a couple o' guns and Rosary beads, again' a hundhred thousand thrained men with horse, feet an' artillery . . . an' he wants us to fight fair!"

In *Forrest Gump* (based on the novel by Winston Groom), Eric 63 Roth's lead played by Tom Hanks is as far removed from the ranks of conventional heroes as O'Casey's. An amiable retardate, he roams a world where all is accident. He falls into one random toilet after another and turns up, again and again, unsullied as a rosebud.

It is bad form and worse dramaturgy to aid and abet your protagonist with undiminished dumb luck because it tilts the field in his favor.

If chance is a factor in the piece, it should always favor the heavy because it then raises the odds against the hero's attaining his goal. Moreover, the most difficult and possibly the most boring hero to write about is a totally decent human being, a perfect, gentle knight without a blemish or even an approximation of an Achilles' heel.

Now it is time to refute the rule; like every other law of drama, it can, in knowledgeable hands, be repealed.

Forrest Gump's unswerving good fortune, totally indifferent to his sweetness, his nobility, and his quintessential innocence pays off with a kind of wry and perverse appositeness. The essential Gump comes with a built-in Achilles' heel of daunting proportions—his retardation. His journey through time and space, in war and peace and work and love is sufficiently chaotic and absurd to accommodate his brand of flakiness. Also, anything goes in comedy and fairy tales when they are as well made as *Forrest Gump*. But to get it made took nine years and constituted a praiseworthy rebellion against accepted form. *Forrest* so violates the classic or the romantic or the realistic mold of a movie that writing it might be said to constitute an aesthetic mutiny against the usual Hollywooden procedures.

If you're prone to rebel against authority, if you have the proclivities of a mutineer, if Aristotle's just not your bottle, or if you seek for whatever reason a road less traveled, you might find yourself a protagonist who deviates from the pattern as much as does witless young Gump. Further, you might even ignore the "law" enshrining unity of action (Aristotle's precept that a dramatic work must embrace a single plot), and find yourself welcome to the excellent company of those who have walked that way before you: Altman, John Cassavetes, Adrien Joyce (Carole Eastman, who wrote *Five Easy Pieces*), and many more. When they rejected "rules" of craft, the results were exciting, arresting, disturbing and exceedingly satisfying. Look at their work and you'll see that the intensity they assign to the conflict between strong and memorable characters overwhelms the niceties of compliance to the rules. There's nothing neat about reality (which goes beyond fictional realism) and that's what they strive for.

There are other writers who deplore the application of any system of rules to the composition of plays and screenplays because they seem to feel that somehow the work is diminished or robotized by it. Why? Possibly because, as each generation acts out its own anxieties, we postmoderns have a tendency to extol spontaneity; any sort of systemic discipline interferes with our expressing it.

Many writers advocate some knowledge of the rules in order to violate them or to make fun of them. Bertolt Brecht ridicules the deus ex machina in *The Threepenny Opera* by introducing a decree from Queen Victoria which out of nowhere delivers Mack the Knife from the scaffold. Woody Allen makes a great joke of the mechanism and uses it effectively to end *Mighty Aphrodite*.

Picasso in his rose and blue periods did representational oils before ignoring the rules of classical realism and perspective. James

Joyce wrote *A Portrait of the Artist as a Young Man*, an immaculate, conventional, autobiographical novel before he went brilliant and radical with *Ulysses*.

Fairy tales like *Forrest Gump* are dandy when you've been around the Horn a few times, but if you're trying to break into screenwriting, it's best, most authorities agree, to write about what you know about yourself and others in your charmed circle. Sometimes it is the others who give you trouble, for writing is a deliberate, often a rude invasion of privacy. A writer will reveal anybody's innermost secrets if he finds them the least bit usable. He not only kisses and tells but he has no compunction whatsoever in telling whom other people are kissing.

Kal Daniels, the baseball player, could never, by his own admission, be a writer. "I want to be good on the field and a gentleman off the field," he said. In one fell swoop of a declarative sentence he eliminated himself from the clan (about which I'm sure he didn't give a good goddamn), for "there never was a good writer who was a gentleman." Thus spake Alexandre Dumas, the Elder, in warning the civilian population of Paris never to confide in a writer unless they wanted to have their private lives unfurled in public like a flag on parade. Civilians, note well: Never confide in a writer unless you're prepared to see yourself in print, onstage or on-screen. So cautioned Truman Capote in Jay Presson Allen's play.

Writers aren't confined to dishing out gossip or violating confidentiality. They draw heavily on what they've lived through, what they've seen, what they've heard about. They thrive on anecdotes and the experiences of others. Even when they adapt a play or a novel to the screen, they're prone to impose their own values and experiences on it.

Good writers, it may be added, are more dependent on their imaginations than on their personal experiences. More good writers are immured in a room with the shades drawn than there are among brawling activists out in the world, kicking up a storm and blabbing about it.

It has also been said that in any artist's experience nothing is ever completely lost; somewhere in the depth of consciousness there resides a remembrance, however inchoate, of the panoramic past. Not true, at least in my experience. To make sure you don't lose it, keep a

65

diary or a journal, or a pad or a tape recorder by your bedside every night. (I've tried them all. Switching on the light beside the bed disturbed my wife's sleep. I thought I could remedy the vexation by resorting to a tape recorder. The first time I talked into it Lorry jackknifed into wakefulness. "What the hell are you up to?" she wanted to know, and that was the end of the experiment. Now I get up and stumble into the adjoining room to jot my notes.)

As regards the keeping of a journal or a diary: It's for your eyes only, and not to be shared with any significant other, including a spouse. Exposing it in an undigested, adumbrated form prompts the diarist to sacrifice his own true and innermost thoughts for the approbation of others, which is inhibiting and can lead only to self-censorship; so when the time does come to draw from it, he resurrects platitudes.

A corollary: Never throw anything away. Dr. Johnson reminds us that "To a poet nothing can be useless." Between "the wild vicissitudes of taste" and the changes that time produce, there is the possibility that there's always somebody out there interested in buying something—a buyer who sees your story in a new, attractive light. There are countless examples of pictures, such as *Platoon*, that took years to get produced, and books, such as *Catch-22*, that took years to get published. And, of course, there is for those of us blessed with the gift of hindsight, the shocking history of *Pride and Prejudice*. Completed by Jane Austen in 1797, it was published in 1813, four years before her death.

Another preparatory step in your career as a screenwriter: See a lot of movies, and don't go only to relax and enjoy them. If a picture whets and inspires, see it at least twice. As Yogi Berra noted, "You can observe a lot just by watching." Consider it work. Think about it, not only whether it was "good," "enjoyable," or "elevating" (or any number of adjectives of positive reinforcement), or "bad," i.e., "boring" or "poorly done" but why it succeeds or fails, at least in your mind. There is to my knowledge no objective formula to define "good" work. Matthew Arnold, perhaps the greatest literary critic in English history, couldn't come up with anything better than "the best that is known and thought in the world." Is his best your best, or mine? Who's to say, when the whole canon, so rich and diversified, is a matter of personal taste?

So see movies and read scripts. Even if you live in a tree or in a town without sidewalks, there should be a video store or a public library available to you. In the stacks you'll find, usually, photocopied scripts, anthologies of screenplays or screenplays in book form, and copies of *Scenario*, the quarterly magazine that publishes outstanding screenplays. Study them. Think about why the writer did what he did. Why does he start the way he does? Why does he end the way he does? How did he get there? How would you have done it differently?

Craft and its mechanics are not self-evident, nor are they acquired by most writers through osmosis. They come through study and application and to each seeker in her own way, just as the creative process itself varies with the individual.

Regardless of individuation, craft and technique cannot be ignored by beginners or anyone else for that matter, although the two groups differ in their approach to them. Veterans apply their craft subconsciously while novices are prone to ignore it out of ignorance or inexperience.

67

Craft can be taught, art cannot. Craft is skill. Art is like a great untamed river. It flows from many tributaries but no one seems able to locate its source. Great talent is a mystery to those who witness it, as well as to those who have it.

Consider Konstantin Stanislavsky (1863–1938), founder and resident genius of the Moscow Art Company. His methods were unusual, and not the least of them was his inclination to open the doors of the theater to anyone who might wander in to watch rehearsals. One day, it is said, a rather nondescript passerby ambled in and, when the opportunity arose, humbly introduced himself to the renowned maestro. He was a shoe salesman visiting the metropolis on business. In his hometown of Odessa he had dabbled in amateur theatricals, and it occurred to him, respectfully, that the great director might allow him to work onstage with actors of whom critics concurred made up the finest repertory group in the Western world.

Stanislavsky was amenable. Rehearsals began; it wasn't long before the stranger's competence confused and confounded the professionals. A member of the cast was chosen to approach the director and raise the disturbing question: How is it that this ungainly shoe hawker from a tank town on the Black Sea, with little training and no professional experience whatsoever, how could this . . . this . . . hick hold his own with the most celebrated actors in Europe?

"Simple," Stanislavsky replied. "He's got talent."

Not all of us are blessed with that sort of dazzling ability, and so we pick up clues about craftsmanship wherever we can. In searching them out, apply yourself to books. I suppose people can live without books, but writers can't. If you don't find them a necessary delight, you're training for the wrong Olympics. Examine novels which have been made into films. You'll find that many of them, as Jean Cocteau said in another context, "are alike except in everything." Why is this? Why are the demands of the camera so different from the requisites of the book? Or is it something else—the improvements or (to use an Irishism) the disimprovements of a producer, a director or a screenwriter? What motivated the changes? Were they logical, dramatic, or the product of an erratic pulsebeat or a cankered childhood?

A vagrant sidebar to our investigation might point out that writers of books and writers of screenplays have been known to differ as regards the utmost degree of adversity encountered, each in pursuit of her chosen genre. Novelists, as would be expected, tend generally to declare that it is more difficult to treat the whole person in a book, not only his surface self but the meanderings of his subliminal and unconscious impulses (those that are dramatically relevant). Playwrights and screenwriters, as a matter of course, usually concur that capturing the complete man within the constraints and confinements of their shared medium makes the work even more demanding.

I see no reason for debate. Both disciplines are tough enough. As for the adaptation of novels to the stage or screen, the list is long and the problems daunting. My adventures in turning *Raintree County* into a screenplay was a long tumble through a spiny thicket without end, and has all the makings of a cautionary tale. The remarkable novel by Ross Lockridge, Jr., more than a thousand convoluted pages in length, did not, I fear, emerge triumphantly on-screen. The picture yielded a plenitude of flaws, not the least of which I inherited: the studio's concept of John Wycliff Shawnessy, played by Montgomery Clift.

There are many times in the making of movies that impediments sprout from the money nexus. The production entity, eager to realize the largest return on its investment, tries to attract as wide an audience as is humanly or devilishly possible by twisting the basic or source material to include a little something for everyone, and to delete anything that might offend anybody. Of course, it can't be done, not even by the masterful Charles Dickens. Of probably the most heart-rending scene in all of nineteenth-century literature, Oscar Wilde wrote, "One must have a heart of stone to read the death of Little Nell without laughing."

The studio ends up, usually, by pleasing nobody and aggrieving all. As a writer, you will at times be invited to eviscerate your own screenplay—to collude with a director or a producer against yourself. A little change here and a little change there doesn't seem like much. What harm can it do to the total canvas?

Plenty. That's how many pictures of bright promise take a half gainer into the toilet. I include *Raintree* among them. In the picture, John Shawnessy marries Susanna Drake (Elizabeth Taylor), who is ravishingly beautiful and mentally unbalanced. During the darkest days of the Civil War she disappears with their small son into the Deep South of her past. Bereft of his wife and child, John joins the Federal forces, as should have been expected, because he has always been an active and outspoken abolitionist. But the lions of M-G-M ruled that if he joined up for political reasons, his behavior would, despite the passage of a hundred years, alienate the unreconstructed Southern market. So they supplied him with what they considered a more ennobling reason for his enlistment: to find Susanna. Which is pretty silly when you regard the larger elements at stake: the freedom of a race, the destruction of a nation.

I've not always succeeded in defying the corporate opposition, but I do try, and I respectfully advise you to resist the candied compromise, the surrendered concession. Try to stick to your muttons as best you can, by all the means you can, for as long as you can. While you'll have to live in some degree of ferocious harmony with the adversary for the duration of the shoot, try not to be overly obedient. It does nothing to ease the relationship and only makes you sore at yourself.

I know from bleak experience that there's just so much defeat you can ward off by defiance. I could not prevail against the studio's executive decision to send Shawnessy off to war to find his poor lost nutty spouse. But I did manage, after many a wrangle, to retain the story's major theme of miscegenation, without which Susanna's psychosis lacked motivation.

When writers do cave in, it usually begins with what can be rationalized as a small point, a midget of a point. It won't affect the overall screenplay, the writer tells himself, i.e., it can't hurt me. This response is termed in psychological circles as "cognitive dissonance," an ungainly locution but a meaningful one, the belief that "I can handle it come what may," the dogged assurance that a threat of calamity will somehow bypass me. It was an attitude held by most Marines in WWII: "They might get the son of a bitch in the next foxhole but they won't get me," or by pack-a-day smokers who believe they'll escape lung cancer.

Director Sam Zimbalist presented a constant challenge to writers attempting to resist his demands. He further insisted that writers follow his abbreviated primer in story construction. It included four articles of faith no good screenplay, he believed, could succeed without—a quartet of scenes that were requisite to any picture under his stewardship. They were 1) a bragus scene (Yiddish, rhymes with Magus), meaning angry, i.e., an impactive conflict between hero and heavy; 2) a piece of pain, i.e., a suffering heroine encouraging audience empathy; 3) a fuck scene, not necessarily literal in the days of heavy censorship, but possibly figurative or metaphysical, sealed or symbolized with a kiss.

All well and good. But it was Sam's fourth element that drove writers mad: a "piece of magic," he called it, and it was, of course, indefinable. Yet what I suppose was so exasperating was that we all knew what he meant. It was that rare, mysterious, just-short-of-attainable *je ne sais quoi* that separates the bad from the brilliant. It was indeed a puzzlement, the kind Luis Polonia complained about when he was released by the N.Y. Yankees. "There's only one thing the Yankees are interested in," he said, "and I don't know what that is."

There are few concessions or compromises in the classics.

Perhaps that's why they've provided the triggering spark for aspiring writers—some aspiring writers, that is. You might look into them and note how with the passage of time the themes, the characters, the plots of every prodigious talent from Aeschylus to Beckett have been repeated, or turned upside down, inside out or ass backwards as generation after generation of hopefuls has applied them to their own times, conceits and concepts, borrowing or, to use a euphemism of fairly recent Hollywood coinage, "paying homage." You can't ignore them because their themes are universal, comprising the elemental verities of Western thought.

There are innumerable ways of giving an old favorite a new configuration. How many haircuts of the Oedipal conflict have you seen?

Many a classic has been lifted in toto, translated to another language without attribution, and played before an audience that wasn't even aware of its provenience.

Louie Calhern, arriving in New York from L.A., was picked up by a cab driver who recognized him from his many fine characterizations in movies. "Mr. Calhern, what brings you here?" the cabbie inquired. "I'm doing *King Lear*," Louie told him.

The cabbie's reaction was so violent he almost slammed his hack into the car ahead.

"In Yiddish?!" he asked.

Not all remakes are drawn from antiquity. Anything that turns a big buck will be copied and revised. Hollywood is a business, its harvest replete with remakes and sequels. Example: All those kick-ass operas numbered like Super Bowls. Not all remakes are forgettable. *The Most Dangerous Game*, a marvelous adventure story by Richard Connell, has been made at least four times. *The Front Page*, by Ben Hecht and Charles MacArthur, has had numerous playings. In one of them, retitled *His Girl Friday*, Hildy Johnson was altered to become a woman because a stellar role was needed to fulfill a commitment with Rosalind Russell. This kind of sex change is known as "switching the testicles."

The most thought-provoking instance of testicle-switching in postmodern pictures is evidenced with *Thelma & Louise*: a unique species of the buddy picture, formerly the exclusive domain of masculinity, but this time two women take to the road and invoke distressing issues about the age-old war between the sexes. What emerges is the iron exigency of establishing a lasting and immediate peace between our two great genders.

And there is no peace for the writer, regardless of gender, who takes her work seriously, who strives to make it true even when it's fiction. Here's how Callie Khouri, who wrote *Thelma & Louise*, discerns the difficulty:

> I have only one or two basic problems with being a screenwriter. Everything else is copasetic. Here's problem number one: I only tell true stories. Even though I've made the thing up out of whole cloth, there is a part of my mind that just flatly refuses to see it that way. It says, "Yup, that's pretty much exactly how it happened," or "No, no, no, it didn't happen like that at all. You want to know the real story? It went like this . . ." Consequently, there's only so much you can change, otherwise it stops being true and starts becoming fiction. And I don't write fiction. I write true stories. Except that I make them up. You can start to see the problem.
>
> It's hard for others to see that the story in my mind is a complete event that occurred a certain way on a particular day, and to change it means you have to lie. Now, I don't mind lying if it helps make my point, but why lie if you don't have to? I like to save the lying for when I tell studio executives that I love their ideas.
>
> It makes it very difficult to watch my movies, because it's like watching someone else portray something that really happened (that never actually happened), so it's only an approximation of the real thing. There are those heavenly moments when an actor so understands the character that they become the truth, they become that character and you forget that they are not the real (totally made-up) person. But that's all too rare.
>
> Problem number two: I have no idea where any of this stuff comes from. Every time I sit down to write,

I'm fairly certain that "it" is not going to be there. Why should it be? "It" is busy. With other good writers. This causes me to approach writing with a certain amount of trepidation. Make that dread. Every time the phone rings I half expect to hear the same authoritative voice of the car alarm going, "Warning! You are a fraud. Step a-way from the computer!" This in no way approximates the positive, life-affirming experience I thought writing was going to be, before I actually started doing it. Every time I finish a script, there is a peculiar feeling of awe, where I have to sit back and say to myself, "Hey, who wrote this?" That was awfully nice of them to put my name on it. I sure hope no one finds out that it wasn't me. I do wish it was a little better, though.

I think it's why people in the movie business who don't write don't understand why we can be such an emotional bunch. It's a very strange process. On the one hand, you have to care more than anybody else in the world about getting the story out straight, true and full. On the other hand, you have to not care too much, so that when it's taken away for others to have their way with, you won't come completely unglued. Which you will anyway.

Mainly, it's hard not to feel like a fool. But everything else is copasetic.

Another genre that until recently was designated For Men Only is the justice, or retribution, picture. It's been a long, hard and bumpy road from the mist-enshrouded rock where the Count of Monte Cristo stood on his treasure island and vowed vengeance upon his enemies, to the lustrous avenues of Manhattan where the three unswerving members of the *The First Wives Club* (screenplay by Robert Harling, based on the novel by Olivia Goldsmith) strike back and score a splendid victory over their porcine husbands who have dumped them for newer models.

The continuous evolution in film that richens and expands the range for women's roles passed another milestone in 1996 with *Fargo*, with a screenplay by Ethan and Joel Coen.

Their protagonist, a stalwart North Dakota cop named Marge Gunderson (Frances McDormand), wins our affection and empathy as she pursues and corrals the killers. Not only is she a member in good standing of what not too long ago was termed condescendingly as the "weaker sex," but she is seven months pregnant.

Despite the fact that I've resorted to examples now and then, an endless list of illustrations has little value. You can learn something from any picture, play or novel, either because it's "good" and thereby supplies something worth your reflection, or because it's "bad" and thereby is a guide on what to avoid. Supply your own examples. They're every bit as valuable as mine.

A final word on the value of reading: You'll find nothing new no matter how far back you go. The character and plot of Oedipus existed before Sophocles went to work on it. The Hamlet saga predates Shakespeare's text by hundreds of years. There are allusions to it in Scandinavian literature at least as early as the tenth century. Nevertheless, if you want to do a *Hamlet* story, go to the best interpretation ever done—Shakespeare's. As writers, we all steal, to use a less delicate term than the euphemistic "borrowing" or the frothy "paying homage to." By reading the classics, at least you'll know who to steal from.

The classics make good reading even if you're not a borrower. They afford that rare, deep feeling we get from all great art. If it's a cathedral or a painting we don't want to leave it. If it's a book we don't want it to end. That goes for just about everybody. But for a writer, the simple act of reading is quite different. You can't read a book for pleasure, although you might get pleasure out of it. You read it to learn (God, that's brilliant!) or to challenge (Why the hell did he do that?) or to criticize (He blew it). The business of criticism extends far beyond the hostility of competition or the salve of ego satisfaction. It can signal an artist's uniqueness. When Oscar Wilde, walking through the deep Parisian night with James Abott McNeill Whistler, admired the stars positioned in the heavens, Whistler said, "I would have done it differently."

6

REWRITES AND CRITIQUES

Arm Wrestling the Muse Is Not Enough

Salka Viertel was a gifted screenwriter who wrote many of Garbo's best films. She held soirees at her home in Santa Monica, as if she were back in her native Vienna before Hitler forced her to leave. It was there one astounding night, when I was young, that I found myself in the same room with Aldous Huxley and Christopher Isherwood. I hung on to every word that passed between them, eager to learn something of technique, of work in progress, some flicker of a whisper of a clue of how they put it together so elegantly. And what did I get? Gossip. Binky was cruising the Greek Islands with his latest inamorata. Lotzi bought a condemned lighthouse on the coast but couldn't work there because Navy combat planes used it as a landmark and buzzed him twenty times a day. And on and on.

There was, I found out later, method to their uncompromising, uncharacteristic tediousness. First of all they were observing the social contract: One simply does not mention casualties at the mess, or talk shop at a bash. Moreover, they were tacitly responding to a couple of trade precepts: 1) the Hemingway advisory that "If you talk about it, you won't write it"; and 2) the paranoid principle that lurks in the shadow of every writer's mind: If you talk about it, some son of a bitch might swipe it. I have since had good reason to believe the two men respected each other as authors of unimpeachable integrity, but there were strangers in the room, including an overly attentive neophyte.

Writers generally have a controlled obsession that extends into leisure hours. They don't enjoy mixing work and play, and they get excessively pissed off by the few who do. Scott Fitzgerald irritated the hell out of Hemingway because he took notes of what other people said at parties.

Writers as a rule are endowed with a high anxiety level. Their fragile egos carry a lot of angst. Unlike most bipeds, however, writers make their angst work for them. *Big* and the Swedish film *My Life as a Dog* explore the pain of childhood. *Postcards From the Edge* examines the despair of a young woman, the shy, show-biz daughter of a brash, intrusive, show-biz mom. *City Slickers* chronicles the wretchedness of three middle-aged drones disenchanted with the lives they lead. *Barton Fink* laughs at rather than cries over the paralytic misery of (who else?) a screenwriter afflicted with an insoluble block. And, of course, there are Woody Allen's odes to self-flagellation, combining guffaws and anguish.

Writers seem to need an external system of validation. Small wonder. It's difficult to make up your mind and reach the apposite decision about plot and character and progression when so many avenues are open to you. And so, because of his insecurity or her need for positive feedback, a writer will seek out a close friend and colleague and ask for a critique. Not, to be sure, in a crowded room, but privately, confidentially.

This sort of thing demonstrates yet another paradox upon examination, for the crit-seeker, notwithstanding Scott Frank's testimony to the contrary and with just the slightest shift in the tides of the ego and id, feels that all his work, every scene, each incident, the placement of a comma, is scintillating and essential to the whole, which makes it well nigh impossible for him to accept criticism of just about anything.

What he wants is not criticism, not epiphanies, but approbation. The kind of praise he can blush at. He's like the self-enchanted starlet who said, "But enough about me. What did you think of my last picture?"

Whenever you have an unquenchable urge to show your screenplay to a friend—squelch it. He'll tell you it's great, to avoid making waves or an enemy, or out of sheer indifference. (Writers are remarkably apathetic to anyone's work but their own—an attitude of intolerant detachment that, I believe, is unconsciously motivated. For we are an envious race, secretly delighted by the shortfall of competition, friends and foes alike. "If there's anything people in Hollywood love," Samuel Goldwyn, Jr. noted, "it's talking about the other guy's bad news." *Schadenfreude*, the Germans call it—malicious joy at another's misfortune.)

Back to your friend and confidant: If for some uncharacteristic reason he takes your request seriously and rips your effort to smithereens, roughly ninety-nine percent of the time you'll ignore his destructive suggestions. "You don't understand," you'll tell him with admirable forbearance as you criticize his criticism. 77

Writers, like most other people, simply do not take well to censure. Helen Deutsch was sharing a celebratory dinner at Chasen's with Kurt Kasznar, an actor in her successful screenplay of *Lili* (from a story by Paul Gallico). He had told her what a fine piece of work she had done, and then he added, "But there was one scene where I thought you kind of missed the boat." Whereupon she poured a cup of steaming hot coffee on his lap.

Producer Sam Zimbalist was a genial, competent gentleman who lived on a Malibu cliff overhanging the ocean. He grew his own vegetables, enjoyed lawn croquet and sparring with Jack Dempsey. He loved movies, and in making them enforced pecking rites with a critical formula all his own.

You wrote the screenplay and you gave it to him. He'd sit down with you in the comfort of his rather luxurious office and explain the rules of the game. "We each take turns making changes in the script," he'd say. "You want to go first?"

I'd say, "Sam, I wrote it. I like it the way it is. I don't want to make any changes."

"OK," he'd say. "But you can't expect me to give up my turn just because you don't want your turn." And he'd proceed, however subtly, to alter the tone, the content, the very existence of what you had in mind with a series of deft and seemingly insignificant strokes, and suddenly the whole damned thing was qualitatively and irrevocably altered.

One day the door of my office opened and in walked Gore Vidal. He knew I was working for Sam, adapting a novel by Tom Chamales called *Never So Few*, and I knew he was doing a new version of the Dreyfus case for Sam.

"How do you handle Sam?" Gore asked. I shrugged, indicating that I couldn't handle him at all.

"I don't know how to handle him either," Gore said. "I swear every line in that screenplay is mine and yet somehow I've been Zimbalized."

How do these things happen? Easily, according to Ben Bradlee, former managing editor of the *Washington Post*, in an interview with Mike Wallace. Referring to the Grahams, owners of the paper, the distinguished editor said, "It's their football, and if they're going to let us play, we've got to keep them happy."

It may well be their football, but writers often feel that it is they, not an inflated bladder encased in pigskin, that gets kicked around. Sometimes the resentment heaped on those who do the kicking is deep and unforgiving. Dorothy Parker expressed the depth of her umbrage as well as anyone in:

FIGHTING WORDS
Say my love is easy had,
    Say I'm bitten raw with pride,
Say I am too often sad—
    Still behold me at your side.
Say I'm neither brave nor young,
    Say I woo and coddle care,
Say the devil touched my tongue—
    Still you have my heart to wear.

But say my verses do not scan,
        And I get me another man!

"The man who is asked by an author what he thinks of his work is put to the torture and is not obliged to speak the truth," Dr. Johnson declared.

Nunnally Johnson, who wrote, among other outstanding screenplays, *The Grapes of Wrath,* discouraged petitioners by posting a sign on the wall of his office at Twentieth Century Fox.

FEES

For reading a story, with one-word comment. . . $5 a page
For same without comment. . . . . $10 a page
For listening to a story while dozing $500
For listening to a story while wide awake $1,000
For listening to a story described as
        just a springboard. $10,000
For listening to stories, plays or scripts written by
        actors or actresses to star themselves $25,000
For attending amateur performances in a converted
        shoe store on Highland Avenue to "catch"
        new material $10,000
For looking at talented children. $500
For talking to their mothers $50,000

As a rule of thumb, show your work only to those who are in a position to buy it (a producer, a studio executive) or to sell it (your agent). A friend's help is like God's help which, as we all know, comes only to those who help themselves. There's no god machine reclining on a pink cloud to tell you what to do and how to do it. You must rely on your own horsepower, on the god or the father within you, and that's an adage.

Writing is a mixed bag of inconstant pleasure, occasional pain, rare triumphs, and small tragedies, all of them, in the face of objective reality, blown grossly out of proportion.

If it can be said, as I said rather dogmatically a few pages back, that you can apply artistry and creativity to any project and derive satisfaction from it, it might be maintained with equal veracity that writing is superior to the general run of jobs, which encourage insanity. It is better than the donkey work designed for most civilians, like pumping gas or buying and selling things. The work is not dangerous, like rough-necking an oil rig, and few writers are powerful enough to be pronounced candidates for assassination, as was Salman Rushdie. (Except for rare occasions the pen, sad to say, is punier than the sword.)

Writing is not hard labor. You can do it sitting down. Or standing up (as did Thomas Wolfe, who used the top of a refrigerator, possibly because of his great height). Or lying in bed, not a bad way to seduce the muse. You're not bound to a nine-to-five desk at a distant venue, which removes your name from the hit list of the freeway kamikazes. You owe allegiance to no crown.

There are other allurements. Some writers believe there is no higher calling in life. When it goes well, when the juice is flowing, you'll walk the high places of the Earth, you'll know exhilaration, it's a hit like nothing else, like a rush of strong sunlight, a release from the thralldom of gravity.

Howard Lindsey, playwright, producer, and actor, was fond of telling young aspirants, "I will give you pain, hunger, and sleepless nights, and also beauty and satisfaction known to few, and glimpses of the heavenly light. None of these shall you have continually, and of their coming and going you shall not be foretold."

Compensation enough. And if you're successful at your craft, it's generally a jammy existence with its supplementary incentives and rewards. You might accumulate a large concentration of money, although your custody of it will be sporadic.

Certainly money has its motivational appeals. It buys big cigars and motor cars and, best of all, leisure. If your sensibility is such that you find materialism embarrassingly crass, you might turn once more to the sensible Dr. Johnson. "No man but a blockhead," he said categorically, "ever wrote except for money."

The wisdom of Johnson's injunction should be noted particularly by writers—men and women—drawn to women and men whose primary impellant is the pursuit of opulence. I had a friend with such a wife. One night, sitting around exploring fantasies, she was asked one of those cliché questions, the kind that crops up now and then in a folk tale: If she were granted just one wish by some ministering spirit out of fairyland, what in one word would she choose? Without hesitation she replied, "Fursanjools."

For a few incandescent years—a precarious tenure but delightful while they last—you may enjoy a modicum of fame, a whiff of power, and easy access to women of spectacular conformity; the flesh times of Hollywood are not a thing of the past. If you happen to be a woman, may I respectfully point out (if only to avoid the stigma of chauvinistic piggery) that there is, here at Land's End, a pulsating world of eligible men, a surprising number of whom look like the better class of Roman emperors, or Praxiteles' sculpture of Hermes. It should be noted, however, that about nine-tenths of them are primarily interested in toothsome actress-types under thirty.

Beyond the aphrodisiacal clout that fame and money bring, there is always the deep gratification of doing a well-made movie. But as a screenwriter, don't expect curtain calls and wild huzzahs. Delirious cries of "Author!" will not be heard to lure you onstage, but a screenplay of distinction may garner an Academy Award or a nomination.

What about the guidance of professional critics? We read them for fun because many of them write well. We might read them to learn how to write a critique. Some of our more mean-spirited colleagues read them to reap a threadbare enjoyment from their excoriations of others. Nobody is immune to a critic's scourge, no towering colossus has always and everywhere escaped a critic's severity. Voltaire called Shakespeare's canon "the ravings of a drunken savage." Tolstoy called him "a feudal snob." And the rhetorical William James: "Was there ever an author . . . whose reactions against false conventions of life was such an absolute zero?"

Writers down through the years gave critics as good as they got, none more so than Lord Byron, who climaxed a combine of cynicisms into a bit more than five scurrilous lines with a final zinger of contempt:

As soon
Seek roses in December, ice in June;
Hope constancy in wind, or corn in chaff;
Believe a woman or an epitaph,
Or any other thing that's false, before
You trust in critics.

As a breed, critics hardly qualify as folkloric heroes. They come across as know-it-alls, seldom weighing alternatives but invariably embracing absolutes. Chances of learning to write a screenplay from the savants who make you walk barefooted over the coals, who have so great a talent to provoke Byron and others, would be close to James' "absolute zero."

We all view the cosmos through the prism of our own peculiarities, so it's rather rare when one of the best of them admits to fallibility.

"A critic," said Kenneth Tynan, "is a man who knows the way but can't drive the car."

What Cliff Temple said about sportswriters also applies to dramatic and literary critics—"Someone who would if he could, but he can't, so he tells those who already can how they should."

Win, lose, or draw, try not to lose perspective. Don't get carried away by good times and orchids, or bad times and weeds. "Success and failure: both of short duration," wrote Robert Bolt, the British playwright and screenwriter, in 1962. "Both unimportant then? No, but neither important enough to knock you off your balance. What holds the balance is that both are brief."

There are other delights along with standing ovations that you should not expect. Perhaps the foremost is inspiration, that good ghost of writers, the mellow, sweet-shining lodestar to stoke your furnace and kindle your fire. A persistent problem for the beginner who has been nurtured (as have so many of us) on all the myths of inspiration, is the false expectancy that some mysterious, miraculous ichor will clear the cobwebs from the brain, electrify the frontal lobes, and deliver genius, sense and wit to full-blown instantaneous fruition. It won't happen. Nor will a guardian angel guide you to glory. Guardian angels, if they exist, are too busy for this sort of low-priority intercession. And no top-gun guru of the precise word is going to take your hand and lead you, as if you were blind, through every bog and thicket of dramaturgy.

The odds against the acquisition of a personal preceptor are, conservatively, astronomical. But accidents do happen in life as well as in bad movies. I had hardly pulled out of the starting gate as a screenwriter before a most unlikely script specialist appeared one dark night outside our modest digs in an East Los Angeles housing project called Aliso Village.

On that occasion, just after WWII, Jacques Thierry's face, flattened against the uncurtained window, would have scared a brace of gargoyles, much less my wife and me. The face seemed fleshless, all bristle and beard with two fierce drooping eyes like black olives under the snap brim of a worn fedora.

How could this apparition possibly have come my way? Turned out there wasn't anything accidental about it. I had been working irregularly for a small animation company called United Productions of America, where I had done a sound-slide film commissioned by the United Auto Workers about blue-collar racism, with an accompanying pamphlet which somehow came to Jacques' attention.

He had worked for Billy Wilder as a "constructioneest"—his designation. Wilder was between pictures and Jacques was out of a job. His English was on a par with my dramaturgy; he needed an American-speaking collaborator in about the same way I needed a constructioneest.

Jacques became my mentor for the following three months. He taught me the trade, I taught him past participles and pluperfects. It was a successful partnership, tempered with a certain splendid goofiness because Jacques was wildly eccentric. Like the Sahara, where he had spent some time, he basked in the sun and was prone to freeze when the sun went down. For the tropical L.A. evenings he dressed in a camel's hair jumpsuit, a bunny suit lacking ears and a tail like those one-piece pajamas from childhood called Dr. Denton's.

Anybody associated with Jacques had to be somebody special who in his elitest mind warranted a superlative. He could be embarrassing, as when he'd introduce me to his friends as the world's greatest unpublished writer. (That C.I.O. booklet didn't count as literature.) When he couldn't find a superlative for a hefty young woman at one

83

of his parties, He said, "This is Janice," and paused and then came up with the best he could muster: ". . . Janice," he repeated, "whose brother was burned to a—how you say?—creesp in a fire."

We couldn't sell our screenplay, a smirky story of arch sexual innuendoes about a traveling salesman. Carried away by Jacques' enthusiasm, I didn't realize that we were banging out bromides, and my partner, in his unfamiliarity with American enculturated values, didn't know they were bromides. What we had come up with was an unredeemable mess, but in the process of writing it he taught me what should have been done technically had the idea been a good one; i.e., the operation was a success but the script died. Jacques, with a Gallic, world-weary shrug, packed up his bunny suit and high-tailed it home to Marseilles.

Writing demands self-reliance and autonomy in a war against the blank page. What emerges is the consequence not of mystical revelation but of cerebral struggle, the "perspiration" of Edison's aphorism, and other such saws about the advantages that only come from the application of seat of the pants to the seat of a chair. You must wrestle the muse; don't wait for her to traipse across the virgin sheet or you're doomed, like an indecisive lover, to wait forever. Put something down on paper, even if it's wrong.

Without a first draft there's nothing to prune, emend, refine, embellish. Good writing is rewriting, the lifeblood of the business. "The name of the game," Hemingway called it. For good reason: So much of what all of us write hardens the next morning into irrelevance. That's when you crank it up and try again. It is disheartening. But "there is discouragement in every life. If you don't want it," advised quarterback Steve Young of the San Francisco Forty-niners, "don't get out of bed in the morning."

Asked about his work, Frank O'Connor told a reporter for the *Atlantic* (January, 1953): "With me it's a difficulty of temperament. Mine is lyrical, explosive. I write a story," he went on, "with a feeling of slight regret for poor Shakespeare's lack of talent and wake up with a hangover that makes poteen look like cold water. Then, having cursed life and forsworn literature, I start rewriting. If I can work up the Shakespeare mood often enough I may get it right in six revisions. If I don't I may have to rewrite it fifty times. This isn't exaggeration."

Not all writers share O'Connor's and Hemingway's emphasis on rewriting. "First thought," Allen Ginsberg said, "best thought."

Whose credo magnetizes you, the gospel according to O'Connor and Hemingway, or Ginsberg's? That's a decision you'll have to make, probably by trial and error. There is a tendency among novices to overestimate the merit of a first draft, and to settle for less rewrite. Further consider the fact that most of us, regardless of experience, find hard work repellant, and so quite often we underestimate the alterations that rewriting might bring forth, to the extent that we reject them before so much as a trial run. Nevertheless, a neophyte's judgment regarding his work is no worse, it seems to me, than an old campaigner's. We all tingle to our own tunes and want to keep them immutable, imperishable, as is, even from our own revisionist forays.

Somewhere between multiple rewrites and "a wise passiveness," as Wordsworth put it, is a compromise you might find comfortable. However, when you write, unless you're an extremely rare specimen, you'll rewrite any number of times before you're satisfied. A reminder from Ginsberg: Rewriting is not in itself an imperative of literary life. While an overwhelming majority of writers regard rewriting as a sacred necessity and the consummation of their best efforts, not everyone agrees that the undertaking is so much as minimally beneficial; some of our outstanding pros do everything they can to ignore its demands. Said William Goldman, an exceptionally sensible, talented, and successful screenwriter, "I hate rewriting. I'm terrible at it, and I've always been terrible at it." Which only proves the point: If it doesn't work for you, forget it.

In any case, whatever you're trying to convey in a script, rewriting will probably bring you closer to it. Nevertheless, there exists no absolute determinant, no set of rules governing its application. But there is a guideline. If you accept the premise that the pith and marrow of a screenplay is emotional, then you try to achieve what best contributes to the affective fires. Foremost among those elements is spontaneity. I find that the more rewriting I do, the more spontaneity is lost. Therefore I try to keep rewrites to a minimum.

Among those whose perspective on rewrites and assorted script concerns are highly operable (for him if not for me) is Michael Schiffer (*Colors, Lean on Me, The Peacemaker*), who views screenwriting as The Art of the Practical:

> Leaving it to others to cover the deep stuff of the craft, I thought I'd offer some practical notions that I try to keep in mind as I tackle each new story—hoping that someday when it grows up, it will turn out to be a film.
>
> 1) If you're writing about reality, research your subject to death. People want to go where they've never been. To take them there, you must first go there yourself.
>
> 2) When researching, tell your story to the experts you're interviewing. See if it passes their bullshit test. Let them, with their years of expertise, help you solve plot problems—according to the way things actually work. The truth is inherently interesting. And people who do one thing for most of their lives love the opportunity to get creative with it.
>
> 3) Get a technical consultant, to give your script that ring of truth. If you're not on a studio payroll, you can offer contingent fees (due when your script gets sold). When you find your technical advisor, make sure you get a signed agreement, specifying his role as consultant. Otherwise, you may find yourself with an unwanted "partner," demanding story credit. If you choose to share your story credit, make that decision consciously, out front.
>
> 4) At all times, no matter how complex the plot, remember these simple words: It's the character, stupid. Write original people. And no matter what type of story or plot, give them a unique voice, and personal dilemmas we care about.
>
> 5) Keep your stars on-screen, and give them all the best beats. He or she will appropriate them anyway. Stars bring the finance money, and in return, demand what made them stars—all your good lines.

6) Reality-test your script by giving it to others to read. Something mystical happens when you finally get a script out of your hands. You start to see it yourself. But first you have to cut the cord.

7) When you give your script to a reader, listen. In almost every reader's reaction there is some grain of truth. If someone suggests a change that you don't agree with, look for the underlying problem that caused them to comment to begin with. Don't assume that everyone's stupid, even when they're wrong. As a professional screenwriter, your ability to synthesize intelligent solutions to others' perceived problems is your ability to survive.

8) Don't watch some lousy movie and think to yourself, "I can do that . . .," then expect to break in by doing that.

9) Write fast and hard. A screenplay is not too long. If you attack it with gusto, you will get to the end. Remember: You can't judge your work until you see it. And you can't see it until it's on the page. If you work fast, you have the luxury of scrapping what doesn't work and replacing it with something better without wasting half your life.

10) Don't write when you're exhausted. Especially in first drafts, it's important to knock off each day, before your writing goes stale.

11) Finish everything. All three acts. What you learn on a lousy script will go into your memory bank, for when you finally have a good idea. Writing muscles, instincts, and intuitions develop only through repeated use.

12) Rewrite tirelessly, and don't be afraid to make radical jump-switches on subsequent drafts. First drafts always feel like they're ready to be shot . . . and almost always suck.

13) Be prolific. What kept me going through the years was the knowledge, that whatever my talent, I was going to outwork the bastards.

14) Don't be intimidated. But set your standards high. In the end, like it or not, we're all up against Shakespeare. That was a guy who could really write.

"Rewrite tirelessly," Michael insists in the twelfth commandment. I've done it and even more often I've not. There are viable alternatives between two polarities: In *Black Rock* my only rewrite was an attempt to intensify a single plot point. On *Raintree* I did a ton of rewrites because the complexity of Ross Lockridge, Jr.'s 1,060-page novel, much of it internalized, flowing through a stream of consciousness—required rather severe transmutations before it could be brought to the screen. Further complications developed as I adapted it, including the head of the studio being fired.

Now it is standard operational procedure in the picture business that when the head of a studio gets axed, all the projects he's introduced are buried with his bones—not unlike the funeral rites for a Pharaoh whose prize possessions are buried with him.

That wasn't the case with *Raintree*. An interim boss with a body of supportive regents took over. Calendar leaves exfoliated and a year lurched by, everybody offering suggestions. Then a new chief was anointed, so-called creative differences were resolved, and we got on with the shoot. What the episode tattooed on my brainpan was the emphatic awareness that the physical time spent writing a screenplay does not necessarily dictate its quality. I was benumbed by a sense of emptiness and loss; with each rewrite I thought the picture had been further impaired.

Nobody's troubles or impairments on *Raintree* came close to matching Montgomery Clift's. Three weeks before we left the sound stages of Culver City to shoot in the Deep South, Monty wrapped his car, himself in it, around a tree while returning from a party at Elizabeth Taylor's home.

He kept working and he endured despite severe discomfort. He never missed a call on location in a long summer of exhausting heat. He delivered a valiant performance for which the media blasted him, although they were quite aware that he spoke his lines through jaws that were wired in place. He never complained. He sat at our table in those self-indulgent days of cholesterol ignorance, and while the rest of us chomped on New York steaks, he sipped broth that Lorry, my wife, brewed for him, more often than not through a straw. He revealed more quiet courage in the reality of his pain than most rawhide heroes exhibit on a fictional screen. He never recovered fully from the crash.

One rewrite I was responsible for, and not particularly proud of, involved a scene in *Raintree*. While on a pre-location reconnaissance in Kentucky, we had signed a number of people in local theatricals to play excessively minor parts. One of them had one line in a scene with Monty and Lee Marvin. But when we were delayed for about three weeks before we left L.A. because of Monty's accident, the young man, a high school teacher contracted to play the scene, got tired of waiting for our arrival and went fishing in the Everglades. The night before the shot was scheduled, I was asked to play the part.

In preparation, I read that single, solitary line and thought, what the hell—why not improve on it? So I added more lines and a joke before I regained my sanity and, realizing with some embarrassment where sheer stark ego had led me, went back to the original with a greater understanding of actors and the demons that possess them.

7

SPEED AND STAGNATION
How Good Are You
at Defrosting a Refrigerator?

Speed is considered a prime asset in the making of a Hollywood movie. It stands to reason that the sooner your picture is out the sooner your money comes in. However, people have been known to apply the velocity yardstick to other endeavors where impetuosity is less than an asset. Producer Harold Hecht, to accelerate his therapy, went to two analysts at the same time, neither of them aware of the other.

There's a hoary question with axiomatic implications that writers are prone to use in an attempt to discourage the stress and pressure that speed imposes. "You want it good," the writer asks, "or do you want it fast?" Sometimes a situation develops in which an equally applicable question might be, "Do you want it good or do you want it slow?"

Not everyone benefits from speeding things up, even in the writing of a picture. I was hired for my first original screenplay, *Take the High Ground*, at Metro on a week-to-week salary. Eager to please by getting off to a flying start, I knocked out ninety pages of a 115-page screenplay the first week. Fortunately, I mentioned my diligence to my agent, Bernie Feins, who had a fit. "Spread it out," he told me, "if you want to grind a few bucks out of the assignment. Give 'em fifteen, at most twenty pages a week. Hide the rest under the carpet." The idea appealed to me. I took my time. The picture prospered with a nomination for an Academy Award.

Pandro S. Berman, an exceptionally talented producer and a man of fine discernment, offered me a crack at *The Brothers Karamazov*, which I unhesitatingly grabbed with both hands. However, there was a tangle of strings attached. The next day he dropped the incendiary: With the Dostoyevsky novel in the public domain, it seemed that Dino de Laurentiis had the same idea and was proceeding with a screenplay of his own. According to Berman, I had three weeks to complete the script or all was lost. Metro's timetable was, to my thinking, about six months out of joint, and there was no way for me or anyone else to set it right. I turned down the assignment. Another writer accepted it. A year passed before the script was completed, and then another six months before the picture was in the can. De Laurentiis never even attempted to make it, but he lost nothing in his abandonment.

The picture, when it finally opened, was a sorry spectacle. Somewhat petulantly I reminded Pan of the absurdity of the schedule—three weeks to write a script which was completed more than a year later, a magnificent novel turned into a weightless, ponderous miscarriage.

He smiled without mirth. "Maybe," he mused, "it would have been better had it been done in three weeks."

But of course that wasn't the point, speed having nothing positive to do with the telling of a tale. Or as Chaucer put it: ". . . no werkman, whatsoevere he be,/. . . may bothe werke wel and hastily."

Somewhat in the same vein, and more than 1,200 years earlier, Plutarch wrote, "Ease and speed in doing a thing does not give the work lasting solidity or exactness of beauty."

A story is told of Billy Wilder on the opening night of *The Big Carnival* which he wrote with Walter Newman. The long shoot was over, the picture finally in the can. As the houselights dimmed he was heard to say, "Now I know how I should have done it."

There are more painful problems than rewriting. What do you do when, at each twist and turn of your story, decisions must be made and nothing satisfies you? Jessie Nelson, who wrote and directed *Corrina, Corrina* says:

> For a long time I struggled with indecision in my writing. My writing has at times been bogged down by indecision. Indecision has at times plagued my . . . The problem was that I could see the validity in every good but not great choice, and consequently for hours would make no choice.
>
> Thank God I have a child and was forced to write more quickly, as she only napped for fifty-eight minutes at a pop. What came up for me was the sense that, if I'm really indecisive, it usually means that the ideas I was struggling with weren't right. I was trying to fit them in rather than really let something true emerge.
>
> Norman Mailer says, "Everything moves toward the right idea." He's right. There's another quote that I love and since I can't decide between that and the Norman Mailer quote, I'll include both. Goethe says that "the moment one definitely commits oneself, then providence moves too." Whether it's projection or truth, there is this rather profound sense of the world unintentionally collaborating with you once you come to that right idea: the song on the radio somehow opens up the scene; the woman in line at the ATM with the too-big hair says something that has to become dialogue; the article my cousin just happened to mention I should read solves the last section. These days are glorious and should be much appreciated, as they don't come around all the time.

Another part of the process that was remarkably affected by having a child was my memory. It's gone. Consequently, one of the stories that had the most profound influence on my writing was about a famous film that for the life of me I can't remember the name of. The writer (why can't I remember his name?) wanted to establish that this couple in the film fought constantly. So he wrote four great fight scenes that would play back-to-back in the beginning of the film. In the last scene, the actor would storm out and the actress would throw her high heel so hard against the door that it would leave a dent. The director (who I think won lots of awards) read the script and said cut the first three fights, have one knockdown–dragout, let him slam the door, let her throw the shoe, then let the camera move in on the door and see that it's covered with dents. That one image will say everything about their dynamic.

After I directed my first film I realized how often in the editing room I would cut out all the extraneous dialogue and try to distill it down to its essence. Now when I write I attempt to do it sooner in the process. It seems to challenge me to take the fat out of a scene and find a more resonant visual image.

I'm having a difficult time deciding how to end this, and I can't remember the brilliant idea I came up with at four in the morning when my daughter woke up. So I'll end with a completely unrelated but wonderful quote that really sums up the whole magilla. I've come to believe that it doesn't matter if the demons take over and the day's work is unmemorable, can't be remembered, or is completely inspired. There will be some of all. Ultimately, as Virginia Woolf says, "The attempt is everything."

What do you do when you chop for days and the chips refuse to fly? When you stare in a kind of subdued desperation at the blank page and have no idea how to fill it, then you've contracted the most virulent bug that writing breeds: writer's block. It comes with the territory, but that awareness affords little consolation when it strikes.

How do you strike back? How do you blast your way out of the sand trap? What do you do with a blank page when you've been watching it closely for two hours and it never gets any less blank?

You might start by taking some seemingly irrelevant action. Write a letter to anybody about anything. Jot down a memo of chores you've been meaning to do—cutting the grass or your toenails, unclogging the sink. Abe Burrows wrote laundry lists. Others have been known to take a drive in the car, a walk, a shower. And somehow, I don't know how, it'll free your instrument. For the mind a magic kingdom is, a mysterious realm without boundaries, where odd things happen. Somehow the unconscious takes over and you'll shift gears into congruity. By embracing irrelevance you'll segue into relevance.

The anxiety induced by the blank page is small beer compared to the terror of staring at a finished scene and knowing that it's wrong but not knowing how to fix it. You've loosed a torrent of energy on the scene. Now you're left sucking big wind in a state of exhaustion. That's what makes you thonk around in the dead of night and wail at the uncaring moon. Hopelessness reigns while Panic, his snag-toothed sister, shrieks that you'd better find some other dodge, like plumbing, where your redactional botchery will handicap you less.

Or you might consider a more constructive stratagem, for it's possible that there's nothing wrong with your questionable pages. They seem to have gone haywire, to tail off like an erratic comet on an undesirable course, but the defect in your carpentry might be nailed to something that has gone before, a scene or scenes that preceded it. You must retrace and review, starting on page one to isolate an earlier, unnoted deviation of plot or character. What needs correction is that previous scene, and not the one you're kvetching about.

Example: In *Bad Day at Black Rock,* Reno Smith (Robert Ryan), the racist heavy, shoots and kills a Japanese rancher named Komoko. At the climax, armed with a rifle, he ambushes John J. Macreedy (Spencer

Tracy), the hero, who has uncovered the crime. They meet by night on an isolated stretch of rimrock; Macreedy has no weapon except his ingenuity. He builds a Molotov cocktail out of a bottle, the interlining of his necktie, and gasoline pumped from the fuel line of a jeep. He throws the grenade. Smith goes up in flames.

Adequate, but despite the rightness of the retribution, something troubled me. I had constructed a pretty good obligatory scene, but a link was missing in the structural chain. A more powerful emotional kick was needed, a deeper infusion of drama, a sense of harmony and closure, with every scene leading up to that less than satisfying payoff.

I reread the scene perhaps a dozen times. Stubbornly it maintained its validity, leaving me without the approximation of a clue as to what was wrong. So I went back to the beginning of the script.

It wasn't until page seventy that I found the flaw.

This is how I had handled the scene (compressed here to the bare synoptic bones): Smith has shot and killed the rancher—workable but hardly riveting. Heavies have the bad habit of knocking off innocents in a lot of pictures. It could stand a bit of buttressing. And then I saw it—a small shift, a waif of a shift: Komoko had to die by burning, for two reasons: Basically, 1) torching the rancher makes Smith truly repugnant and a jewel among sociopaths (like Richard Widmark a decade earlier in *Kiss of Death* when he threw the old lady down the stairs); and 2) killing by fire he later is killed by fire. The parallel action, inverted, is stronger in a dramatic sense if for no other reason than it's more unusual, more interesting (or so it seemed to me) and therefore more memorable.

The rewrite (again in shorthand): Smith sets the rancher's house on fire. The man staggers out, engulfed in flames. Then Smith shoots him.

Another type of writer's block, perhaps the most maddening, occurs when you have all the components of your craft lodged in the mind's eye but an immovable barricade of steel and stone is set up somewhere on the arterial road between head and hand. Chemical traffic gridlocks the brain cells and you can't put the goddamn thing down on paper. The trigger refuses to be squeezed, the valve will not open, and the speeding kaleidoscope spins on.

There is no inoculation to resist its ravages. The genius suffers along with the hack—probably moreso.

"Nothing would induce me to lay down my pen if I felt a sentence—or even a word ready to my hand," wrote Joseph Conrad to his friend David S. Meldrum in 1898. "The trouble is that too often—alas!—I've to Wait for the sentence—for the word."

You never know when the dreaded jabberwock will strike. Conrad, so far as I'm aware, never recorded what steps he took to combat writer's block. Perseverance seems to provide the only remedy for riding out the storm. There is nothing you enjoy while it lasts, with the possible exception of weekends and holidays. They make you feel less deviant, moderately normal, because nobody works on the weekend, nobody therefore expects you to, so you can enjoy a feeling of almost belonging. The anguish of a block is compounded, I think, because the stoppage has little or nothing to do with writing per se. It seems to derive from a preoccupation, on the edge of consciousness, with the outside world, its pernicious pressures and wearisome demands, the build-up of welts and bruises that every once in a while overwhelms. Free association sometimes helps.

There is an equally destructive form of blockage that is lodged in the subterranean recesses of the mind. The goal here is conscious procrastination. The writer carries out a devious program of approach-avoidance to shun the finality of commitment. Anything that keeps him from work he finds mesmerizing. He does research whether it's necessary or not, further to forestall what by title and definition he's supposed to be doing. It is easier than writing; there will be times when you'll think anything, like diving from a hundred-foot platform into a tub of water, is easier than writing.

Research isn't the only outlet for indolence. There are many others, some of which take a physical toll. I know a writer who showers ten times a day, another who shaves a dozen times. A third washes his socks, for Christ's sake. Hemingway had his own specific for sneaking up on his subject by temporarily ignoring it. Asked by an aspiring young man how to become a novelist, "How good are you," Hemingway replied, "at defrosting a refrigerator?"

Sometimes the luxury of an undemanding time frame encour-

97

ages the kind of procrastination that can implode into a world-class blockage. TV writers who are required to knock out their work on a tight schedule don't seem to be as pandemically infected by the blockage virus.

Most of us talk a good game, admonishing youth to work long and hard at the trade—blah blah blah—but we seldom practice our own preachment. Johnson again: "I have, all my life long, been lying till noon; yet I tell all young men, and tell them with great sincerity, that nobody who does not rise early will ever do any good."

Thing is, writers, like just about everyone else, enjoy dawdling. And like all addicts we are full of self-hatred whenever we yield to it. Coleridge was a great procrastinator, a "tomorrower," Wordsworth called him. Shakespeare bewailed his own "dear time's waste."

When Anatole France exhibited a tendency toward sluggishness, as was his wont, his mistress Arman de Caillavet padlocked him in his study to force him to write. Johannes Kepler, whose discipline as scientist and mathematician we might assume to be superior to that of your average, quirky literary genius, noted about himself "two opposite tendencies: always to regret any wasted time, and always to waste it willingly."

He is not alone. Alan Zweibel (*It's Garry Shandling's Show, Bunny Buuny,* and *The Story of Us*) heads to the local stationery store:

> Perhaps the most frequently asked question of any working writer (with the possible exception of, "Look, my sixteen-year-old nephew wrote a screenplay and I think it's pretty good but what the hell do I know I'm just a dermatologist so could you do me a favor and look at it and give him a call?") is, "Where do you get your ideas?" It's an understandable query that may very well have as many answers as there are writers who've taken the time to find out exactly where their specific muses dwell. For me, they hang out at stationery stores.
>
> I love stationery stores. Not the big kinds like Staples or Office Depot. They're too big. Cavernous. High ceilings and wide aisles lined with really tall shelves stocked with thousands of pencils and tons of paper—

still, these places curiously don't remotely smell like stationery stores. Stationery stores, the proper kind that is,
appeal to the same olfactory receptors that the proper
kind of bakeries do. But in order for the subtle aromatic
mix of composition books, reinforcements, pencil cases,
and protractors to effectively evoke sense memory the
way old songs do, they must be contained within more
personal, more intimate confines so their magical scents
cannot dissipate. Places that can only carry six com-
passes, not six hundred. Where pens that cost more than
$4.99 are locked inside a display case, as opposed to liv-
ing in big bins. And where the smell of blue looseleafs is
not polluted by the plastic emission of those impostors
which are made of fake leather and referred to as
binders. It's comparable to the way a baseball game
smells at Wrigley Field as opposed to how it smells at
one of those huge new stadium complexes. One smells
like baseball; the other like a building.

So whenever I'm blocked, I head to a real stationery store about a mile from my house. A small place
called The Stationery Store which is sandwiched
between a Blockbuster and a Circuit City—both of
which I hate. For when I step into that place, I smell
first grade. And Mrs. Kasarsky's hair. And my crush on
Barbara Graber. And state capitals. And the phrase
"cursive writing." And how in junior high I wrote
Nancy Edelman's name a thousand times on a book
cover that said "Green Bay Packers" on it—which makes
me now able to smell Nancy Edelman and Vince
Lombardi and Super Bowls and Januarys and ski trips
with the family and my parents arguing in our car and
my wife and I arguing in front of our kids in our car
and how my children think I'm insane when I tell them
that I can smell my entire life when I go into that store
and that my family may very well starve to death if it
ever goes out of business.

Phil Alden Robinson, the writer of *All of Me* and *Field of Dreams* says,

This is my writing routine. I follow it religiously and I highly recommend it.

I do not get up early on the days I write, as I don't want to be groggy. In fact, to prevent grogginess, I sleep as late as possible, then feed the dog, exercise (very good for clearing the head before writing), take a long shower (good thinking can be done here), eat a healthy breakfast (very important to prepare you for writing), read the newspapers (sharpens your mind), make some phone calls, and do all the assorted little things around the house that have piled up to get them out of the way, so they don't give you an excuse later for not writing.

Now it's time for lunch. I make it a point to go out to eat, having found that getting out of the house is an excellent way to clear the mind for writing. Lunch invariably leads to an errand or two, maybe a little shopping, sometimes even involving the purchase of items without which one cannot write, such as paper, a nice pencil, or a book that you may someday need for research.

When you get home, there's mail to answer, and phone calls to return, all of which are very important to get out of the way so they don't interrupt your writing later. By late afternoon, you're faced with a dilemma: start writing now, only to have to interrupt it for dinner, thus losing valuable momentum and focus . . . or put it off until after dinner. I highly recommend you not start writing at this point. Most people are not at their peak in the late afternoons, and there's nothing worse than getting a head of steam going only to cut it off prematurely. So now's a good time for catching up on magazines, one of which might actually contain a nugget that inspires or informs your work.

After dinner, you realize there's a movie you've been putting off seeing, and let's be honest here: how can we be so presumptuous as to write movies if we're not seeing them? It is absolutely crucial that we learn from our peers, profit from their mistakes, and experience first-hand what the audience likes and dislikes.

Okay. The movie lets out at 10 and home you go. Now, finally, there are no more distractions, all the possible procrastinations are gone, you're primed and inspired to start writing.

But here's the thing. If you start writing now, you'll be up until 2 or 3 in the morning and that's going to screw up tomorrow something fierce, so I urge you to go right to bed.

The next morning, be sure not to get up too early, as you don't want to be groggy on a day when you're writing . . . and repeat all the above steps.

I do this for weeks—sometimes months—on end until I feel so guilty and fraudulent that I drop *everything*, turn off the phones, and do nothing but write from morning till night until I'm done.

When I asked Larry David (*Seinfeld*'s co-creator and head-writer) for a couple-of-hundred words on his approach, he responded deftly, and skillfully as might be expected from his fine writing, but not immediately:

As soon as I got off the phone with Mr. Kaufman, I cursed myself. I curse myself as a matter of course, but this time it was actually justified. I had just agreed to write something for his book about the writing process. Why? How could I have been so stupid?! Even though I've made my living as a writer, I've always tried to avoid it whenever humanly possible and now I'd gone ahead and opened my big mouth. I called him back to try and worm my way out of it when he started singing the praises of *Seinfeld*.

"I can't tell you what a welcome diversion this is," I replied.

My deadline was next Wednesday. One week. Well that should be plenty of time. I'll start tomorrow.

When I arrived at my office Thursday morning, I noticed that my knee was bothering me a little. I write in long hand with my feet up on my desk and that position seemed to aggravate the condition. Sure I could have written it with my feet on the floor but I was worried it might not turn out as good. After all, if you're used to writing one way, with your feet up, how could I be expected to suddenly switch and write with my feet down? The very idea of it gave me the shudders. I thought, "Let's see how the knee is tomorrow," and headed for the golf course.

On Friday, I got into the office around ten and immediately tested the knee. Much better. The golf must have helped. "I'll knock it off today," I thought, "Get it off my mind." I picked up my pen, put my feet on the desk, said my customary prayers and was just about to get started when, wouldn't you know it, the phone rang. It was a wrong number. Anyway, we got to chatting and as it turns out, we both went to summer camps in states that started with the letter "M." Small world. The guy was quite a yakker, so by the time I got off the phone I was starving. Can't write on an empty stomach. I need food, bro!

Two hours and forty-five minutes later, I returned. Those macrobiotic places sure take their sweet time. (All right, if truth be told, I did stop at a bookstore on the way back and read about a hundred pages of Mia Farrow's autobiography.) When I arrived at the office, it was around two-forty. I gazed out the window and noticed all these people leaving the building across the street. Of course. It was Friday— people getting an early start on the weekend. How could I be expected to sit here and work while everyone else was clearing out? Why should I be the only idiot left in the building? Whatever it was, it could wait until Monday. Who was this Kaufman guy anyway? I wasn't about to let him ruin the start of a beautiful weekend.

Monday was not a good day. I was up most of Sunday night because the smoke detector went off at three o'clock in the morning and the only way I could stop it was to beat it with a bat. I was so shaken I couldn't get back to sleep, so I spent most of Monday napping on my office couch. (And what a couch it is—almost eight feet and *sooo* cozy. Does the word "chenille" mean anything to you?) When I woke up, I suddenly remembered—the Pontiff's here! Nothing like a papal visit. I turned on the TV and I have to say, the man is looking good. I could watch him wave all day.

103

Now it's Tuesday. This piece is due tomorrow. I haven't written a word yet. No problem. I'll knock it right off, as soon as I take this call.

We persist in this sort of schizophrenic ambivalence—eager to get the writing done and erecting every barricade to make doing it difficult. For our actions and inactions we supply an abundance of sound reasons, and just as many false justifications.

From the dawn of history, the human race has striven mightily to survive. Yet there have been times when we struggle just as laboriously to overcome that elemental laziness which implores so many of us to put off for tomorrow what might, with far less anguish, be done today.

Second, and a not inconsiderate propellant for writers, is the striving for perfection. Achieving that sort of mastery is certainly one way of making your own little ding in the world. Although we know it's unattainable, we mull and fret in our pursuit. Paralyzed, we stare off into the horse latitudes. Rather than put something less than perfect to paper, we put down nothing. But something must be put down, if only to jump-start the recalcitrant engine, even if you're weaving out of the gate on the wrong horse.

To stare at a blank slate is to turn to stone—the eye of the Gorgon is upon you. No magic short of a miracle will fill that emptiness. Only you can do it, to induce a willing suspension of disbelief in your ability. It comes only by writing the damned scene. And then it's always back to the midnight oil that gutters low until finally, satisfied with it, you can move on.

No picture has ever been made that wasn't rich in problems. Even when the action and the dialogue are eminently and acutely workable, there's always some element that defies logic and emotion, authenticity or warmth, excitement or whatever you're striving for. Such was the situation with a key character in *Never So Few*. We thought we had Sammy Davis, Jr. to play the part, and suddenly we didn't. It seemed that no one could come up with an actor to convey the kind of brash dependability the role demanded. And then one night when Lorry and I were late in getting to where we were long past due, she asked me while I was shaving to check on the kids' progress through dinner.

I found them before the TV set entranced by a brash, dependable performer. I watched with them, equally mesmerized until Lorry wanted to know where I had disappeared. The actor on the tube that night, and who was signed for the part, was Steve McQueen.

Another exasperating problem can come out of a scene that simply refuses to work, as was the case in the Broadway version of Leonard Spigelgass' comedy *A Majority of One*. Gertrude Berg, the charming and rather large Jewish lady from the Grand Concourse, dresses as a geisha out of respect for her gentleman caller, a Japanese industrial tycoon. Nothing in the scene played, not the jokes or the progression or the chemistry between the two principals.

The difficulty, which took days to solve, was Berg's exotic kimono. Everybody thought it would be hilarious to have the Bronx yenta caparisoned as a Nipponese dancing girl—possibly the world's oldest and stoutest. But the costume made her a figure of ridicule when she should have been a pillar of dignity. There's a hoary adage out of burlesque quoted by generation after generation of top bananas: Never wear anything that's funnier than you are. It certainly applied in this case.

Sometimes it becomes necessary to change an actor's lines or his business or both because his lack of expertise is such that he can't cope with them. In *Take the High Ground*, whatever we tried didn't help a peripheral player hired for one day's work. He simply couldn't synchronize his lines with the action. There was no time to get another actor. Take after repetitive take skyrocketed beyond cost-effectiveness. The sequence was jettisoned.

Onstage, with ample time allotted for tryouts and rehearsals, the actor would have been canned, as was the case with *The Bird Cage*, by Arthur Laurents. The actor in question was an ex-prizefighter seeking a new career. As a waiter, his brief assignment was to balance a head-high tray on one hand and toss off a funny line as he proceeded cross-stage. Every time his only line was due, he stopped before he produced it. Laurents explained again and again that the line was to be delivered *en passant*, without breaking stride, but again and again the ex-pug took off on his perilous journey from wing to wing, paused center stage, threw the line and then continued. Finally, in frustration, he turned to Arthur. "Look," he said, "I can walk and I can talk, but you can't expect me to do both at the same time." Of course, that was just what the playwright expected, so the man's brief, untriumphant career was over before it started.

The Script: Basics

8

FROM GREECE
TO HOLLYWOOD
Why Aren't You Home Writing?

Let's look at the three-act form in toto, e.g., the dramatic composition that is the sum of its tripartite structure.

Immediately we face another anomaly: Plays, from which film
and its specialist vocabulary derive (viz. "three-act form") are presented in segments and divided by intermissions. Physically, they number
anywhere between one (subdivided, possibly into a number of scenes)
and seven acts.

In Greece, where it originated, drama was continuous theater,
with all the action incorporated in a single act. So it was with Roman
plays and the compressed repertories of the Middle Ages when
logophilic nuns and priests wrote "mystery" plays (based on biblical
tales, usually those relating to the life, death, and resurrection of

Christ), miracle plays (the lives of saints and martyrs), and morality plays (allegories featuring personified abstractions of the theological virtues and the seven deadly sins).

Pre-Elizabethan theater resembled cinema in that the action was continuous, except for the filmic intermissions that afford merciful but temporary relief when they bisect those rare, bloated, interminable movie epics. Pictures are unique, however, in one peculiar aspect: They run perpetually in a hard-top house. The viewer shows up at any old time, sees the flick through to the end, remains to see the beginning up to her point of arrival, and then splits. It can be said with a certain degree of truth that movies make up the only ass-backwards medium of entertainment ever devised by a moderately civilized society.

All of Shakespeare's plays—tragedies, comedies, histories—had five acts. So did the work of his peers and colleagues: Jonson, Marlowe, Kyd, Beaumont, and Fletcher. The same with playwrights of the Restoration and of the eighteenth century. Henrik Ibsen wrote four plays in three acts, three plays in four acts, and four plays in five acts. Show time on Broadway meant three acts until quite recently. Now there are two. As spectators, a passive state of grace we all shared before we became writers, we know that an episode for a TV dramatic series runs four or five acts, while long-form, or two-hour made-for-television movies, have seven acts or breaks in the on-screen progression, to force-feed the viewers like geese with as many commercials and promos as the F.C.C. will tolerate.

The wide variation in the number of acts assigned to a play is arbitrary and artificial as regards to aesthetics. It is determined by no iron law of God or man but by convention, and by the imperatives of culture and commerce.

The Greeks, as noted, served up the three-act form in one uninterrupted, undivided totality. Theater gratified the theistic component of Attic life. Drama was an intense religious experience for the people, drawn from the undertakings and enterprises of their demigods and goddesses, heroes, and heroines (heroes in Hellenic usage were beings of godlike prowess and beneficence who often were honored as divinities). Playgoers comprising the congregation, so to speak, would not tolerate the disruption or division of the liturgy onstage any more than devout Catholics would condone intermissions during the performance of their sacred mysteries or with the highest drama of all, divine services.

The stories enacted onstage, celebratory or cautionary, were therefore anchored in theology to a degree that no significant deviation from the essential character of the gods and godlings was acceptable, any more than the canonicity of Moses, Jesus, or Muhammad would allow for any basic departure from their fundamental natures, respectively, as seen by doctrinal Jews, Christians, or Muslims. When a society refuses to tolerate heterodoxy, its playwrights are severely limited in depicting the nature and temperament of their high and mighty and often hubristic brainchildren. It followed that the key ingredient of Greek drama was plot, as Aristotle stressed. Moreover, the idea of character was a mystery. In that remote, pre-Freudian age, Aristotle with all his polymathic brilliance still had no tools to explore the metaphysical question of why people act the way they do. Aristotle thought that what people did determined their characters, and not the other way round.

Consider too that Greece was a political incongruity, a democracy of city-states built on slavery, with each estate interacting much of the time with indelicate disaffection, to put it mildly, against the other. Yet both citizen and slave could empathize with Oedipus. He might have been above the drab and at times painful dailiness of life, but he wasn't beyond the reach of capricious fate and its scalding ramifications of pity and fear. And if all this awfulness could happen to him, it could happen to you, baby.

Elizabethan audiences were predominantly male. Multiple intermissions gave them more time to troll for hookers.

Broadway and off-Broadway plays, habitually running three acts, allowed for a little socialization, boozing, and deference to the human bladder. The three became two when theaters began drawing wads of customers from the suburbs, particularly lower Westchester and upper Long Island. To get patrons back home at a relatively decent hour, management jettisoned an interval in order to meet earlier and more convenient train schedules, and to ease the fatigue of long, late chartered bus rides back to the manicured boondocks.

All this has nothing to do with art. The divisions, however, might have something to do with the human psyche and its reliance on that ". . . insidious aspect of our tendency to divide continua into fixed categories," as scientist Stephen Jay Gould has noted in another but not wholly unrelated context. Thus, perhaps, we become the victims of a false trichotomy.

There might be other reasons, based on the hoary but imperishable assignment of magical power to certain numerals. Three is such a digit; so are seven, ten, and twelve. They seem to hold greater mystical appeal and staying power than just any old lackluster number even when, quantitatively, the designated choice violates simple arithmetic. We accept an aggregate Ten Commandments without bothering to count them, although Old Testament scholars dispute the number. We subscribe to the First and Second and Tenth in conformance with custom, but do each of them embrace one or two precepts of the coda? In like manner we discuss the Twelve Tribes of Israel (when was the last time you discussed the Twelve Tribes?) when exegetes tell us they totalled eleven or thirteen. (The number twelve possibly connects with the lunar months of the year or the signs of the zodiac, both imports from Babylon, or from Solomon's partition of the land into a dozen parcels.)

Seven's magical and majestic fire emblazons the Seven Seas, Seven Wonders of the World, Seven Sages of Ancient Greece, the heroic Seven against Thebes, the Seven Hills of Rome, Seven Deadly Sins, the Seven Heavens of Islam.

Enough of magical persuasion, although one final inference may possibly be drawn from it: Whenever some matter of human interest or consequence is stamped as true over a long period of time, and even when its falsity is clearly demonstrable, habit patterns coupled with our own peculiar resistance to change dictate that we might as well accept the errancy so long as it does no harm, and for the sake of convenience.

All of which, after a detour of some 2,500 years, brings us back to the so-called three-act form which endures despite its many masquerades. What propels a practicable screenplay from start to finish is not the neat demarcation of acts but the vigor of the conflict between warring forces, served up with heaping great gobs of suspense.

Let us therefore amend the traditional definition of a screenplay into a more utilitarian and comprehensible instrument:

A screenplay is a dramatic composition
1) told on film
2) in the present tense
3) establishing early the time, place, and action, and
4) focusing on the conflict between two or more principal characters, protagonist and antagonist.

It runs somewhere between 90 and 120 pages. Usually. *Raintree County* ran 206 sides, causing many an audience to wish that it didn't. Long pictures seem to embrace irrelevant elements, thereby losing concentration on the heart and core of the enterprise. *Jefferson in Paris*, written by Ruth Prawer Jhabvala, is a study in that sort of diffusion. It ranges far beyond the basic love story, if that it can be called, between the troubled ambassador to France and his slave-mistress Sally Hemmings, to include the quackery of Dr. Mesmer, the extravagance of Marie Antoinette and the dawn of the French Revolution. All these disparate elements (to name but a few) might have converged to forge the character of the hero, but Jefferson has matured, or petrified, before the curtain rises, as a rigid and monumental founding father of the U.S.A. Hemmings does invigorate the pageantry, but she doesn't appear on-screen until the picture is half over.

Unlike *Jefferson*, which runs two hours and twenty minutes, most long pictures generate excitement in the beginning and wilt from sheer exhaustion in the second half. When Ivan Goff and Ben Roberts were writing *Captain Horatio Hornblower*, the British Navy epic, for Jack Warner, he asked them how long the picture would run.

"It'll run about forty minutes," Roberts told him, "and crawl the rest of the way." Goff and Roberts were straight-away fired.

Mainstream, homogenized pictures often carry the synecdochic imprint of "Hollywood" even when they're made in Cleveland or Sevastopol. Yet the people who write them are constantly influenced by the experimental, non-narrative mavericks. Their output serves as an imperfect but enthusiastic clinic from which the at times stodgy and calcified film establishment learns, drawing ideas and techniques from the counterculture, recruiting brisk new talent from the fringe.

Breakthrough pictures made with spit, Scotch tape, and short dough have enjoyed aesthetic and financial success. Their creators have been known to use the ends of raw stock spliced together, remnants wheedled from a lab, with a neighborhood cast and crew. They shoot with an 8 mm camera, hand-held or fixed on an improvised mount. If their text or the texture works, the writer and/or director (usually one and the same in these enterprises) is on an upward spiral. She'll know the galvanic power of being wanted by the Caesars of Quake City. They might be eager to father her next project—a picture that commands interest for any reason has a dozen fathers lined up to welcome the next offspring (while a bomb is forever an orphan).

The Coen brothers offer a positive case in point. *Clerks*, written and directed by Kevin Smith, is another example. The static unorthodoxy of talking heads—all schmooze, no action—like *My Dinner With Andre* and Virginia Woolf's remarkable *A Room of One's Own* got wide metropolitan distribution. At times an entire genre on the edge hits a responsive chord, finding a niche among traditionalists and altering dominant cultural perceptions. Orson Welles came out of the East via the avant-garde stage and sci-fi radio with *Citizen Kane*, screenplay by Herman Mankiewicz. Another explosion was detonated by film noir with its somber stress pattern of disillusionment, pessimism, and despair.

It seems that writing, whatever the form, has an irresistible attraction for a large number of young people eager to learn from those professionals who might take the time and the trouble to teach them.

There is a story, probably true, about Sinclair Lewis, vintage novelist of the Midwest and the first American to win the Nobel Prize in Literature (1930), who, strapped for cash, a predicament that most writers find themselves facing at one point or another, took a job teaching a seminar at Columbia. When more than 400 students appeared for the first session, the author, an immoderately private man, was a bit confused by the sheer quantity of young people who showed up.

"How many of you would like to be professional writers?" he asked. Hands shot up, attached to just about everybody in the class.

"In that case," Lewis asked, "why the hell aren't you home writing?" And he walked out.

Lewis wasn't the only Nobel laureate who believed practice, not tutorials, make a writer. Faulkner didn't think much of the idea that theory and technique (whether in the classroom or between the covers of a book) could be taught, and he was even more emphatic about it than Lewis.

"Let the writer," he thundered, "take up surgery or bricklaying if he is interested in technique. There is no mechanical way to get the writing done, no shortcut. The young writer would be a fool to follow a theory. Teach yourself by your own mistakes; people learn only by error."

He has a point, and he makes it so well that the fledgling writer might be tempted to respond in total agreement.

"What's good enough for William Harrison Faulkner and for Harry Sinclair Lewis," you might reflect, "is good enough for me."

Don't kid yourself. Faulkner and Lewis were men of certified genius, colossi of talent who could ignore just about any conscious learning process other than that mysteriously dictated by the circuitry of their own unassailable brains.

Certainly it is true that you learn to write by writing—by following some indefinable internal imperative. But sometimes you can be pointed in the right direction by taking council from those who have struggled down that rocky road before you. I know of no writer who wasn't a reader before he took a whack at a word processor.

In *Antigone* Sophocles says:

The ideal condition
Would be, I admit, that men should be right by instinct
But since we are all likely to go astray,
The reasonable thing is
To learn from those who can teach.

9

CATECHISM BEGINNING WITH THEME
Stick to It
Like Grim Death

The Faulkner–Lewis doctrine is, of course, at polar variance with the accepted persuasion of the how-to manuals. However, there is, I believe, a way to combine both: to develop the potential of the tyro without robotizing her in a plethora of rules, paradigms, and absolutes while encouraging the aspiring wordslinger to sound off in her own unique voice. As we sashay down the yellow brick road toward a workable screenplay, there are certain guidelines and principles that can be called upon to free your instrument, as method actors say. The approach is Socratic; the method is catechistic, incorporating a series of self-directed questions whose answers could excite scrutiny, encourage flexibility, open doors of exploration and discovery, and stimulate a meaningful analysis of your work.

Sounds a little too much like the promises of a con artist or a snake-oil salesman? Particularly when, before you start, you recognize in yourself a tendency to brood about the possible negative aspects of your upcoming endeavors, or to enthuse too intemperately and too soon over its glowing potential?

Self-doubts, interior quarrels, bare-knuckle infighting assail many a writer, the veteran as well as the novice, as soon as she sinks into her uneasy chair. If you feel this way, you are by no means unique. There is no success without suffering in any dodge worth pursuing, whether the goal was Andrew Jackson's or Michael Jordan's.

Faulkner's professions of distrust for how-to punditry might be lodged in his belief that a theoretical understanding of principles is not enough. You can comprehend a theory but you cannot apply it unless you process it, and to process it you must do it, in praxis; you must fill your own blank pages.

The beginner's approach should be that of any professional. As he mulls over his unborn screenplay, outlines it (if that's a step in his m.o.), writes it and rewrites it following the advisories suggested, he might with luck and some talent hit the mother lode.

We'll start with theme, not because of its primacy but to dispose of it early. Theme is defined by various dependable dictionaries as a unifying or dominant or central idea or motif in a work of art. There is about it an underlying significance and solemnity, deriving as it does from Themis, a Greek goddess and the personification of law, order, and justice. Every story has a theme, it being impossible to write one without it; just as it is impossible to entertain a thought about nothing. It can be expressed as a principle, a maxim, a universal law, an approximate truth; it might even embrace a strong and toxic prejudice. But it remains an abstraction, and you don't record an abstraction with a motion picture camera.

There are all kinds of writers and they're all over the place. I'm sure some start work by first considering the theme they want to explore. But not many. Writers write stories, they don't write themes. The determinants of what is on the page are visual and visceral. They spring from our conscious and unconscious wiring until, somewhere in the middle of the piece and in some sneaky and mysterious way, the theme emerges. It is possible but hardly probable that novelist Winston Groom decided first to address the theme that Good Guys Finish First and then banged out the biography of Forrest Gump to confirm it. Or was he amplifying a richer, stranger theme?: The world is in such an absurd state of chaos that only a deviant, a retardate, a huckdummy dingbat can make his way successfully through it.

A theme can compress and crystallize an idea, and, if you're so inclined, propound with equal facility its opposite. The wages of sin, according to Goethe's *Faust*, is death and the eternal torments of hell; the wages of sin, as Federico Fellini saw it, is *La Dolce Vita*. Just about any witticism can be cast into a theme. The list of quips and cranks invoked to capsulize films is endless and familiar: He who lives by the sword, etc., power corrupts, etc., love is blind, etc., etc., etc. Just about all of them are so excessively simplistic and vague that they are meaningless. Perhaps the broadest and most simplistic of them all is the most thought-provoking: The immortal mythic theme of every narrative, according to Joseph Campbell and other explorers of humanity, is the endless search for the meaning of our lives.

But mankind is complex; a life has many themes, and so does any movie that imitates it.

The multiple facets of Whit Stillman's *Barcelona*, for example, might include: Nice Guys Finish Last, and To The Shitheels Go the Spoils, and Postmodern Young People Are Sick But Irresistibly Attractive, etc.

The Lion King is *Hamlet* with a tawny mane, and the theme could be interpreted as Vengeance for a Father's Death. It might with equal facility be Coming of Age in Africa, or Overcoming Guilt in Order to Function Responsibly.

It's because of the multiplicity of themes that individual pictures of substance appear at times to lack unity, and come up with set pieces that seem more or less extraneous to the sequence of on-screen events. Example: Jack Nicholson's explosive burst of rage as Robert Eroica Dupea in *Five Easy Pieces*. Unsuccessful in getting the breakfast he orders from an uncompromising and unimaginative waitress, he upsets the table. Yet the scene is integral to the picture's themes, and symbolic of a man sinking in the prosaic quicksands of life, becoming increasingly and inextricably involved with an insignificant other, a middle-aged son seeking a father's love that was never given. Shattered in his frustration and despair, lost in a lunatic world of inflexibility and misunderstandings, he turns on that stern goddess of unresponsiveness, the waitress.

The multiplicity is further compounded when, as so often happens in Hollywood, you're assigned to develop a screenplay from somebody else's work, whether it's a novel or an earlier draft of the script. You inherit the theme or themes, but then a curious subliminal conflict is joined as your very own idiosyncratic self takes over. As you tangle with the material, you change the theme.

Only once was I consciously aware of changing the theme and redefining it before getting on with the story.

It was many years ago. Gene Kelly and I were hired by Universal, he to direct, I to write a movie based on *Beau Geste*, Percival Christopher Wren's celebrated novel that glorified brotherly love and Western aggression as practiced in the French Foreign Legion. I detected what I thought was a considerable opportunity to strike a blow for the wretched of the Earth. The fraternal love I retained but my screenplay blasted colonialism and the F.F.L. and I transformed the three charming and romantic Geste boys into less-than-thoughtful tools of imperialism.

Wren's book was published in 1926, a time when a sizable number of solid citizens, with their assumptions of innate superiority, justified sordid aggression over people of a different race or color. Pious euphemisms flourished, expressions like "the white man's burden," and along with them disparaging and offensive terms like "wog." "To us English," Sir Austin Chamberlain said publicly, "wop begins at Calais."

And then, in 1965, with the unfailing vision of hindsight, I put my novel spin on Wren's novel. How I ever imagined that the U.I. front office would applaud my unorthodox surgery, I do not know. I do know that they kicked my presumptuous ass off their lot, but my insensitive treatment of Wren's book did focus their attention on the inappropriateness of his message. Instead of killing me, the studio killed the project.

Theme is hardly paramount to the writing of a screenplay. It might possibly change as you proceed with fresh insights and new ideas that demand at least an audition. Sometimes in the early steps of writing, your theme will be difficult to pin down, but sooner or later it will emerge. To encourage clarity and its emergence, ask yourself a few additional questions: Have I stuck to it? Does it express what I'm trying to say?

Somewhere, usually toward the middle of the first act, your theme will emerge (as in *Hamlet*) in recognizable although limited and perhaps inchoate form. Possibly you had known it earlier and subliminally while your computer screen was still bathed in blankness. Such a case is rare, despite the fact that writers, critics and civilians have been barraged with a great deal of cosmic blather emphasizing the imperative that a play/screenplay delivers one basic idea, that everything in the vehicle should be unified, that it should follow the lodestar on which our attention must be fixed, and that it appears, before you write "fade-in," full blown and as unmistakable as Venus springing from the thalassic foam. Somerset Maugham's insistence on "finding your subject and sticking to it like grim death" is worth stressing, yet the greatest play in the English language, most critics concur, violates the injunction. Hamlet, according to Bernard Shaw, "is six characters rolled into one." The Prince of Denmark, so much larger than life, can be depicted the way he himself describes the earth and the sky as "a congregation of vapors."

And there's Aristotle's admonition that your protagonist should not be deranged or a drunk, for then his actions would lack the rationality that an audience demands. But is Hamlet mad? Or isn't he? Much could be said in support of either conviction. As regards alcoholism, both *The Lost Weekend* (screenplay by Billy Wilder and Charles Brackett from the novel by Felix Jackson) and *Leaving Las Vegas* (screenplay by Mike Figgis, from the novel by John O'Brien) trumpet zonked-out protagonists who are attractive and empathic.

To Aristotle, the emotional breakdown of a protagonist was unthinkable. When a hero (like Oedipus) went mad, it came at the end of the piece as divine retribution for his sins. Quite a removal from *Shine*, released in 1997 (screenplay by Jan Sardi from a story by director Scott Hicks), a deeply moving and effective biography of a musical

121

genius who early on suffers a psychopathology that prevents him from functioning and who retreats into his interior world.

Most themes, distilled to their irreducible essentials, are anchored to the archetypal myths of humankind, the nursery, folk, and fairy tales that cut across geographical, social, and psychological boundaries, such as *Little Red Riding Hood, Jack and the Bean Stalk, The Ugly Duckling, Cinderella,* to name an easily recognizable few. *Cinderella* is the oldest of the international folk classics. Its first version appeared in China around 900 A.D., its most famous on an American screen in Walt Disney's 1950 animated feature. It has been made many times, and will be, indubitably, served up again in the future.

Regarding that glass slipper: In or around 1697 Charles Perrault wrote the first Occidental version of the tale. His story, *Cendrillon*, in French, featured a *pantoufle en voir*, a fur slipper which was mistakenly transcribed into English as *en verre*. Glass. Which supplies us with a rather rare case of cross-cultural alchemy, and which was accepted incontestably. And so it remains.

There are highly competent writers who stress the value of theme and its early definition as an exponent in story-telling. On the subject of theme in craft, Robin Swicord (*Little Women, The Perez Family*) says:

> Action may be character, but theme is the quiet engine that drives the plot. "What is this story about?" informs the content of every important scene. Theme and character create the story's "logic," that quality of inevitability the narrative must have if the audience is to remain engaged. We enter drama through direct representation: We *are* the character(s), and we know ourselves through the words we say, the decisions we make, and the actions we take. In watching films, we all experience moments in which we find ourselves at odds with what happens next, when the scene at hand suddenly feels "out of left field," as if the new event or decision has been inserted for plot convenience. "I don't believe that a character would do that," we scoff, and from that moment we stand at a distance from the story.

In screenwriting, "What happens next?" is not a decision the author makes at random. In dramatic narrative, one scene pushes the action of the next. Whether we are adapting or inventing a story, each narrative event pushes the next into existence. The simple reporting of linear events might be described as "And then . . . and then . . . and then." Dramatic action requires more cause and effect. "Because of this, that happens . . . Because of this, that happens . . . Because of this, that . . ." and so on, with each scene determining the necessity for the next. I find that *theme* is a lifeline during the early stages of thinking about the narrative and outlining, when theme reminds me that "What happens next?" depends upon "What do I mean to say?"

When theme informs what happens from scene to scene, the story feels firmly grounded, which helps the audience "give over" to surrendering the self and becoming the characters. With theme directing the action, narrative becomes a playing-out of hidden forces—and they *must* be hidden. For this reason, subtext is the ally of theme. When theme surfaces and overtly drives the action, "inevitability" becomes predictability and scenes feel contrived. Similarly, when theme is too closely aligned with character, characters seem schematic. Theme must be invisible, surfacing in dialogue only obliquely, understood mostly in retrospect. When only one theme is at work, a story seems thin and single-minded. To make a story rich and characters complex, various forces must be at play. The dynamic interplay of multiple themes creates a shimmer and boil beneath the surface of the narrative. When these forces are finally brought together in the culminating scenes, the effect is one of catharsis.

10

THE THREE-ACT FORM
Surrender and
We'll Give You a Second Act

The rules, rubrics, and definitions for just about every aspect of screenwriting are fraught with paradox. Nothing is absolute or carved in stone. Confusion reigns even in the simple arithmetic of counting acts, and what goes into each of them is interpreted with a certain amount of dissidence.

Scholars and cineasts do concur that in the first act the dramatist should present the situation to be explored—should "set forth the case," as noted by Lope de Vega (1562–1635), founder of the Spanish National Theater and the reputed author of more than two thousand plays, most of them, according to critics, without structure or subtlety. De Vega and many others of stature and renown insist that you introduce your hero early, for the sooner you establish him and his goal, the sooner you can hook your audience into identifying with him.

It should be noted that in the first four or five minutes of a film, the audience will accept just about anything except tedium. In the opening of *The Fugitive* (written by David Twohy and Jeb Stuart, based on characters by Roy Higgins), a distinguished physician, Dr. Richard Kimble (Harrison Ford), with an income commensurate with his eminence in the medical community, is accused, tried, and, on circumstantial evidence alone, convicted and committed to prison for the brutal murder of his wife. Not a single, solitary member of the worldwide audience challenged the verdict. Yet we are all aware that Dr. Kimble, being of sound mind and substantial income, would have fought saw and scalpel for years and years through every appellate court in the nation before succumbing to the verdict.

In *Coming to America* (written by David Sheffield and Barry W. Blaustein, based on a story by Eddie Murphy), Murphy plays an African prince, presumably bored beyond solace by the plethora of beautiful women vying for his favors. He comes to Queens, U.S.A., to find a wife. His quest makes as much sense as Itzak Perlman's going to Zimbabwe for fiddle lessons.

In a well-made first act, it is not unreasonable to expect the imminent appearance of hero and heroine, who'll start throwing off the kind of interactive sparks that make them marketable stars. But Ingrid Bergman doesn't show up in the celebrated *Casablanca* until three-quarters of an hour have elapsed. In *Sleepless in Seattle,* by Jeff Arch, Nora Ephron, and David S. Ward, hero and heroine are introduced early but not to each other. They don't meet until the final minutes of the picture.

Your second act focuses on the developmental confrontation between hero and heavy. Once the conflict between them is joined, the obstacles set up in your hero's path by the heavy and his bravos should be increasingly formidable—more difficult to overcome—as the story progresses.

Turn up the burners, fore and aft. Stomp every drop of wine from the exploitable grape. Pour it on. Squeeze it out, as in *Bonnie and Clyde,* by David Newman and Robert Benton: With every twist of the plot, the ill-fated lovers veer closer to destruction.

Complicate each complication, intensifying the tension as in *The Bridge on the River Kwai* (novel by Pierre Boulle, screenplay by Michael Wilson and Carl Foreman) until the end of the act allows your protagonist neither a point of retreat nor a safe, triumphant haven in the future. Box your hero into such deep trouble that it seems impossible to extricate him, as in *Deliverance* (novel and screenplay by James Dickey).

As you proceed, always honor one of the rare but gem-like absolutes of story construction which de Vega stressed. "At all times," he admonished, "trick expectancy," i.e., surprise the hell out of the audience.

Historically, formulaic usages and conventions have been assigned to each of the customary three acts that constitute a play or a screenplay. In the first act the vital elements and the essential information are presented. In the second act the clash between hero and heavy intensifies as they contend for the prize at stake.

Struggle is the pith of the second act, as the thrusts and counterthrusts of your belligerents collide with increasing force. It is the arena in which your gladiator faces insurmountable obstructions and surmounts them until, at the end of the act, in what is aptly termed the second-act climax, catastrophe looms and appears inescapable.

The second act challenges our inventiveness in progressing the story. The writer must come up with new and different plot points to keep hero and heavy locked in combat.

Unfortunately there is no formula, no quick and easy index for this (or any other) application of creativity. Science has yet to find a way to induce "divergent thinking"—the ability to discover solutions to previously unexplored and highly individuated predicaments, literary and otherwise.

No one doubts that a certain creativity is required in turning out each part and parcel of a screenplay. Why a second act is so demanding derives from the awareness that the scenes preceding it deal with who's who, and who wants what from whom, while the scenes that follow supply the resolution and its consequences. It is the second act that keeps things jumping from the time your leads are established to the moment of maximum impact, the decisive instant of climax that is the final major turning point of the plot.

Middle European playwrights have long noted the devilish preeminence of the second act. Particularly Ferenc Molnar. He was a dazzler, overwhelming in his ability to fit together the dramatic pieces of a puzzle and to build, stone by stone, the complex bridge of a second act. Hungarian writers treasured his second acts although they, like everybody else, sometimes had difficulty unriddling their own.

Producer Joe Pasternak, the spiritual and intellectual leader who hired many of the Hungarian émigrés of WWII, gathered his flock together during a downsizing period at M-G-M.

"Fellas," he began—he called everybody fellas, even when they were alone—"Fellas, it's no longer enough just to be Hungarian," he told them, "you've got to have a second act."

According to Lotzi Vadnoy, a talented and successful comedy writer from Budapest, Allied airmen on bombing missions dropped leaflets on the city which read, "Surrender now and we'll give you a second act."

Pasternak was the uncontested champ of barbarisms. He wanted a songsmith to write him "an Irish diddle." "The first time you see Lanza," he told me about a picture in progress, "he's wearing blue gungadins."

Regarding a game in the Rose Bowl: "S.C. won't feel so bad losing if it's a tie."

"How are things going?" I once asked him. He shrugged and said, "Comme ci, comme su."

At the end of a long day, "I'm tired of all of this rigamajew."

Describing an on-screen action of Robert Taylor: "He works his way back into her good gracious."

Of course, he spoke English a hell of a sight better than I'll ever speak Hungarian.

To stress the dominance of a second act over what precedes and what follows it is probably a function of misguidance. Every line in a workable screenplay is hard to come by; it must have consilience with the piece in its entirety.

A viable screenplay is one that an audience responds to emotionally. The emotion reaches apogee, the zenith of intensity, in the third act as your heroine and her antagonist are locked in a final conflict that cannot be resolved until one or the other is destroyed—defeated, never to rise again.

It is where she faces the supreme challenge, the greatest jeopardy. Even if she is victorious—all's well that ends well, right?—she dies a little, but temporarily or, in a tragedy, winds up totally and permanently dead.

Your third act climax is the high point of the action, and not a war of words. The clash is cataclysmic. It should set your neurons atingle as the hero struggles to survive (*Boyz 'N the Hood*, *Thelma & Louise*, *High Noon*); to right a wrong (*Shane*); to avenge a death (*Hamlet*); to save the world from the forces of catastrophic darkness: the anti-Nazi gamut (*The Guns of Navarone*); and all those chronicles that require doubles and stuntmen as the hero fells the arch-fiend who possesses an H-bomb and is eager to drop it.

Your third act is where your plants pay off. The progression must be rational, credible, and not pat or contrived. In *Four Weddings and a Funeral*, by Richard Curtis, the hero's charming manner and trivial mind brand him as a legitimate offspring of Bertie Wooster. His rash advances toward a rather unappetizing young woman is planted early, and it comes back to haunt him deep in the third act, when he is afflicted with feelings of misplaced remorse and compassion, with a heaping side order of guilt. His decision to marry her hoists him high on the horns of a sticky dilemma from which there appears to be no reprieve. His deliverance comes about through a cruel and callous decision to abandon her at the altar in order to pursue his true love.

The deed is out of character. It would have worked more gracefully had it been carefully planted. It would have worked best had the situation been inverted, i.e., she forsakes him, possibly out of revenge, for treating her so shabbily earlier.

The business of inverting a plant to bring about a desired conclusion is most evident in mysteries; it happened in every episode of *Murder, She Wrote*. Something seemingly extraneous, or relevant only in another context, is said or shown en passant and becomes the keystone clue that solves the puzzle.

129

Woody Allen is a master of the inverted plant. In *Bullets Over Broadway* (co-written by Allen and Douglas McGrath), there are many astute and highly operable inversions. One will suffice: As the picture opens, the first words said arrogantly by the protagonist-playwright, who is about to take the New York cognoscenti by storm, are, "I'm an artist!" In the final scene, he admits sadly and humbly that he is somewhat without talent, and returns to Pittsburgh.

As does the brash young playwright in the opening scenes of Allen's film, we all see everything through our own kaleidoscope. Our very own screenplays we see as towering accomplishments and never as blights or doorstops, as a targeted producer might see them.

"The salutary influence of example," said Dr. Johnson, "is always more efficacious than precept." So let's look at *The Fugitive* and the deadly chess game played out between the hero, Dr. Richard Kimble, and the man opposing him, in this case not a villain but an implacable cop, U.S. Deputy Marshal Samuel Girard, who is resolute on returning Kimble to custody. Portrayed with power and intelligence by Tommy Lee Jones, he is an impressive fusion of M. Javert, Jean Valjean's nemesis in *Les Misérables*, and Porfiry Petrovich, the resourceful detective of *Crime and Punishment*.

The film uses a venerable device that has proven effective in a multitude of thrillers: The hero is assigned a dual role. He is pursued by the relentless marshal and at the same time he must with equal steeliness pursue the killer—finding him and turning him in is the only way to prove his own innocence.

Never has the union of hunter and hunted been more skillfully handled than by Sophocles in *Oedipus Rex*, the world's first detective story. Oedipus must find the murderer of King Laius, whom he has succeeded to the throne of Thebes. Perhaps the most mesmerizing aspect of the masterwork is the hero's search for the felon, who turns out to be himself.

Turning back to *The Fugitive*, the basic conflict is introduced in the first act. What Dr. Kimble must accomplish is made clear, as is who opposes him, and why. Then we get to the meat of the second act, dramatizing the struggle as protagonist and antagonist vie for the victory. Each thrust by the hero toward his goal is met with a counterpunch by the heavy. Consider the capsulated metaphor of Paul Schrader's and Mardik Martin's *Raging Bull*, with Jake LaMotta and Ray Robinson in the ring, kicking the bejesus out of each other. Each shot landed by Jake (Robert De Niro) is returned with staggering impact by Sugar Ray (Johnny Barnes). Mayhem promising eventual destruction of one by the other increases in the flurry of furious fists.

In their first act of *The Fugitive*, the writers Stuart and Twohy, establish that Dr. Kimble has been railroaded to the Illinois State Prison, but they make sure he never gets there (or they wouldn't have had a picture, or the picture they wanted). The high-security bus transporting him and others goes off the road and down a heavily wooded hill.

Now the complications of the second act take over, shifting with the progression as Kimble and Girard each strives to outfox the other: the doctor to escape capture and find the one-armed "perpetrator" of the crime he's convicted for, the deputy to run Kimble to earth. With each unexpected twist of the plot, first one man and then the other achieves what seems to be a telling advantage, only to see it evaporate, to swing back in favor of the other.

A précis, blow by blow:

Kimble and another convict escape from the wreckage of the bus an instant (in movie time) before it is smashed to smithers by a barreling freight train. Each goes his own way. Advantage Dr. Kimble.

Samuel Girard arrives at the scene leading a reinforced regiment of heavily armed cops, a mechanized cavalry of souped-up police cars and a helicopter. They fan out over the rough terrain in a dragnet it seems impossible for Kimble to escape. Advantage Girard.

Kimble eludes cops by fording river, despite nasty wound sustained in bus wreck. Infiltrates hospital for self-treatment, stealing necessary medication. Reversal of fortune, advantage Kimble.

Cops enter hospital with an injured guard from ill-fated bus. Advantage Girard's team.

Kimble hides in sleeping patient's room. Manages to shave beard, eats patient's dinner. Advantage Kimble.

Guard recognizes Kimble. Cops tear after him. Advantage Girard's team.

131

Kimble steals ambulance to evade cops. Advantage Kimble.

Ambulance spotted, chased by cops in patrol cars and by Girard in chopper. They close in. Ambulance trapped in tunnel with cops at both ends. Advantage Girard.

Kimble escapes through sewer, regains advantage.

Kimble trapped in sewer. Girard armed, trails him, closes in. Advantage Girard.

At brink of spillway, Kimble has no choice but to leap into white water of a river that looks to be about 10,000 feet below. Climbs out, bedraggled but undamaged. Advantage Kimble.

Kimble manages to hitchhike back to Chicago. Phones his lawyer for help. Advantage Kimble.

Phone call traced. Background noises identify source of call as Chicago. Girard et al. go after him. Advantage Girard.

Kimble accesses prosthetics lab at Cook County Hospital, makes some inconclusive progress in identifying the one-armed man who escaped after killing Kimble's wife. He cross-checks computer for an amputee with a criminal record. Advantage Kimble.

The son of Kimble's landlady, arrested for dealing drugs. Tries to cut a deal by telling Girard of his suspicions about Kimble. Advantage Girard.

Kimble goes to Cook County lockup, posing as a visitor of an amputee prisoner. Advantage Kimble.

Wrong man. Meanwhile, Girard realizes that Kimble might be seeking a convict with one arm (Kimble had always insisted on his innocence and had repeatedly told authorities that his wife was murdered by a one-armed assailant). Girard therefore pokes around jail, spots Kimble. Advantage Girard.

Nota bene: In any conflict, a blatant accident or coincidence, as in the above paragraph, with hero and antagonist converging in the same place at the same time, is only acceptable to the audience if the results favor the heavy or his equivalent, thereby adding another obstacle to the thorny path of the protagonist. If the situation favors the hero, the audience feels cheated and dismisses your construction as fraudulent and cheap and contrived. One or two such bungles and your whole screenplay self-destructs without any contribution from

a

The author at work, 1959.

Above: Whipping up a breeze for Elizabeth Taylor in period armor during a summer shoot in torrid Kentucky, *Raintree County*.

Below: In a cameo as a Union officer with Lee Marvin and Montgomery Clift, *Raintree County*.

Above: Millard Kaufman (right) with studio head Dore Schary in M-G-M's Iron Lung.

Below: With Charles Bronson, *Never So Few*.

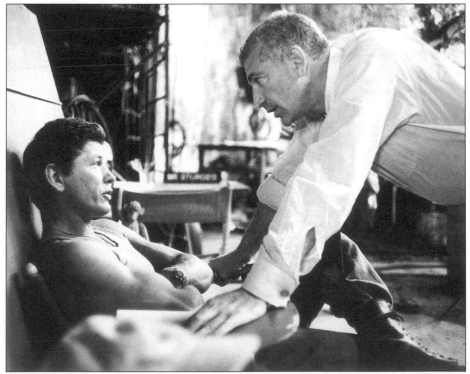

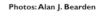

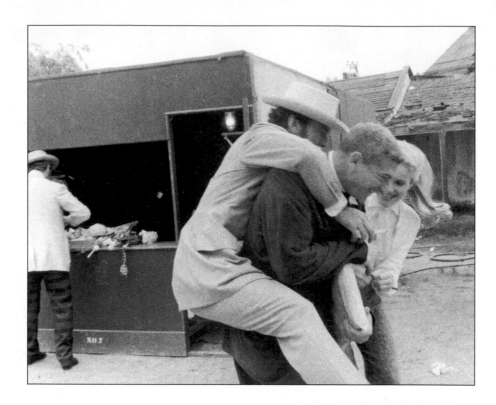

Above: Rod Taylor, the writer, and Eva Marie Saint clowning around on the set of *Raintree County*.
Photo: Bob Willoughby

Right: With Montgomery Clift and Eva Marie Saint on the set of *Raintree County*.
Photo: Bob Willoughby

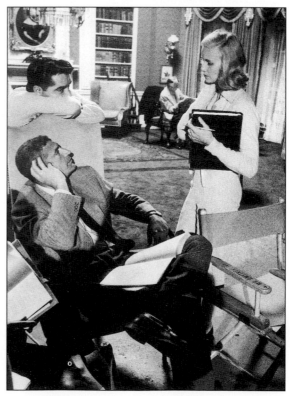

e

Director John Sturges with the writer on the set of *Never So Few*.   Photo: Alan J. Bearden

Montgomery Clift and Kaufman "blowing smoke" to create atmosphere for a scene in *Raintree County.*

Photo: Bob Willoughby

Left: *Never So Few* star
Gina Lollobrigida with
Millard Kaufman.
Photo: Alan J. Bearden

Below: Millard Kaufman,
columnist Hedda Hopper,
and Elizabeth Taylor chat
while dialect coach
Marguerite Lambkin
looks on.
Photo: Bob Willoughby

g

Hollywood writers featured in the August, 1958 issue of *Cosmopolitan*. Left to right: Edmund Hartman, Karl Tunberg, Michael Blankfort, Millard Kaufman, Ray Bradbury, Ken Englund, Ernest Lehman, George Seaton, James Poe, John Lee Mahin, Rod Serling.

h

Clift and Kaufman going over lines in the actor's trailer, *Raintree County*.

the director or the actors, but not without the irritation and hostility of the audience. Disadvantage everybody.

After Kimble is spotted by Girard, a chase ensues. Kimble escapes capture, swallowed up among the massed anonymous humanity marching in a St. Patrick's Day Parade. Advantage Kimble, who gains further advantage when additional investigation discloses the one-armed killer as a Mr. Sykes. Kimble breaks into Sykes' apartment. He finds pictures of the amputee in the company of a distinguished physician whom he identifies as the medical spokesman for a mega-powerful and opulent pharmaceutical firm for which Sykes handles security.

Now we are well on our way toward a driving showdown, with a series of decisive confrontations leading to the climax and resolution. Who of our principals will succeed or fail, live, or die?

The third act:

Kimble phones Dr. Charley Nichols, his closest friend and the administrative chief of pathology at Chicago Memorial. Having found the killer, he needs Charley's help in determining the relationship between Sykes and the distinguished physician in the photograph. Kimble learns the physician has died recently.

133

Sykes gets a mysterious phone call, immediately leaves his apartment armed with a pistol.

Kimble puts the pieces of the murderous puzzle together: Here we revert to a plant in the first act when he had been tapped, as a pillar of the medical establishment, to lend his name and approbation to a new "miracle" drug whose side effects of which he discovered were disastrous. Kimble's findings, if made public, would have ended the flow of millions to the drug company; thus he had become a prime candidate for assassination, a killing engineered by Dr. Nichols, who had succeeded the dead physician as the company's laudatory spokesman.

Sykes had broken into Kimble's house to kill him, but with the doctor out on an emergency, Sykes had to silence the only witness to his intrusion—Kimble's wife.

Now Sykes goes after Kimble, his primary target from the outset. In a confrontation on an elevated train, Kimble disarms Sykes and handcuffs him to a stanchion. Kimble goes to a hotel convention where Charley is the keynote speaker. On the board of directors for the pharmaceutical firm, Charley announces that the life-endangering drug (with falsified data) will be approved by the U.S. Food and Drug Administration.

Kimble confronts Nichols. Girard appears. Kimble saves the cop's life. In the ensuing vicious fight between the two doctors, Nichols falls to his death. *Sic transit malus mundi.* At least cinematically.

In synopsizing the three-act form, subtleties and segues inevitably disappear in a void of oversimplification, as demonstrated in perhaps the most famous of such glosses, the triadic Boy Meets Girl, Boy Loses Girl, Boy Gets Girl. Or in the immortal shorthand of George M. Cohan who committed the first act to getting his hero up a tree, the second to throwing rocks at him, and the third to getting him down.

When a non-professional sees a picture or reads a screenplay, each zig and zag of the plot and each fluctuation in which the heavy and then the hero, trade the advantage back and forth and surmount the reversals, it seems quite simple—the obvious way to go.

It is not. Each deviation is subjected to trial and error. It has to be thought out and fleshed out and integrated with every other scene that preceded it, and in sync with what follows. It must be created, and that's a difficult task, for the process has been known to put a bit of a strain on that locus of the nervous system we least like to use: the brain. To pound away at the obvious, if only because it's worth repeating, not one speech or sequence in *The Fugitive* or any other workable script sprang full-bodied from the computer. A writer had to hit on it, develop it, and probably rewrite it more times than he cares to remember. Perhaps now it might be worthwhile to x-ray the bare bones of the summary, and reflect on how each operational procedure was sutured to the next. In other words, how do you keep the zigs and zags coming?

You might approach the subject in the shifting geometry of still another paradox, one that is perhaps fueled by the Hegelian dialectic which, like Caesar's Gaul, is divided in three parts.

It goes something like this: An established proposition—the thesis—is contradicted by a second proposition—the antithesis—and then the two are reconciled in a third—the synthesis.

134

In our analogy, the first proposition or principle for the development of any given scene is the conceptualization of the wildest, most impassioned, most impossible, spellbinding, eye-catching action that you can come up with.

The series of escapes engineered by Dr. Kimble in *The Fugitive* include:

. . . disentangling himself from a bus wreck an instant before it is demolished by a freight train.

. . . stealing an ambulance parked at the heavily populated emergency entrance of a hospital.

(Why is it in pictures that whenever an actor needs a vehicle to escape capture and to progress the story, one is readily available with a key in the switch? To carry the non sequitur a bit further, why is it that most actors enter a strange house through a conveniently unlocked door and, when leaving, very seldom shut it? And why do actors on the go carry suitcases which their body language tells us are obviously empty?)

135

Back to Dr. Kimble:

. . . leaping into a raging torrent from a precipice, the visual equivalent of a free fall from the gates of heaven to the river Styx. . . .

There are many more such examples, far beyond the confines of *The Fugitive*. One might think that this sort of hyperbole belongs under the heading of fantasy and outside the bounds of dramatic realism. Not so. Max Beerbohm tied the two genres together in an inextricable bow when he said that "All fantasy should have a solid base in reality." Thus we apply the antithesis of the dialectic:

Every outrageous situation invented or devised must be couched in a way that the audience finds acceptable. In conformance with the thesis we are extravagant and unrestrained in molding a scene, yet at the same time we must be plausible. Photographic realism on-screen depicts a world of the possible and not of the probable. You must induce the audience to endow your "shadows of imagination [with] that willing suspension of disbelief for the moment, which constitutes poetic [i.e., dramatic] faith," as Coleridge so famously put it. The scene must flow from the sum total of all the scenes that have preceded it, twisting and thrusting the story forward by shifting, as we've seen as we explored the progression of *The Fugitive,* the dominance from hero to heavy, and back again, and yet again through 120-odd pages of recombinations and ramifications, switching, scene to scene, the polarities of attainment and adversity.

Easier said than done. Another hint on procedure: Work backwards. Determine where you want to go (how to end the scene or the act or the play) even before you know how to get there. Then figure it out.

The above-cited examples from *The Fugitive* are paradigms of playable scenes, not because of their realism or logic, both of which they lack, but in being so well done that they allow the audience to "suspend disbelief." A well-made comedy or drama responds to the same extreme and radical approach as mainstream action-adventures.

Exaggeration is alluring and stimulating; therefore, exaggerate in building a character as well as in formulating a plot. A character can be made memorable regardless of how minor the part or how ordinary the individual. If he is vain, make him a gigantic bonfire of vanity. If she whines, make her a monarch of malcontents. If she is ordinary, make her the absolute quintessence of ordinariness. In dealing with mediocrity, mold your character into the most spectacular, most remarkable mediocrity you can dream up. Albert Brooks as Aaron Altman is such a character in *Broadcast News,* by James L. Brooks. So is Paul Newman as Mr. Bridge in *Mr. and Mrs. Bridge* (screenplay by Ruth Prawer Jhabvala, based on the novel by Evan S. O'Connell), and Kevin Kline in and as *Dave,* written by Gary Ross. When characterization is so well-delineated, *mediocrity* seems hardly the blanket or generic term that applies. It seems, rather, to be a misplaced circumscription and gives way to memorable and a fascinating unordinariness.

Sometimes it is impossible to exaggerate the outrageousness of a living, breathing, irredeemable individual. Such a person was W.C. Fields who was also a fine, funny writer who ventured far beyond the limits of propriety. Even his righteous name was as bizarre as any moniker he gave to an on-screen persona: William Claude Dukenfield.

In an interview granted to a woman representing the *Christian Science Monitor,* during which Fields continuously drank martinis, the reporter asked him, with some understandable exasperation, "Don't you ever drink water?"

"No," he answered.

"And why not?" she asked.

"Because fish fuck in it," he told her.

One Christmas Eve, at home with a companion, he took to musing about the lack of charity and justice in the world.

"Here I am," he said, "an old drunk alone with my millions while most of the children on Earth are sick and hungry and penniless. I've been thinking about doing something for them—giving them money, setting up a foundation. I thought and thought and finally I decided, the hell with 'em."

11

PLOT AND SUBPLOT
Thirty-Six Situations
Including
The Horse Will Help Her

Plot is the development of your story line, the flow of the action in detailed continuity. It is what people and other animals (as in animation) do in a literary or dramatic work, and what happens to them. It is the progress of the possible rather than the probable.

Many writers, critics, and scholars concur with Aristotle that plot has primacy over character. Others, including Bernard Shaw and Mark Twain, do not. Shaw, with his tendency to pamphleteer, emphasized social factors in his plays. His leads, and many of his peripherals as well, symbolize the human attempt to surmount an inhuman environment.

"Plot," he proclaimed, "is the curse of serious drama." He was all for the abandonment of neatness and precision under the proscenium arch. A master of inconsistency and irregularity in his presentations, he dispatched his plays in two-, three-, four- and five-act forms. Plus further diversifications: *Saint Joan* is six scenes and an epilogue; *Fanny's First Play* contains an introduction, three acts and an epilogue. All of which demonstrates how the divisions of a play are at best arbitrary, unstable, and inconsistent.

Mark Twain, too, saw his characters struggling in an inelegant morass of randomness. Of *Huck Finn,* he threatened that "persons attempting to find a plot in [this book] will be shot."

Linear screenwriting, i.e., the homogenized Hollywood product, requires some degree—if only a soupçon—of a plot, particularly if you'd like to see your work made as a movie.

But not all Hollywood plots are linear, and not all linear plots are lucid and rational. Plot progression can be firmly anchored in the vagaries and randomness and absurdities that ensue outside a predictable chain of events, deviations in human behavior that veer off wildly, inexplicably like the erratic tail of a comet, violating order and reasonable expectations. A good example: *Pulp Fiction* (stories by Quentin Tarantino and Roger Avary), an episodic film of outrageous black humor, a violation of classic morality. The picture has a satanic bite in its dialogue and the vitality of unbridled wickedness. Its thrust depends more on accident than most of us who do not cherish ugly surprises would like to accept.

Usually the dramatic conflict explored in a plot pits the forces of good against the forces of evil (as in *The Usual Suspects*). In *Pulp Fiction*, good does not exist. The conflict is joined by the more charming forces of evil (if you'll tolerate the oxymoron) and the more despicable and thoroughly uncharming forces of evil in a circuitous plot.

Life, it can be said, is circuitous. But for the most part it is, happily and luckily, more boring than pictures which depict it as a repetitive and terrifying assault of violence.

Reality deals many times with the implausible, situations so incongruous they could only take place in nature, and nature herself would be embarrassed to put them on-screen. Life can also be accidental and chaotic, while drama allows for neither, except for situations when randomness or coincidence work against the protagonist to make her goal that much harder to achieve. If chance solves or circumvents her problem and snaps her out of a pickle, the audience views it with suspicion and distrust. They consider such lucky intervention an inartistic cop-out.

A resolution that derives from accident occurs when we the audience, are shocked or surprised not by what we might have expected—indirectly presaged by a well-integrated plant—but by some happenstance we couldn't possibly have imagined within the confines of rational predictability. A coincidence is usually unpalatable and always unplanted. It storms out of a deep, dark, unfulfilling corner of nowhere.

In reality, the fickle fingers of fate do seem at times to spin the plot. But good writing doesn't sanction that kind of irresponsible behavior to benefit your fictional hero. Toil that produces so happy a coincidence will bring nothing but trouble. The thrust of *City Slickers II* declines and dies unmourned in the denouement when Curly's (Jack Palance's) conscience (until that moment, we aren't aware that he has one) triumphs over avarice, and he reveals to Mitch Robbins (Billy Crystal) that he owns a map pinpointing the gold mine that they have, throughout the proceedings, been unable to locate.

Breathes there a movie fan with a critical faculty so impoverished and insensitive that he hasn't heaved a sigh of despair when the on-screen hero is saved from a savage death by the Bluebellies of the Seventh Cavalry? Or when the adorable child is snatched from the grave by a miracle drug flown through a howling storm from Johns Hopkins or Vienna, and in the nick of time?

The answer unfortunately is "Yes." It isn't that most moviegoers have eyes that see not, and ears of the purest tin; they'll accept a picture's poor construction when no better fare is offered at their friendly nabe playhouse. They'll bop over, eager to swallow the good it might offer and at the same time resigned to the bad that goes with it. Just as, with equal resignation, it seems, the consumers among them bought cars with those hideous fins on their rear fenders at a time when little else was available.

In pictures, as in most other endeavors, artistry is rare but hogwash abounds. Small wonder that we've become habituated to story construction that far too often falls short of diligence. We are never quite sure when sloppiness will strike. We expect it more times than not, but we don't know what form it will take until it pounces. When it does, we are left with a feeling of depression and dissatisfaction that starts in the pit of the stomach and spreads to the brain. Most adults flinch from the strained artificiality of senseless third-act bail-outs, unlike children, who are more open to fantasy and the absurd.

Recently, a friend remembered taking his six-year-old daughter to a revival of Disney's *Cinderella*, the child accepted the benevolent intervention of the Fairy Godmother, and was full of hope that further assistance would be rendered the beleaguered heroine, somehow against all odds, from other sources. So when Cinderella bolts from the ball at the stroke of midnight, losing with her slipper all hopes of a match with the Prince, the child turned tearfully to her father.

"Don't worry, Daddy," she solaced him, "the horse will help her."

Didacts and technicians of theater have long tried to find a system for cataloging and quantifying the sum total of plot variations, for purposes of tracking or research, to aid and stimulate writers, or possibly just for the hell of it. We're all familiar with the deck of cards that, after a hearty shuffle, enables the shuffler to come up with a plot by plucking cards and melding them into three acts of high-intensity progression. Any combination of pasteboards in the pack, however, could hardly be expected to span the inexhaustible spectrum of story lines, and certainly no such mechanical or architectonic approach could encapsulate all the plot possibilities that have evolved through a painstakingly slow passage of ideas across the millenniums.

Perhaps the oddest and certainly the most economical and famous attempt at plot classification was made by Count Carlo Gozzi (1720–1806), a Venetian dramatizer of fairy tales. He reduced the grand total of possibilities to a scant three dozen. His taxonomy was resuscitated in 1916 by a fellow countryman, Georges Polti, in a slim volume forthrightly entitled *The Thirty-Six Dramatic Situations*. In it the divisions are so broad, so loose and so incongruous that they afford little enlightenment for those who would take them seriously.

For example, in the Second Situation, classified as "Deliverance" under the subclass of A: "Appearance of a Rescuer to the

Condemned"—is *Don Quixote,* by Cervantes. The Third Situation encompasses "Crime Pursued by Vengeance"; its subclass C: "Professional Pursuit of Criminals" includes Conan Doyle's *Sherlock Holmes.* Goethe's *Faust* is sufficiently complex to land in two categories: the Sixth Situation with the stark yet unrestrained title of "Disaster," further broken down under D (1), "Abandonment by a Lover or a Husband," while it also merits a partial listing in the First Situation, "Supplication," where in C (1) "Supplication of the Powerful for Those Dear to the Supplicant," is a reference to Margaret in the denouement.

Charles Dickens' *Great Expectations* falls under the Twenty-First Situation, "Self-Sacrifice for Kindred," subdivided in A (2): "Life Sacrificed for that of a Relative or a Loved One." *Madame Bovary* by Gustav Flaubert finds a slot under the rubric "Adultery," which says it all for the Twenty-Fifth Situation. Adultery is further explicated in C (7) as the act committed "For a Commonplace Rival, By a Perverse Wife." Dostoevsky's *Crime and Punishment* is assigned a place within the Thirty-Fourth Situation, called "Remorse," and refined under A (3) "Remorse for an Assassination." Finally, *Julius Caesar* by Shakespeare is categorized in the Thirtieth Situation, "Ambition," subsumed in A (2) "By a Relative or Person Under Obligation."

143

In a corollary even more curious than *The Thirty-Six Dramatic Situations,* Georges Polti, in his introduction to the work, announced his own "discovery that there are in life but thirty-six emotions . . . and no more"—presumably one for every plot his predecessor had assembled.

Other Gozzi-Polti categories include "Pursuit" (5), which would embrace *The Fugitive* and *Les Misérables;* "Revolt" (8), involving tyrant and conspirator, as in *Spartacus;* "Daring Enterprise" (9), with its yarns, epics and sagas of adventure, war, and westerns; "Abduction" (10): *The Sheik, The Wind and the Lion;* "The Enigma" (11): murder, mystery, mayhem, tales of crime and detection. "Disaster" (6) also hosts "Natural Catastrophes" like *The Johnstown Flood* and *The Raging Inferno.* "Crimes of Love" (26) would house *The Graduate;* while "Obstacles to Love" (28) and "An Enemy Loved" (29) share *Romeo and Juliet* as well as the feuding, passionate, and disorderly conduct of the Hatfields and the McCoys in *Roseanna McCoy.*

Regarding plot, ask yourself:

What is the subject of your story—the kernel, the gist?

Examples:

Pursuit by the hero of the heavy, or vice versa, as in *The Fugitive*.

Vengeance by the hero on the heavy, or vice versa, as in *The Count of Monte Cristo, Ben Hur*.

Vigilante films like those starring Charles Bronson.

Tales of daring enterprise: *Guns of Navarrone, Thirty Seconds Over Tokyo*.

Stories of revolt: *Battleship Potemkin*.

Once sufficient thought and writing have been exerted for the theme to emerge, a subplot may surface if there exists a need for one. That underplot or counterplot is the secondary action of the screenplay. It might be needed to express the theme of the screenplay, once the writer has identified it. The subplot may be unallied to the main thrust of your story, but, as it stresses the theme, it is not irrelevant or inconsequential to it. It may reinforce the plot, as does the subplot in *Sense and Sensibility*, by Jane Austen with a fine, surgical screenplay by Emma Thompson. The mystifying and frustrating rejection of Marianne Dashwood (Kate Winslet) by the profligate John Willoughby (Greg Wise) sharply accentuates the painful vicissitudes that characterize her sister Elinor's (Emma Thompson) relationship with Edward Ferrars (Hugh Grant). It stresses the theme of the story as it delivers a variation on it.

Jerry Seinfeld, the hero of what was perhaps TV's zaniest and most amusing show, introduced each episode with what amounts to a brief subplot in the form of a monologue; the theme often parallels what we're about to enjoy for the next twenty-five minutes.

A subplot can take the form of a counterplot, which is not a reflection of the mainstream action but that which progresses in contrast to it. Shakespeare was big on counterplots, which comprise key elements of *Hamlet, King Lear*, and *The Tempest* among others.

At some point, usually in the second act, the subplot intersects and fuses with the primary story. Minor characters, generally used to express the theme, are the connecting rods that bridge the gulf.

Does your subplot fall into one of the following categories? Examples:

A subplot unrelated to the main action, used to supply comic relief: The pair of cricket buffs in *The Lady Vanishes*, screenplay by Frank Launder and Sidney Gilliat.

A subplot that is by contrast or comparison reflections of the plot: The young lovers in Arthur Laurents' *Summertime*, adapted from his play *The Time of the Cuckoo*. Their relationship, smooth and sexy, punctuates the difficulties that Katharine Hepburn faces in her romance with Rosanno Brazzi.

Subplots to reinforce the main plot: *My Man Godfrey*, screenplay by Morrie Ryskind and Eric Hatch, adapted from Hatch's novel, in which a pauperized William Powell prospers during the Great Depression. Parallel to his story runs that of the homeless and jobless with whom he lives in a garbage dump.

Subplots that reinforce or substantiate or identify your theme once you find it: Jane Austen's *Pride and Prejudice*, screenplay by Aldous Huxley, in which Elizabeth Bennet's mother and four sisters manifest variations on the same theme, viz., a deep and irrefutable belief that every rich young bachelor is badly in need of a wife with the kind of credentials they are willing and able to supply.

Possibly the most important question arising from the use of a subplot: Do you need one?

12

CHARACTER
Heroes and Heavies
Raising a Fist Against Fate

Art in all its forms has been described from time to time as a merciful delusion of reality. Or, to put it inversely, the suppression (if only temporarily) of reality might be interpreted as a merciful delusion of art. No one has expressed the notion better than John Steinbeck in *The Grapes of Wrath*. A minor character, one of the hungry, landless, jobless army of Okies in California, has managed to amass ten cents—one dime. He spends it on a movie rather than on a loaf of bread. The unnamed picture referred to in the book appears to be thematically identical to *Sullivan's Travels*, by Preston Sturges. What makes this communion between the two all the more curious is the fact that the book was published in April, 1939, two years before the movie was released. Whatever the chronology, it serves as a good example of a minor character being used to express a pet notion of the author's, the indispensability of art.

Movies can supply something that bread cannot, even to a hungry man. A great plot excites because it recounts what interesting people do; a great character is unforgettable because he "disturbs and arrests," as Maugham writes in the opening paragraph of *The Moon and Sixpence.*

Producer Edmund Grainger was, at times, disturbing and arresting because somewhere in the deepest recesses of his mind there was a severance between words and their meanings.

We had finished, one afternoon, talking about plot.

"Now," I suggested, "let's talk about character."

"Don't be metaphysical," Grainger said.

Too many heroic characters, in "disturbing and arresting," are sleazy symbols of the triumph of sour aggression over sweet reason, of disorder over harmony. Too many so-called heroes smash too many mouths, wielding weapons that stick and slash and puncture. The punk brutalities of the *Rambo* movies (based on characters by David Morrell) fade mercifully before the complex melancholy of *Hamlet.* *Rambo* is explicit, unambiguous; in contrast, an element of mystery surrounds and enhances *Hamlet.* You always know that Rambo is on the verge of kicking some evil bastard's ass. You never know what Hamlet will do next. Brigid O'Shaughnessy finds Sam Spade fascinating (as does the audience) in John Huston's screen adaptation of Dashiell Hammett's novel *The Maltese Falcon,* calling him the "most unpredictable man I've ever met." Similarly, the Coen brothers create mysterious characters who are mesmerizing in their eccentricities.

Both Hamlet and Rambo (what a pair) stand alone. Each in his own way has "composure, awareness, and concentration—vision," which Bernie Kosar, one of the more articulate quarterbacks in the NFL, declared that all great field generals must have, including the "ability to accept all surrounding stimuli and utilize it."

Your principle character, like any fine quarterback, must not only join the struggle; he, with the progression of the screenplay (or the ball game), must lead it. Your hero and Bernie Kosar must change, must forge ahead when they learn something new which qualitatively alters and advances the progression. Example: Deep in the third act of *The Front Page*, the dual heroes, Hildy Johnson and Walter Burns, are in trouble for "harboring a fugitive from justice," an innocent schlemiel named Earl Williams. All seems lost for Hildy, Walter, and Earl when Irving Pincus delivers the governor's reprieve for the fugitive whom both the mayor and the sheriff were hell-bent on hanging to win an election on a law-and-order/root-out-all-radicals ticket. Earl is saved from the noose, and Hildy and Walter triumph over the forces of municipal corruption.

The definition of a primary character as a man (or woman) who likes to suffer has in postmodern pictures been modified to include the hero who likes to inflict suffering on others. Example: Stallone as Rambo again, with his immeasurable capacity for dishing it out.

Why is violence on-screen so magnetic? Is it possibly because we, in our social contract, must hold ourselves in almost constant restraint, and we find it frustrating? Whatever the reason, there's nothing new about it in our fiction. "The American hero," D.H Lawrence observed, was "cold, hard-eyed, isolate and a killer," functioning where "there is too much menace in the landscape."

John Wayne, in the scripts he chose, was invincible, indomitable, capable of anything. Even when he died at the squeeze on *Sands of Iwo Jima*, his spirit lived on, inspiring lesser men to hold high the torch of machismo.

The late producer Nicky Nayfack perhaps best verbalized why Wayne was so totally unbeatable. "He had the quality," Nayfack said, "like when the heavy covers him with a .45, Duke says evenly, 'Give me that gun or I'll kill you, and the audience and the heavy believe him."

The hero can be the man who knows—he knows what's wrong and how to fix it, as does John Travolta in *Get Shorty* (screenplay by Scott Frank, based on the novel by Elmore Leonard) or Clark Gable/Marlon Brando as Fletcher Christian in *Mutiny on the Bounty*, screenplay (1935) by Jules Furthman, Talbot Jennings, and Carey Wilson; remake (1962) by Charles Lederer, from the novel by Charles Nordhoff and James Hall. He can be the man who stands alone, the Byronic hero, like Robert De Niro as Neil McCauley in *Heat* (screenplay by Michael Mann), or the eponymous *Nixon* (screenplay by Stephen J.

Rivele, Christopher Wilkinson, and Oliver Stone). Or he can be the man who learns, changes, and grows, as does David Shayne (John Cusack) in *Bullets Over Broadway* or Mario Ruoppolo (Massimo Troisi) in *Il Postino (The Postman)*. The hero, according to Clark Gable, was the man who had the last word—at least that was how he evaluated his own heroics. "I don't give a damn what happens in a scene," he declared, "who has the most lines, where the camera moves, but I want the last word. I want the camera on me when I say it, and I want to be the first to exit." (Leaving the rest of the cast, presumably, with lots of egg on their collective face.)

According to Konstantin Stanislavsky, the hero is the actor (you're writing for actors, remember) who enjoys the most respect and deference, hardly a notion that quickens the pulse of a democratic society in which, at least in theory, respect and deference must be earned. "How do you know," Stanislavsky asked, "that the man up onstage is a king? Not because he wears a crown or sits on a throne—a jester can do that—but because he's treated like a king."

How do you build character? By assigning a feature or a trait to illustrate a quality or qualities of an individual. In *The Fugitive*, Dr. Kimble is cornered in a hospital by his pursuers. Yet he risks discovery to save a child's life. In *Boys Town*, written by Dore Schary and Eleanore Griffin, Spencer Tracy as Father Flannagan takes a sip of water, pauses, then crosses the room to share the rest of the glass with a plant. Symbolically, he tends the fern as he nurtures children.

Character can be exaggerated eccentricity. Tracy's character, Gunner Sloane, in *Test Pilot* chews gum and plants a wad on the fuselage of an airplane before he climbs in for a perilous trial run. When for once he doesn't, suspense is heightened. Is this a sign that he will be killed? (Note use of gum and its consequences as plant-payoff.)

Early in *Lawrence of Arabia* the hero lights a match and, as it flares, extinguishes it between thumb and forefinger. "What's the trick?" a colleague asks. The "trick" is his willingness to accept the pain. In what seems to be an irrelevant and completely remote context, Michael Wilson and Robert Bolt, the screenwriters, have established Lawrence's ability to endure the hardship he later overcomes in the desert.

In *Driving Miss Daisy* (script by Alfred Uhry from his play), an insight into the character of Hoke Colburn (played by Morgan Freeman) establishes early on that he is more interesting and more complex and more learned than just another handsome automaton behind a steering wheel. Applying for the job of chauffeur for Miss Daisy at her son's factory, he finds the staff in a state of agitated confusion because the only elevator is fritzed, and nobody on the payroll knows how to unfritz it. Hoke Colburn does.

In *Shirley Valentine* (screenplay by Willy Russell), the heroine of the same name talks to a wall, to a rock, directly to the camera, revealing the depth of her loneliness and isolation. Some of these examples appear to be no more than a detail or a gesture, what is designated in N.Y. and L.A. as shtick, Yiddish for "stage business." No more, at times, than a brief movement or a limited action, they are handy little gadgets capable of expressing anything you might want to convey.

In the pantheon of heroes, honorable niches are occupied by a wide variety of luminaries. The nomenclature for character classification is rather picturesque and is used by professionals not academically but practically, to communicate in an easily identifiable sort of verbal shorthand. A few examples:

The Doom-Eager Hero who looks for trouble. A prime specimen is *Hamlet*.

"The time is out of joint:" [he muses]

"O cursed spite,

"That I was ever born to set it right!"

Other Doom-Eager Heroes include:

Gentleman's Agreement, in which Gregory Peck goes off to tilt against country-club anti-Semitism.

Mr. Smith Goes to Washington, with James Stewart taking on the U.S. Congress to save the republic from corruption.

In the Line of Fire, with Clint Eastwood seeking a confrontation with death by exposing himself to mortal danger for not exposing himself to mortal danger earlier in an analogous but equally ugly predicament.

It should be noted that the Doom-Eager Hero at times seeks out a perilous situation in which he had suffered a previous and devastating defeat, confronting jeopardy in order to redeem himself. The procedure might be termed the Ploy of the Second Chance, the first chance having been botched early in the story or revealed as an action that took place before the curtain rises.

A variation on the theme is struck in *Bad Day at Black Rock:* Doc, the undertaker, presses his friend Tim, the sluggish sheriff, to take a whack at saving Macreedy's life after another life in an earlier parallel situation had been lost due to apathy:

> TIM
> (angrily)
> Lemme alone, I tell ya!

> DOC
> I can't let you alone! I can't let myself alone! Don't you understand that?
> (madly, fiercely)
> Four years ago something terrible happened here. We did nothing about it. Nothing. The whole town fell into a sort of settled melancholy, and the people in it closed their eyes and held their tongues and failed the test with a whimper.

Tim sighs, running a thick hand over his forehead.

> DOC
> Now something terrible is going to happen again, and in a way we're lucky because we've been given a second chance. And this time I won't close my eyes, I won't hold my tongue, and if I'm needed I won't fail.
> (harshly)
> And neither will you!

Another durable specimen is the But-For Hero, consciously seeking to right a wrong. Such as:

But for Henry V, England would have become a vassal state of France.

But for Joan of Arc, France would have become a vassal state of England.

But for the Pony Express, we would have lost the West. And on and on.

Another familiar figure of distinction is the Reluctant Hero whose destiny and difficulties are thrust on him by outside forces. Thus, the linguistics student who preferred the musty quietude of the archaeology stacks becomes Lawrence of Arabia.

And:

Destry Rides Again, wherein a shy and dovish young man straps on his six-guns when all else fails, and resorts to the violence he hates in order to restore tranquillity to the town he loves.

And:

The lanky, laconic sheriff of Carl Foreman's *High Noon,* who on his wedding day must take up arms to defend himself from the murderous onslaught of an outlaw band.

The Mistaken-Identity Hero, of the "What-They-Really-Don't-Know" picture, who gets in a mess because he's acknowledged to be someone else, as in *The Inspector General, Charley's Aunt, Sullivan's Travels, The Prisoner of Zenda.* To which might be added the genre of the Heroic Masquerade, as in *The Scarlet Pimpernel* (screenplay by Robert Sherwood, Sam Bermann, Arthur Wimperis, and Lajos Biró from the novel by Baroness Emmuska Orczy), in which a limp-wristed British fop saves French aristocrats from the guillotine. Or as in the *Zorro* series wherein a scion of the nobility wars on the evil oligarchs who have taken over colonial California. The long list includes Schindler, a card-carrying member of the Nazi party, who saved more than a thousand Jews from the camps and the ovens. The category wouldn't be complete without *Superman,* the aerodynamic vigilante.

Some heroes have the added attraction of being Strangers Out of Nowhere who drop in to right a wrong and then disappear back into Nowhere: that epitome of valor as played by Alan Ladd in *Shane* (by A.B. Guthrie, Jr.), so virile that when he strides across the pasture his balls clank on the soundtrack; or the vagabond-philosopher played by James Cagney in Louis Bromfield's *Johnny Come Lately* (screenplay by John Van Druten); or Nick Nolte's bum in Paul Mazursky's *Down and Out in Beverly Hills*; as well as every tramp Chaplin ever wrote. Their roots are never disclosed.

A spin-off is the Mysterious Hero. Sometimes he is lost and trying to find himself or is escaping from the obstructive past and seeking renewal, as in *The Quiet Man* (screenplay by Frank S. Nugent, from a story by Maurice Walsh), whose presence in Ireland is an enigma until his motivation for leaving the U.S. is explained in the third act; or as in *The Mark* (screenplay by Sidney Buchman and Stanley Mann, from a novel by Charles Israel), whose protagonist holds a horrifying secret that threatens to destroy him. Sometimes he seeks a new and better life, usually in a fresh, exotic climate in darkest Africa or in the early West, as in *The Immigrants*. Or he takes remedial action to rectify an earlier character flaw, as in *Lord Jim* (screenplay by Richard Brooks, from the Joseph Conrad novel).

154

Another subspecies is populated by the kind of hero who crashes into town hell-bent on exploiting it, and through the love of a good woman, gets all married up and settles down, as does *The Music Man* (by Meredith Willson), and *The Sheepman* (by William Bowers).

Then there are the great adventurers including the accidental and reluctant voyagers motivated by an unswerving drive and longing to find their way back home. The list is impressive—from Ulysses to Dorothy marooned in the Land of Oz to E.T. These are Mythic Heroes, the epic overachievers, the searchers and seekers of some precious Grail, the progeny of the Argonauts and the Knights of Camelot. They include the Saviors, from Gandhi to Superman; the Town Tamers on a planetary scale (Alexander, Joan of Arc); and those who changed the world (Lincoln, Curie, van Gogh); and its royals (Anne, Elizabeth, and Victoria).

If you're dealing with a hero who is "cold, hard-eyed, isolate, and a killer," he will still incite the empathy of an audience so long as the heavy opposing him is worse, infinitely more heinous than he is.

Example: *The Godfather*, in which the hero's savagery is mitigated by a lovable alter ego. Coppola and Mario Puzo, who wrote the novel, surrounded the godfather with children who adore him and by neighbors whom he aids and defends against a greedy, corrupt, and totally noxious predator, like a Robin Hood unwittingly transplanted to an East Side ghetto.

In structuring character, begin with your protagonist, for he is the vortical figure of any story. It isn't enough that he joins in the struggle; he must, as the screenplay progresses, ramrod it. Other characters turn to him for leadership.

Your hero must be, as the French say, *engagé*, entangled in the gears. Writers at times have been taken by a tendency and a temptation (because it is easier, i.e., requires less intense plotting) to have a hero stand above the madding crowd, as in the eye of a hurricane, while turmoil and catastrophe rage around her. To be untouched, aloof, and uninvolved is to assume a stance that is coolly cerebral and philosophical, two admirable qualities which at best have at best a subordinate place in the persona of a hero. A protagonist might be motivated by cognitive logic, but the core and substance of her psyche is her effective capacity to feel and act out love, hate, joy, sorrow, fortitude, fear, etc.

There are modifications. The protagonist of *Der Blaue Engel—The Blue Angel*—(screenplay by Robert Liebmann, based on the novel by Heinrich Mann) is both professorial and philosophical, but the stick that stirs his fire is emotional: his obsession with the tarty chanteuse played by Marlene Dietrich. A more bizarre and pathetic misalliance would be hard to find. Yet we can empathize with professor Immanuel Roth (Emil Jannings) because none of us is immune to the pain and futility of unrequited love.

Our identifying with a protagonist can be swiftly vitiated when those around him are in physical danger and he is not. He can suffer in his sympathy for those in peril, but his sensitivity to their plight does nothing to increase the flutter of our hearts. It is the people in deep trouble with whom we empathize.

A basic weakness of this sort, anchored in an otherwise fine picture, emerges in *Paths of Glory* (Stanley Kubrick, Calder Willingham, and Jim Thompson's adaptation of the Humphrey Cobb novel). Kirk Douglas suffers and sighs to no end as a French Army officer of World

155

War I when he is called upon to defend three scapegoated enlisted men accused in a court-martial, and on the flimsiest evidence, of cowardice in battle.

It is the defendants that we root for. As the story unfurls, it isn't long before the audience gets fidgety over an issue the picture refuses to face: Why is Colonel Dax so heroic and long-suffering when the other three unfortunates will soon be stood before a wall and shot dead?

Then there is the hardy type of hero who flat-out refuses, come hell or an army of adversaries, to be shot dead: the Invincible Hero. He is, in the late twentieth century, the easily recognized no-brainer who wipes out a cast of thousands in the mass-murderous canon of Sylvester Stallone and all those martial artists and humanoid stencils who have proliferated since the enshrinement of Bruce Lee and John Wayne.

In the pre-Wayne history of drama, the "invincible" hero lacked absolute impregnability because he possessed a tragic flaw, a defect which led to his downfall. It came in two handy packages, each of them freighted with unlimited possibilities. One was cognitive, an error in judgment which Aristotle called *hamartia* (meaning error). Thus the tragic flaw of Oedipus is lodged in his fatal unawareness that the man he killed was his father, and the woman he married was his mother.

Othello's error in judgment is, like that of Oedipus, twofold. He is jealous of his innocent wife, Desdemona, and he believes with naive fervor the lies of the malcontent and mess-maker Iago.

The second defect can be physical rather than judgmental, a part or particle of the hero's anatomy that is especially or solely vulnerable. Today, the Achilles' heel gambit is exercised for the most part to invoke empathy (we are all symbolically flawed or wounded in one way or another), or to aggravate the hero's difficulties by planting obstacles and adversity for him to overcome. Thus John Macreedy's paralyzed arm in *Black Rock* becomes his Achilles' heel, as does Philip Carey's (Leslie Howard's) club foot in *Of Human Bondage*.

The impairment can be a character or a psychological disorder: greed in *The Informer*, booze in *The Lost Weekend*, compulsive womanizing in *Shampoo*.

Hamlet procrastinates, losing all volition, wallowing in self-doubt and indecision. When finally he takes action, stage and screen are strewn with corpses, including his own.

Another permutation of the Achilles' heel: a characteristic that ultimately defeats the hero and in so doing invokes the admiration of the audience for his audacious and uncompromising integrity, and arouses their fears for his well-being. Among these Doom Seekers is Sir Thomas More, who defies the Crown and dies for his faith; the chain-gang impenitent called *Cool Hand Luke* (screenplay by Frank Pierson and Donn Pearce); and the refractory inmate of a mental hospital in *One Flew Over the Cuckoo's Nest* (screenplay by Lawrence Hauben and Bo Goldman).

In Sinclair Lewis' *Arrowsmith*, the Achilles' heel of the doctor-protagonist is his humanity. He sacrifices the objective detachment to which he has dedicated his life of "pure" science when he prescribes his bubonic antitoxin to everyone who needs it, rather than to half the island population, thus ruining the value and losing control of his experiment and his prospects for fame.

The tragic flaw in its diverse aspects and modifications has been all but exterminated in the past few years.

Problems facing Invincible Heroes like Wayne and Stallone stem not from some internal or personal weakness which might be construed as wimpy in this sick era of malignity and drive-by shootings. The tragic flaw as an instrument of opposition to the hero's realizing his goal has been supplanted by the multitude of villains determined to liquidate him. The excessive beastliness of these rotters is such that Sly and the Duke must kill, kill, kill them all to preserve goodness and mercy, godliness and decency in the world. Count the corpses in a Stallone epic and you'll run out of numbers. Try to find just one Achilles' heel in his copy-cat battalion of celluloid tigers and you'll come up empty.

A man becomes a hero by raising his fist against his fate, but every time he does he stands at the crossroads and risks getting knocked on his ass by the heavy. The antagonist must be worthy of your hero's steel. He must not be a patsy, never an easy conquest, for the harsher the conflict, the more glorious the triumph. And, inversely, your hero is only as strong as the scoundrel who opposes him. "A

157

delight it must be to face an opponent of some worth," Sherlock Holmes says in *The Adventure of the Noble Bachelor*. Which brings us to the question of antagonists.

A few vagrant thoughts that stray from technique to pure theory regarding heavies:

Unless your work is honored by a command performance before a crowned head, a prime minister or a president, your audience, in all probability, will be made up of people who haven't achieved the goals they aspire to, simply because most people don't. They've somehow fallen short of the jackpot and the rewards they feel they deserve in a meritocracy. Or they suspect they are the victims of enemies or society, of injustice or an unsympathetic randomness. In a word, underdogs on some fair and frabjous day that has yet to dawn will rise up and claim their rightful stake on Celebrity Row.

We the audience unconsciously root for ourselves when we identify with the hero as underdog, someone of as-yet-unrealized character and virtue who is prefigured to lose the impending conflict because the odds are stacked overwhelmingly against him.

Casting your hero as an underdog is best accomplished not by making him a clod of ineptitude, but by throwing him into the ring against a power-packed, seemingly invincible adversary. It was Goliath who made David a biblical luminary. It was Sonny Liston who made Muhammad Ali the idol of fistiana some five thousand years later. In between, it was the depth of Iago's unmitigated malignity that made Othello a colossus of tragic splendor. Without him, the Moor is just another misguided honcho with a bent for uxoriousness.

It was mentioned some pages back that every writer is the hero of his own fantasies. To which may now be added a corollary: He is also the heavy. Virtue and vice can, and sometimes do, dwell concurrently in the same body. The co-existence of opposites that rule our own passions is essentially a Freudian notion, but in dramatic and literary interpretation it was noted by many of his predecessors— Aristotle and Horace, Coleridge and Hobbes, to name a few. Indeed, the duality of mankind, the fusion of two sides of the same coin in each of us, is one of Jung's four archetypes of literature (the others being the Hero's Quest, the Fall From Innocence, and the Fertility Cycle with its never-ending repetition of birth, death, re-birth, and so on). Perhaps the most extravagant instance of internal warfare occurs in R.L. Stevenson's *The Strange Case of Dr. Jekyll and Mr. Hyde.*

We all write out of personal experience. Our fiction is in one way or another autobiographical. To mold an antagonist we reinterpret and refine our layered trove of subutaneous recollections, our id impulses and instincts. The juices churn and ferment without our giving so much as a mumbling thought to the archetype from which they possibly spring. We syphon them off, jerk them free and then, finally, imprison them on paper. What emerges may be so camouflaged and distorted that it becomes unrecognizable even to us.

In *Witches and Other Night Fears*, Charles Lamb wrote, "The archetypes are in us." He died forty years before Jung was born.

The characterization of the bad guy can evolve as an adult expression of a fear or a hatred toward something or somebody reflexively evoked from a childhood memory, even when it's irrational; it is a stimulus that excites a literary or a dramatic response in a writer's later life. An awareness of evil becomes a depiction of evil.

Additionally, there is an attempt on the part of some writers to assuage our moral or ethical failures and nastiness by consigning them in a somewhat disguised form to the black-hatted scoundrel we've created to prey on the part of us that's all spiffed up under the white hat.

A final foray into the structure of heavies: There are writers whose bad guys are the potent ghost-surrogates of themselves—phantoms of terror who lurk deep in the unconscious. They can at times be drained off and put to rest, vanquished by the hero with whom the writer consciously identifies. This is possibly the writer's attempt to defeat a specter that terrifies and dominates him.

Many pictures fall apart in their conclusions, it seems, because we as writers don't know how to dispose of our suppressed ghosts, or because we are unsure of how to conclude the relationship between the ego and the id of our own makeup. The way a writer deals with his hero's antagonist could be an innocuous outlet for the writer's inhibited aggressions—possibly an attempt to resolve them.

159

Who constitutes the opposition? Who crosses swords with the hero? Consider antagonists in terms derived from a makeshift series of telescope phrases invented for swift communication among the makers of early Westerns.

The Brain Heavy:

The intelligence behind the gang, the syndicate, the Mafia (originally cattle rustlers). A leader of high standing in the unsuspecting community—a banker, perhaps, or a lawyer. A figure of respect or authority. His number-one lieutenant is:

The Dog Heavy:

The sociopathic killer, the enforcer, so-called because in the dawn of Westerns he'd be established early when he'd get off his horse and swagger out of his way to kick an innocent dog. Conversely, the hero, wearing his signature white hat, would be introduced, or shown shortly thereafter, feeding his horse a few cubes of sugar, which established him as a splendid fellow.

The Cad Heavy:

Not evil but weak; a follower, a bed-wetter. Possibly the errant brother of the heroine. Killed not by the hero but often by a stray or ricocheting bullet from the Dog Heavy's gun. The Cad has metamorphosed into a libertine, a gigolo, an exploiter of women.

The variations on all these bad-ass stereotypes are infinite. They're found everywhere. Shakespeare incorporates strong elements of the devil and vice in morality plays of the Middle Ages: Iago (*Othello*), Aaron the Moor (*Titus Andronicus*), Richard of Gloucester (*Henry VI* and *Richard III*), Don John (*Much Ado About Nothing*), Edmund (*King Lear*), Iachimo (*Cymbeline*).

If the theme of a story is delivered by a primary character, it sounds pompous and self-serving. The character is sounding off about what he will accomplish; indeed, what he must accomplish to make the theme work. Therefore a secondary character is needed to present the theme.

It has become acceptable and legitimate for a secondary character to progress the story with voice-overs, incorporeal narrative delivered on the soundtrack that supplements action and developmental segues. The technique is infinitely easier than writing dialogue or sharpening the progression of a story. It takes less time, so it costs less money and it can be satisfactorily executed by a subordinate in the cast, who might only participate in this capacity—a sort of narrative voice of God.

A secondary character is usually one whose interaction and dialogue with the protagonist will clarify and advance the lead's actions and motives. He is the hero's (or the heavy's) confidant, for example. He basks in the reflected glory of a star, thereby emphasizing the star's luster while lacking the star's excitement and charisma himself.

To Jack Warner, Ronald Reagan was a competent secondary-role player. When he learned that Reagan was being groomed for President of the U.S. as the star of the Republican Party, Jack was dumbfounded.

"No," he said, "it can't be. Ronnie for Best Friend, Dennis Morgan [a firm-jawed actor who, briefly, was nurtured by Warner for stardom] for President."

A tertiary character is further removed from the action as it unfolds. Her function is that of the secondary character but with a smaller part and less money. She can be used as the frame who introduces the story and gets the hell out of the way until she reappears to give the piece closure at the squeeze.

Example: Mr. Lockwood, who periodically relates the story of Heathcliff and Catherine in *Wuthering Heights*.

Secondary and tertiary characters are used to support opposing principals, represent opposing principles, explain and progress your story.

Make sure that every actor's connection to the plot is more than tangential, even if it's momentary. Sometimes, and at first glance, a brief set piece might seem irrelevant, but even a cursory examination of the scene might reveal that it isolates or clarifies the picture's theme, as does the tired and snotty waitress in *Five Easy Pieces*. At other times it moves the story forward when it flounders. Example: *The Love*

Parade. Halfway through the picture Jeanette MacDonald and Maurice Chevalier are married in a colorful and elaborate ceremony, which meant to preview audiences that the picture was over. They got up and left the theater. To keep them in their seats, Ernst Lubitsch inserted a shot of a diplomat, the Turkish Ambassador, who shakes his head emphatically to nobody in particular. If furtive memory serves, he said something like, "It will never work." And the members of the audience, realizing that the leads are not about to live happily ever after, happily sink back into their seats. This brief but brilliant ploy of using a minor character to revive the flagging interest of an audience has thereafter been known in the trade as "the Turkish Ambassador." The aforementioned Irving Pincus of *The Front Page* is a Turkish Ambassador.

Everybody needs somebody, the old song goes, and so in the history of drama, as in the writings of St. Paul, we have the figure of the Paraclete.

162   Does your hero need a helper-intercessor when he's in a jam, a comforter to support him, a staunch spear-chucker to follow him anywhere and, along the way, to explain your theme to the audience? Someone to talk to, to trade expository secrets in the role of best friend? The peripherals also discharge the duties assigned to the chorus in ancient Greek or classical Renaissance theater by interpreting, reinforcing, criticizing the principals in the mainstream action.

Heavies get lonely too. Does your heavy need any of the paracletean input?

Why and how do your secondary but necessary characters aid, abet, counsel, and console? How do you make them, if not unique, at least memorable? You might try making them a trifle eccentric, a bit peculiar. Lesser or supporting players have "quirks and little guilts," said Alfred Hitchcock. Such characters do enrich a screenplay. They are its very salt and pepper.

13

ANATOMY OF A SCREENPLAY
Emotions Are the Only Facts

For hundreds of years, the three unities—of time, place, and action—were attributed to Aristotle. Despite the fact that critics, in their worship of Classicism, considered them inviolate, Aristotle never advanced two-thirds of them.

The first tine of the trident—that the time span of a play should not exceed the duration of a single day—and the second—that its locus be limited to one venue—are no longer accepted as ironbound laws of stagecraft. They are, rather, considered oppressive, restrictive, and capricious. Even more disturbing in pictures, strict adherence to the unity of place deprives an audience of the rich brocade that a wide-ranging camera can weave.

Academics sleuthing over the last three centuries have yet to disclose internal evidence that the unity of time was but vaguely indicated by Aristotle, nor is there substantiation that he even mentioned unity of place.

When, however, the greatest savant of ancient times wrote in *The Poetics* that "A plot that is well constructed should be rather single than twofold," he was invoking unity of action. The other two unities of time and place were somehow extracted from the old master through a doozie of a misperception by Ludovico Castelvetro, a sixteenth-century pundit, in his *Theory of Poetry*. Other scholars and critics accepted his skewed pronouncements, particularly in his native Italy, and in France with the neo-classicist Pierre Corneille, although the putative Aristotelian dicta never took fire in England despite the adherence of Dryden, Addison, and Ben Jonson.

However, the three unities have their advocates among playwrights and screenwriters today, so if you wish to comply with Castelvetro's bobble, sail on, forge ahead, and welcome to the company of those authors who have preceded you in honoring him. A sampling of their work includes *All My Sons*, *Arsenic and Old Lace*, *Broadway*, *Cat on a Hot Tin Roof*, *Dead End* (time span: a day and a few hours), *Detective Story*, *Dog Day Afternoon*, *The Front Page*, *High Noon*, *Idiot's Delight*, *The Lost Weekend*, *The Male Animal* (three days), *Of Mice and Men* (four days), *The Petrified Forest*, *The Philadelphia Story*, *The Time of Your Life*, *Tobacco Road* (one day plus a few hours), *The Voice of the Turtle* (two days), and *Who's Afraid of Virginia Woolf?*. And, I might add, *Bad Day at Black Rock*.

The compaction of time and place may or may not be observed, according to your fancy and the length and breadth of the story you're telling. Only unity of action is essential to the organic construction of any fruitful play or picture. Without it, randomness and confusion reign. A unified story line cannot serve two masters, nor can it be haphazard or helter-skelter. Maugham's enjoinder that you must "find your subject and stick to it like grim death" seems sensible and easy enough to follow—nothing arcane about it—but beginners often find it difficult to discharge. Remember, your progression is a horse with a single purpose, and not like the beast Stephen Leacock described, which the rider "flung himself upon . . . and rode madly off in all directions." Bear in mind the significant words of the world's greatest sculptor of elephants who (so the joke goes), when asked by a throng of admirers to explain his m.o. said, "What I do is I take a chunk of wood and a mallet and a chisel, and then I chip away everything that doesn't look like an elephant."

A sculptor chips away. A writer deletes. "Cut out anything that does not belong to the emotional development," said Joyce Cary.

It is the "emotional development" that integrates John Sayles' multifaceted screenplay *Lone Star*, a rich and complex tapestry of racial tension, the immutability of love, the conflict between fathers and sons, the solution to a murky homicide, the interrelationship of business and politics—all of which compound to unify the action and entangle the lives of the people in a Tex-Mex border town that is more prototypically American than most of us would care to admit.

It's generally predictable (and easy) to say that your work will improve if you cut your most gorgeous constructs, your gems of exultation, purple passages, most adjectives, unrelenting solemnity in a drama, and unrelieved hilarity in a comedy. However, all this is exceedingly hard to do. Just about every writer (and this includes you, regardless of your experience and training) loves to the point of sanctification every syllable he writes. Secondly, the keenest logician in the screenplay dodge may employ his critical gifts to somebody else's work, but he is a purblind source of prejudice to his own.

Aristotle doesn't seem to have been purblind or prejudicial in his analysis of drama, possibly because he never wrote a play of his own. We don't know enough about his life to apply a Freudian or any other kind of intrusive scalpel to it, but we know that his *Poetics* was the fountainhead from which all Western dramatic criticism sprang. It still dominates; only in the past century or so has dramaturgy deviated from his 2,000-year totalitarian sway. His genius makes it inconceivable that Western culture, so long as it remains more or less intact, will ever be completely free of its incisive influence. However, dramatists of the stage and screen continue to explore and experiment.

Aristotelian analysis held that action, which to him meant plot, was the fundamental element of a play, thereby relegating character to a subordinate position. Therefore, a hero to Aristotle was a man victimized by circumstances, on the bitter receiving end of what he termed "undeserved misfortune." Quite a while later Scott Fitzgerald maintained, inversely, that "action is character," that what a person does is determined by what he is, that character is destiny or, as Heraclitus said a century and a half before Aristotle, "A man's character is his fate."

Maybe, maybe not, for there's no way to test the hypothesis. It might as readily be said, and again without ironclad laboratory evidence, that action is genes or testosterone or toilet training. It's only worth mentioning because the premise worked for Fitzgerald. May whatever literary theories, even prejudices, you hold work as well for you.

Each camp has its adherents, but the debate, which at times can get heated, seems to me, academic. Teachers and practitioners of screenwriting invariably divide the two components. Like Aristotle or Fitzgerald, they emphasize the primacy of one ingredient over the other in the dramaturgic stew. But they are not immiscible. Conjoined and inseparable as Siamese twins, they should enjoy an egalitarian relationship, one never lording it over the other, for with any specific plot, a distinct and matching character is needed to best tell your tale. I don't believe a story analyst can whip up a sampler of plots that work solely because of the character of his protagonists. And if your jumping-off place is a character, then he must be plunged into a story that can best enhance and stimulate his persona.

A story can therefore start to percolate with a character or an incident, which is a piece of a plot. In the beginning, neither the peripaties of the plot nor the fullness of a character emerges full blown on the page. They develop more fully in the rewrite as you hone and expand and, at the same time, eliminate all the unnecessary furniture.

Let's take a look at *The Fugitive* from another angle. In it, a certain kind of character is essential to maximize the plot. He must be a medical doctor whose negative testimony about a forthcoming "miracle" drug will assure its rejection by the F.D.A., its failure on the market, and saddle the giant pharmaceutical corporation which manufactures it with a crippling financial loss. To find the murderer of his wife, Kimble must be a certain kind of doctor—a man brilliant in his profession, one whose mental and physical competence enables him to find the culprit and solve the mystery for the audience before it can digest the clues served up like a series of exotic and unfamiliar dishes on a groaning board.

In *Black Rock*, John Macreedy is an Army officer and a combat veteran of WWII, with an abiding sense of indebtedness to a Nisei soldier who had died saving his life in Italy. He seeks out the young man's father to give him the posthumous medal won by the son and in doing so uncovers the racist murder of the old man. The action calls for a man of uncommon courage and quiet strength, with a repository of martial skills in order to cope with the anfractruosities of the plot. It should be added that Macreedy's paralyzed arm, a relic of combat, is in no way an impediment to his deftness for inflicting punishment on those who deserve it, just as the wounds of Frederic Henry in Hemingway's *A Farewell to Arms* in no way interfered with his sexual gymnastics. It should also be mentioned that the idea of a protagonist with a gimpy arm was contributed by producer Dore Schary. The notion that the hero's impairment (without tasteless, unattractive scars or blemishes) might encourage an audience to empathize with him in his vulnerability had nothing to do with Dore's proposal; rather, it was founded on his unshakable conviction that no actor could resist playing a cripple. (Director Henry Hathaway harbored a not dissimilar fancy. He told me once that no actor could resist playing a pimp.)

167

Scratch any writer and you'll find a student of sorts, i.e., a nosy, omnivorous animal who explores and investigates. The student in me, such as it is, would like to know what the great practitioners between Aristotle and Fitzgerald had to say about craft—Emily Brontë, for instance. Did she bare her immaculate mind to her brother and sisters?

Did she say, "I got a notion for a rather bizarre character—call him Heathcliff—with a wild and stormy nature in which gentleness and savagery are combined. Now I've got to work out the plot. . . ."

Or did she say, "I've been thinking about a story of a Gypsy stray, raised on the moors in the north of England. He falls in love with the daughter of the man who found him in the squalor of Liverpool. He is cruelly treated by her brother. Although she loves

Heathcliff, Catherine marries a neighboring gentleman, while Heathcliff, out of revenge, marries the gentleman's sister. And then, a generation later. . . ."

The point again is: It makes no difference where she began or whether she thought plot was an accessory to character or the other way round. She probably didn't fret over it, she just started writing. In any event, *Wuthering Heights* achieves a seamless, symbiotic bonding of plot and character. She, and then Ben Hecht and Charles MacArthur, who wrote the screenplay a century later, made it work.

Scenes that on the surface appear to be no more than irrelevant episodes can contribute to the totality of the finished product. Linking dissonant and disconnected elements to the main story adds tone and color, strengthens the values, and sharpens the images.

A character in a viable script must be judged, with few exceptions, entirely by his behavior. Only in narrative fiction does the author enjoy the luxury of exposing what his brainchildren think.

Even as a character changes, his characterization must remain consistent with the aggregate of features and traits endowed him by his creator. What he is and who he is, is demonstrated to the audience through the self-evident expedients of deeds and dialogue. Feelings are voiced, the action is external. Seldom is the interiority of the players laid bare, but occasionally it happens, and when it does, we have grown accustomed to the techniques employed: the voice of a character in an aside, lines supposedly not heard by others onstage, directed to the audience, or the voice of a character who doesn't appear to speak on-screen but is heard on the soundtrack. Eugene O'Neill, in an attempt to overcome and to extend the dramatic limitations of dialogue, peppered *Strange Interlude* with "voice-overs," streams of consciousness and private thoughts to reveal what is usually unspoken. *Our Town*, by Thornton Wilder, employs another familiar device in the on-stage presence of the Stage Manager, a one-man chorus who explains, interprets, and comments on the action.

No tale lives by its characters or its plot alone. What propels a story line is the harmonic convergence of the two, inextricably wired together, and the texture that holds them in place is emotion. "Emotions," said Havelock Ellis, "are the only facts." They are expressed primarily through conflict, the clash of wills that unleashes the action, the linchpin of the drama.

There are three customary ways of deconstructing a screenplay by analysis of its essential parts. The first is a breakdown of that familiar trichotomy comprising a first, second, and third act (beginning, middle, and end), perhaps the most elementary divisions a script can bear. It is, however, too simplistic to furnish much guidance beyond the rudiments of the boy-meets-girl, boy-loses-girl, boy-gets-girl, or the get-your-hero-up-a-tree, throw-rocks-at-him, get-him-down school of segmentation.

A second approach is the venerable diagnosis that defines in generic terms the items that go into the work. The difficulty here: We all are familiar with the meaning of these components as words which are substantively defined in any unabridged dictionary—words like *plot, character, exposition, progression, construction,* etc., etc., but their connectedness, their impingement on each other, is seldom if ever examined.

Between the covers of a screenplay, from fade-in to fade-out, is lodged a third approach—a five-pronged linkage of content that can be parsed to measure the efficacy of your dramatic structure. But again be forewarned: No matter how dedicated you might be in following this or any other advisory, you never know how the picture will turn out. Nevertheless, here is the organization of the screenplay in five parts:

1) The Introduction discloses the time and the place of the action, the plot and the principal performers, friends and foes.
2) The Rising Action, with an increase of pressure on the hero and his response to it.
3) The Critical Point of Conflict, the inexorably approaching crisis leading to the conclusive settlement of the issue(s) at stake.
4) The Relentless, Precipitate Train of Events peaking to the climax—Aristotle's "Catastrophe."

169

5) Winding Down of the Action, including the obligatory
scene (more about it later).

These are the five bare bones in the anatomy of a screenplay. They need a massive infusion of blood and a solid integument of flesh which only you can supply. In building conflict, the antagonism between hero and heavy and their respective cohorts usually evolves in five concatenated stages:

1) an airing or an exchange of views, followed by
2) a sharp difference of opinion, leading to
3) the determination to take action, climaxed by
4) the action itself, and finally
5) the results of the action taken.

The purpose of each stage is to propel your protagonist ever closer to his goal.

Within the five-fold configuration, how does your hero go about getting there?

An analogy, strained perhaps but relevant, might be made with a football team in possession of the ball on its own one-yard line. With the entire field before it, the offense is loaded with options. But the farther the team advances, the more its area of operations is narrowed, and the more limited is its range. To wit, the farther you march, march right down the field until you as a writer reach your personal goal line, the more restricted is your focus.

What measures will your protagonist effect to cross his goal line?

Goals are not always affirmative. In film, however, a negative goal can be disastrous. In *The Brothers Rico*, a wonderfully disturbing novel by Georges Simenon, the protagonist avoids action, knowing that the aggression his racketeer bosses demand of him will cause his brother's death. The effort was a dismal failure on-screen.

The Beast in the Jungle, a novella by Henry James, and perhaps the most astounding and brilliant story ever told about paranoia, was never even attempted as a picture. The Beast in the hero's fantasies is a formless, fearful and oppressive force that will at any time savage him irrecoverably with some "rare and strange" affliction. He avoids its terrible destructiveness by doing nothing, only to realize in his declining years that the Beast is his own inaction and the fate he suffered was the passive, impoverished existence of a man to whom nothing ever happened.

A play about man's deplorable estate which never made it to the screen, possibly because of its negativism, is *Waiting for Godot,* by Samuel Beckett. In it nothing is attempted by the protagonist to attain his goal. Indeed the goal is mysterious and undefined, as are the dual leads who dangle in a vacuum of passivity between an ever-abiding hope that Godot will show up, and an indestructible despair that he will not. Who Godot is (God plus the standard abbreviation of Old Testament?) and why they are waiting for him is never made clear. Didi and Gogo are a reduplicated pair of lost souls, alienated from this world, possibly seeking spiritual grace and deliverance which might be associated with Godot's arrival.

A goal can be paltry in its genesis, but it can grow and change into something exalted and fine. Stephan Elliott's *The Adventures of Priscilla, Queen of the Desert* opens frivolously on three shabby drag queens off to the outback of Australia to play a series of gigs. It becomes wondrously poignant when the doyenne of the group, an over-the-hill transsexual, hooks up with a meaty, melancholy car mechanic whose tacky wife has run out on him. As it has for millenniums, love conquers all.

Ed Wood (screenplay by Scott Alexander and Larry Karaszewski) kicks off with an ineffectual and spectacularly unsuccessful director trying to put a B-minus movie together without a budget—a dismissable project at best. It becomes a touching, bittersweet study of an aging director as poverty and senectitude overtake him.

As regards your hero's moves to attain his objective:
1) Do they induce retaliatory or antagonistic moves by the heavy?

2) Does each of their strokes and counterstrokes add depth and strength to their struggle?
3) Does each move additionally contrast and vitalize the warring characters, and vivify their conflict?

The quintessential goal of a dramatic hero is the same as it is off the sound stage: survival. As conflict is the life blood of a screenplay, so struggle is the perpetual state of mankind caught in a vise of turmoil. Jeopardy is a constant in a script, and all of the players are passionate.

Drama from the pre-Shakespearean, Roister-Doister-swagger-dagger school to the heavy-weapons-lumbering-tanks assaults of Oliver Stone has always been confrontational. The writer sets up obstacles, his hero knocks them down, the heavy resurrects them and launches another attack, more formidable than the last. The hero responds in kind, but moreso, stoking the boilers, opening the throttle, punching fast-forward.

IV

The Script: Making It Rich

14

A PIECE OF THE ACTION
Invoking the Worst Calamity

"Waste not, want not" is an aphorism that might be applied to the writing of scenes. Or put another way, in the form of a reciprocal question: Does each of your scenes, and the characters in them, have a reason and a purpose for their inclusion in the total screenplay? If they do not, discard them in conformance with that radical axiom propounded by fourteenth-century scholastic philosopher William of Occam (1300?–1349?). Occam's "razor," as it was called, declared that all unnecessary constituents of the subject being addressed were to be eliminated, i.e., don't be windy or repetitive, and don't clutter your work with irrelevancies.

Another famous argument against *excess* in a scene is found in a metaphor coined by José Ortega y Gasset (1883–1955), the Spanish essayist and critic, when he explored redundancy and too-muchness in the field of fashion. He admired the newfangled modishness of pleated skirts when he first encountered them. "The things that could be more and are content to be less," he wrote with approval.

A fine-tuned and functional scene can still deliver more than one action or explore more than one idea within its parameters. Matter of fact, the major thrust of a scene integrated with a minor action can strengthen its primary focus.

Example: *Nixon*, wherein the former president in the Oval Office, and with a lethargic golden retriever at his feet, directs a bitter monologue at his Secretary of State, growing increasingly pissed off at the U.S. electorate. The American people, he whines, have no affection for him; they don't understand the weight of his office and its punishing responsibilities. Suddenly he turns his vitriol on the handsome beast that ignores him. It is both sad and funny when Nixon (Anthony Hopkins) zeroes in on the poor dumb animal, and it gives greater substance to the scene by showing the depth of the man's paranoia.

Synchroneity—two actions or two voices each ignoring the other—can also remind the audience that the principals on-screen are part of the "real" world that for the most part doesn't listen—the rich broth of life bubbles and boils over for the leads while the rest of the uncaring planet is oblivious to their plight. Engrossed in their own solipsist lives, civilians have plights of their own.

In *Gypsy* (by Arthur Laurents), the leads interact backstage (foreground) while the audience is aware of what is transpiring in the polyphonic background, the stage, as the burlesque show plays on—a not unfamiliar technique used in show-biz stories. Chazz Palminteri as Cheech, the bimbo's bodyguard in *Bullets Over Broadway*, is killed by hoods in the flies while the play within the screenplay progresses on-stage.

In *Corrina, Corrina* (screenplay by Jessie Nelson) the child whose mother has died hides under a table laden with the funeral meats while the adult mourners act out the rueful clichés above and about her.

In *The Front Page*, reporters snarl into phones and at each other, scuffle at penny-ante poker, sharing center stage with the mainstream action.

In *Searching for Bobby Fischer* (screenplay by Steven Zaillian) much of the intellectual passion evidenced by the principals for the lordly game of chess is counterposed against the frenetic background of chess nuts and hustlers in Washington Square, N.Y.C.

In *Four Weddings and a Funeral,* a joyous marriage celebration is transformed into despair when a beloved guest is stricken with a fatal heart attack.

Another form of creative synchronicity: the half-hour sitcom *Seinfeld* (co-creator and head writer: Larry David). No one does it better within an extremely limited time frame. Each of the four main characters takes off on separate, goofy tangents, drawing the others, sometimes screaming, usually resisting, seldom listening, into whatever zaniness is on the burner. Not always is the plot resolved, but it is sufficiently entertaining to be addictive.

To make your scenes sharp and tight doesn't mean that you must make their every facet, their every nuance and innuendo crystal clear. You must guide the audience so that they see only what you want them to. Put blinders on them to shut out unwanted light. Limit them to tunnel vision. By endowing them only with what you want them to see, your screenplay is enriched by their putting their own interpretation on it. Example: the climax of *The Bridge on the River Kwai,* when Alec Guinness, mortally wounded, stumbles into the dynamite detonator and destroys the bridge he had built for the Japanese enemy. Is it an accident, or does he with his last breath make one final conscious and courageous effort to strike a blow for Britain? Audiences mulled over the incident long after they left the theater.

If deception or intentional obscurity is your goal, make sure your evasion of clarity leaves nothing to chance. There are times when the writer pays imprecise attention to the development of a character who must exhibit traits that are less than admirable—boorishness, perhaps, or pomposity, or sycophancy. Such a portrait should be drawn with as much thought and anguish as you'd apply to a character attesting to more worthy attributes. Droll Henry Fielding alludes to such a writer in *Tom Jones,* "who told the public that whenever he was dull they might be assured there was a design in it."

A monitory tip: Beware that in putting blinders on your audience, you don't put them on yourself. Self-inflicted blindness seems to have its origin in an attitude many writers assume in overestimating their own endowments, particularly their ability to make swift and felicitous decisions. They're not unlike those magicians who suffer from a case of "shut-eye," the psychological phenomenon in which the thaumaturge performing "psychic" tricks begins to think that he is indeed endowed with preternatural powers. Some psychics and some crystal gazers and indeed some writers do have a kind of super-charged acuity. Among writers it gives rise to another paradox: People who depend on their intellects to turn a buck can be decidedly anti-intellectual, if anti-intellectualism can be defined as hostility or opposition to academic theories, coupled with a distrust or a disregard for the learning process—the epistemology—involved in creative writing courses or in manuals and how-to's generally. The attitude seems to be particularly applicable to the young and inexperienced who contend that there is no need to learn their chosen craft—it will come to them instinctively, or by osmosis, or by divine mercy and favor in a vision perhaps—certainly without the impediments of musty book-learning. They seem to subscribe to the Wildean postulate that nothing worth teaching can ever be taught. Some wise and veteran practitioners agree with them, adhering to another principle: Only by writing does one learn to write.

Another form of shut-eye: the writer who is totally incapable of shedding the faintest ray of light on her own work. Leni Riefenstahl is a confusing example. She could no more explain her formidable artistry than she could her politics. "Like many a first-rate artist," Stephen Schiff wrote in *Vanity Fair* (September, 1992), "she doesn't really know what she's doing, she only knows how to do it." In constructing a scene, when the tiniest parcel was deleted, she could not explain why or how the whole megillah would suffer from it. But buried deep within her visceral complexity she somehow knew what would work and what would not.

A scene can also be fulfilling without revealing everything, whether about plot or character. By holding back a pivotal dollop of information for later divulgence, interest can be sharpened, suspense created. In Act III, Scene ii, Hamlet refuses to allow Guildenstern access to his privacy, to "pluck out the heart of my mystery," Shakespeare might be speaking for any writer who declines to divulge all before the time is ripe.

"A bore," Hitchcock noted, "is somebody who tells you everything at once." Joseph Conrad holds to the "delight and wonder" of restraint in limiting the revelations of a scene. "The artist speaks," he wrote in *The Nigger of the Narcissus,* "to the sense of mystery surrounding our lives."

In terms of character, there are times when the protagonist of a drama is best left unexplained. Who was Shane? Where did he come from? Pictures are heavily populated by heroes whose roots are buried in hallowed, impenetrable ground. Even a classical Freudian analysis—a fifty-minute hour, five days a week—doesn't clarify a hell of a lot.

What motivates Iago's evil? "Unmotivated malignity," Coleridge called it. Was it genetic, if there is such a thing? Or the way he was raised? Or was it a flare-up of sixteenth-century racism?

Next questions: With each scene does your conflict intensify the action, sharpen the excitement, heighten the urgency? Does each step toward the climax build antagonism and make the confrontation increasingly unavoidable?

In scene after scene do you apply additional pressure, constantly turn up the heat? Have you released your exposition gradually, not in great encyclopedic gobs but a bit at a time, hoarding the best jolt for last?

All stories, as has been observed, are tales of mystery and detection. Scene after scene, the writer piles up clues and surprises, shocks, alarms, and red herrings. Unfolding events seem to point us in one direction when we are destined for another.

The correct interpretation of all the helter-skelter is hidden as if in a labyrinth of double meanings and Aesopian language. The analogy is even more evident when we are lured to one or more false conclusions before we're presented in the squeeze with the correct one. Exemplars here are abundant. Any picture that delights and arrests will provide a specimen.

Another scene-by-scene progressional format is the accumulation of isolated, incidental, and seemingly unrelated plot points. Once the

179

piece is completed, they produce a unified, indivisible, and integrated whole recognizable to the audience only when the writer finally wants to reveal it. As in *The Usual Suspects*.

In a jigsaw puzzle of the classic mystery-detective variety, we the audience are made to realize when the revelation comes that while the protagonist has the same information (clues) we have, he has diagnosed the facts correctly (as in *The Maltese Falcon*) while we—through misdirection and legerdemain—have bungled them.

Do you develop each succeeding scene on the foundation of what has preceded it?

Consider the opposite: A haphazard sequence of disconnected events which cannot possibly contribute to the screenplay's unity of action, and instead plunges it into a wayward and capricious randomness.

Every scene should contain some fusion with what has gone before to assure the indivisibility of the complete work. At the same time (another paradox) each scene must be different to lend variety to what otherwise would founder as a repetitive bore. Each scene advances the story, departing from the past as it digs deeper in the present to explore and to challenge what lies ahead. A scene is an individual link in time, place, and action that gets you from where you were to where you're going. It can involve an astonishing interrelatedness of isolated realities—a slew of seemingly disconnected incidents—that vault, once they're arranged in a harmonious manner, into an intelligent and unified pattern. Examples: *The Usual Suspects, Pulp Fiction*.

The ultimate test of a scene: If it is deleted from the text, will the screenplay be incomplete without it? "A thing whose presence or absence makes no visible difference," Aristotle noted, "is not an organic part of the whole." If on the other hand an essential scene is expunged, the audience is left with a feeling of confusion and irritation, of emptiness and discomfort.

The laws of life outside the realm of physical science are generally accepted as unfathomable. "It is impossible to know the outcome of an action," contends an old Japanese proverb. The art of writing in any genre has been examined endlessly by comparing and contrasting it to reality. Many postmodern critics and many skeptics without spiritual security seem to believe in the inherent purposelessness of the universe. All is random; most people in actuality seem to rely on a series of accidents to attain an objective.

Not so in drama, with its necessary dependence on causality. Cause leads to effect, and while the effect may be wildly different from what was expected, the final scene of a screenplay has its own eschatology and a solution that gives the fictional march of events a neatness, a roundedness, and a relevance that is seldom evident in life.

Another analogy: Science sees the Earth as host to humanity but not to humanism. It is a field of interplay for impersonal forces. Man and his needs and aspirations appear to be completely irrelevant. It is only in art that man and his needs and aspirations are treated as totally relevant, while on-stage or on-screen a star assigns to himself even greater solipsistic significance.

A star likes to put his own spin on personal relevance. Remember the histrionic philosophy of Clark Gable: All he claimed he wanted in a scene was the last line and the first exit, an existentialist approach to his craft not unlike that of a psychoanalyst friend (of mine, not Gable's). The doctor was reminiscing about his practice in the days when orthodox Freudians were notoriously silent. At the end of the fifty-minute hour he would say something pertinent and revealing, a gem-like little morsel that would progress the analysis a small step forward. Just like Dr. Gable.

In building scenes, a screenwriter should have at least a vague idea of where she wants to go, some inner bardic voice or some guiding flicker of light that draws her to the end of the journey. Perhaps it's no more than a scrawl on a map. The creative act of writing will fill in many of the blanks once you get going. A curious and indefinable (to me) cranial tool takes over and turns up the burners. (This is what some practitioners refer to as "the story writing itself.")

You may be cruising on automatic (or holding the conviction that you are); but by conscious design you must progress the action, further complicating the complications and intensifying the tensions, with the antagonist increasing the pressure until your hero's ability to extricate himself from the mess he's in seems impossible.

The name of the game is jeopardy; the rising action peaks at the climax when all seems lost—what Aristotle called the catastrophe. How do you get there? You must set up a brace of insurmountable obstructions for your hero and then maneuver to have him overcome them. With each increase in pressure, ask yourself, "What's the worst possible calamity or reversal of fortune I can inflict on him?"

Pick the punishment, no matter how absurd or outlandish it at first seems. Then figure out how to make it tenable. When the hero responds, the heavy tries something else, ever more combative. And so on, no matter how radical; a series of reciprocal unrestraints and high-voltage immoderacies is what constitutes an engrossing plot. And of course, if it doesn't work after giving it a good shot, move on to something else.

Pouring it on: Examples, in many molds, include *The Fugitive*, examined earlier. In *Sense and Sensibility,* a series of scenes makes it increasingly impossible for the two couples, Marianne and Colonel Brandon, and Elinor and Edward Ferrars to be together, and they remain hopelessly lost to each other until screenwriter Emma Thompson, and Jane Austen before her, remove the barriers. In *Mighty Aphrodite* the possibility of Mira Sorvino's finding happiness—a transition from whoredom to housewifery—seems unattainable until Woody Allen, using a vastly satiric deus ex machina, makes it all possible.

As a scene develops, a noteworthy, if superficial, means of increasing tension was employed on-stage (it works in pictures as well) by P.G. Wodehouse. Keep actors on their feet, he advocated. It's crisper when they're vertical; on their bums, actors lose energy—a letdown for them and the audience.

When a scene works, you don't need a critic to tell you. Here again, something visceral makes it known, and once more our analogy persists, coupling two facets of the entertainment business—sports and plays, whether they're for the stage or the screen.

On the night of June 1, 1994, in a playoff game that Reggie Miller of the Indiana Pacers will never forget, he sank five three-point baskets in the fourth quarter. When your stuff is going well, "Everything feels like slow motion," Miller said. "You see the plays before they happen."

Which is another way of saying, when you're hot you know it. But don't get carried away. The quality of human comprehension is faulty; there are times when you think you're hot but you're not. To compound the issue, you can go from torrid to frigid swiftly. Consider what many textualists esteem as the greatest story ever told: Jesus was sensational on Palm Sunday. He bombed a week later. On a far less sublime but a more personal level, in less time than it takes to tell a friend, you, too, in one misbegotten scene, can go from a full house to a busted flush.

Audiences must know what motivates the characters in a screenplay. Exposition is what tells them—the divulgence of information about their lives and relationships in the past—what they were up to before the fade-in. Direct, declarative exposition is invariably boring. There is neither artistry nor craftsmanship involved when the characters on-screen tell each other what they already know for the enlightenment of the audience.

Exposition works best when it is indirect and inverted.

In *The Heiress*, by Ruth and Augustus Goetz, the audience is told indirectly that the heroine's father is dead when a secondary character says, "We've asked you [to visit us] every year since your father died."

Good exposition can be compounded to include more than one idea, as when the heroine of a TV drama says, "With all the young men off in this wretched war, I have to run the farm myself."

Exposition can answer such metaphysical questions as why and how by elucidating the back-story. Why does Colonel Nichols, a courageous British Army officer of WWII in a Japanese prison camp, cooperate with his captors in building a strategic bridge that can only benefit the enemy's war effort? The back-story of *The Bridge on the River Kwai* tells us.

How did that uncommunicative and inscrutable young man, known among his fellow denizens of the jungle as *Tarzan, King of the Apes*, get there?

Why did John Macreedy crop up in the dismal, almost invisible hamlet of *Black Rock*?

These are questions that must be addressed sooner or later.

Sometimes it works best to save the answer for a shocking revelation deep toward the end of the piece—a tendency in most murder mysteries.

Alfred Hitchcock was a vigorous proponent of the early disclosure. He said that it was better to let the audience know the murderer and have a minimum ninety minutes of delicious suspense building to his discovery, rather than hold off the unmasking until the conclusion and maybe achieve two minutes of surprise. Yet he himself on occasion violated the principle, as in *To Catch a Thief* (screenplay by John Michael Hayes).

In *The Usual Suspects,* Christopher McQuarrie ignores the master's injunction. McQuarrie's arch-criminal and killer is exposed not more than a minute before the fade-out. The writer, moreover, makes brilliant use of exposition, exploiting it in a new dimension by creating a labyrinthine thicket for a back-story and planting it with semi-truths and outright fabrications, thereby concocting a wild tale told mostly in flashbacks by an inspired liar who pretends to be an abject fool, but who is far from it.

Another kind of exposition is extremely well done in *Apollo 13* (by William Broyles, Jr. and Al Reinert from the book *Lost Moon* by Jim Lovell and Jeffrey Kluger). To keep the physical action from becoming totally incomprehensible to the audience, Tom Hanks (as Lovell) first explains the science, the technology, the mysteries of cosmology—indeed, the astronaut's gnosis to his children. Then he and his fellow travelers hold forth to tourists, to the media, and to their flight controllers in Houston via public or closed-circuit TV and radio from deep space.

Exposition can take still another guise. When a screenplay (or any other fictional form) bogs down in its thrust toward a desired conclusion, it might be necessary to ignite the afterburners by introducing information not previously known, as does the heralded Irving Pincus of *The Front Page*. In *Sense and Sensibility,* the confidential information buzzed in the delicate ear of Elinor Dashwood by stalwart Colonel Brandon, changes her sister's attitude towards handsome John Willoughby, enabling the impulsive young woman, the personification of *Sensibility* in the title, to see, finally, the fashionable young man for what he is—a cruel and uncaring rake.

To continue the catechism: How is your exposition maximized?

In dialogue, with discord? When two principals spark a verbal conflict by comparing notes or attacking each other, as in *The Usual Suspects*? Or without conflict, providing that the material being examined is so intrinsically valuable or sufficiently engrossing that it can be disposed of simply and directly, without artistic embellishments, as in *Apollo 13*?

Or with humor as in *Mighty Aphrodite*, in which Woody Allen delves into the past, trying to identify the natural mother of his adopted child? And in *Aphrodite*, there is exposition in action, through a series of scenes of physical confrontation or sexual contretemps.

Or does your exposition work best en passant as the answers to who and what and where and when are revealed, which, at the time of the delivery, registers little more than throwaway lines? In *The American President* (screenplay by Aaron Sorkin), we see that Michael Douglas has a daughter but no wife. We learn in time that the child's mother has died of cancer before the curtain rises.

Can you get across what you want within the chronological order of normal progression, or must you insert a back-story to clarify uncertainties and confusions? Unless, as is the case of *The Usual Suspects*, your calculated point is to create or exploit them.

Most back-stories are less convoluted. In *In the Line of Fire* we learn in snatches and installments but without curlicues what is destroying Clint Eastwood, why he is an alcoholic, why his wife left him, why he is so hostile and mean-spirited.

In *Black Rock*, we learn what happened to John Macreedy in WWII, how he lost the use of his arm, why he is searching for Komoko, and what happened to the Japanese farmer.

Although exposition enlightens and instructs almost anytime, it usually surfaces somewhere during the screenplay's *rising action*, a related series of scenes that build toward the point of greatest conflict.

But before a picture can reach its point of highest intensity, scenes of lesser voltage must lead to it. First, chronologically, incontrovertibly, and quite obviously is the inauguration: the opening scene.

In the history of Western literature one of the few great works that begins in the beginning is the Bible. The telling of most other tales has a back-story. Therefore writers subscribe to Horace's mandate known in dramatic trade talk as *"in medias res"*—begin in the middle of things—which appear in his *Ars Poetica*, counseling dramatists to "hasten on to the event," to "hurry away" the audience "into the midst of interesting circumstances," relegating preceding events to expository dialogue or to a flashback—a scene or scenes showing what happened before the fade-in that dictates or explains the present action.

There are times when the body of an entire film, excluding only the opening and closing scenes, is a flashback. Usually the flashback is employed when exposition is overwhelming—necessary but boring. Therefore, start at the high point of the action. *Double Indemnity* (screenplay by Billy Wilder and Raymond Chandler, based on the novel by James M. Cain) opens with hero Fred MacMurray, mortally wounded, careening through a city in the dead of night. A flashback running the length of the picture tells us how he got that way. *Citizen Kane* opens with the demise of the protagonist whispering that one enigmatic word, "Rosebud." *Sunset Boulevard* starts with William Holden lying dead in a swimming pool. His voice comes over the soundtrack: "I always wanted to own a swimming pool."

Billy Wilder was the undisputed master of the flashback. Yet it was he who cautioned writers and directors on the hazards of being too spectacular in opening a picture. "How will you ever top it?" he asked.

There are some opening scenes that can never be topped, but the writer in each case obviously wasn't disturbed by their clout. Arguably the grandest, gaudiest, and most staggering zinger of all time is the opening scene of Mozart's *Don Giovanni* (with libretto by Lorenzo da Ponte) in which the protagonist seduces Donna Anna, rejects her and kills her father in a duel. Instead of wringing her hands, she belts out a vow of vengeance. Stallone can never top that.

Another audience-hooking curtain raiser seems to derive from some constituent of the human psyche, a kind of homing instinct, that finds fascination in a place or a situation revisited.

Think of all the books and plays and pictures that begin with the return of a native son or daughter. A random sampling might include:

Death of a Salesman by Arthur Miller. Curtain rises as Willy Loman returns home from an exhausting and unprofitable trip peddling his stock in New England.

In Lillian Hellman's *Watch on the Rhine,* the heroine, Sara Muller, returns to her ancestral acres on the Potomac with her anti-Nazi husband and their children.

In *The Best Years of Our Lives,* by Robert E. Sherwood, three veterans return to their hometown to resume with difficulty lives disrupted by WWII.

The fireworks of plot and the wondrous insights of character in *Hamlet* tend to diminish our awareness that the play kicks in with the return of the prince to the Danish court from his studies at the University of Wittenberg.

The homecoming of Clym Yeobright to the Wessex village of his birth is recounted, as the reader might expect, in Thomas Hardy's unequivocally titled *Return of the Native.*

Why the prevalence of this opening gambit? Because it heralds a new and qualitative change that is about to befall and probably engulf your protagonist and all others who line up with or against him.

Another favored variant you might consider in jump-starting your screenplay: The arrival of your hero at a new and unfamiliar place rather than returning to it.

Still another: the start of a journey.

The setting can be anything you want it to be—strange and unworldly as in science fiction or futurism; ominous as in *King Kong, The Most Dangerous Game, Black Rock*; a micro-cosmic island or some long-lost land that requires, for survival, a social change from class privilege to a meritocracy, as in Barrie's *Admirable Crichton*; a soothing and enchanting enclave (at first sight) as in *Death in Venice,* by Thomas Mann. It can be mysterious as in *Lost Horizon,* by James Hilton; fantastic as Alice's Wonderland. There are all those cowboys, including the Australian from the outback who tamed New York, and all those tenderfeet who won the West, the greenhorns who floundered into America, and the Yankee who ventured into King Arthur's court.

In the case of writing an adaptation to the screen from a book or play, aside from the inherent legitimacy assigned to a story with previous recognition, it is at the very least an interesting exercise to "let air" into the vehicle, to exploit the photogenic vastness of space, whether the vistas are the handiwork of nature or of man. Ernest Lehman overwhelms us with the panoramic grandeur of the Austrian Alps in *The Sound of Music*. The practice is not limited to material derived from another medium. Woody Allen staggers us with the establishing shots of New York's steel canyons in *Manhattan*, an original screenplay. It's an eloquent way to open a picture unless, of course, the mood you want to capture is claustrophobic confinement as in *The Cabinet of Dr. Caligari*, by Carl Mayer and Hans Jankowitz, or Arthur Laurents' *Snake Pit*.

The Lillian Hellman play *Watch on the Rhine* takes place within the walls of a living room. The curtain rises a few minutes before the arrival of the Muller family, allowing supporting members of the cast to supply the essentials of exposition before Kurt and Sara and their three children appear on-stage. The movie opens on the Mullers, tracking them over a wide expanse of geography before they reach Washington.

There's a problem in this introductory sequence with its additional and quite unnecessary dialogue. While the play is terse and energized—excellent qualities for a dramatic work—the movie is debilitated even as it begins with all the extraneous talk that must be exchanged to fill the awkward pockets of silence that would otherwise dominate the journey.

In restructuring a film from a novel, the screenwriter tries to retain the depth and the tone of the book while bringing its interiority, its introspections, and possibly the undercurrents of its stream of consciousness (assuming it exists) to the surface. The reader knows what a character in a book thinks and feels because an author devotes a lot of time to it. In contrast, what a character thinks or feels in a play or a picture is expressed in overt speech and action, or by using voice-over exposition.

Techniques such as an incorporeal voice on the soundtrack to communicate thoughts and feelings to an audience have never been universally comprehendible. Total incomprehensibility prevailed not long ago in Tahiti, where an interpreter stood on-stage in the dark at the side of the screen not only to translate the dialogue but to untangle as best he could the reasons why the characters of a foreign culture behaved the way they did. Points out the limitations of the so-called language of film.

15

CONFLICT AND EMPATHY
The Cardinal Virtues

Conflict is one of two cardinal virtues that shape a screenplay. The other is empathy, the factor that snaps an audience out of its doldrumic indifference and instills in it a deep emotional identity with your hero.

It applies as well to an antihero. *Macbeth*, for instance, with his comminglement of conflicting traits, gives an audience much to identify with. He is ruthless, he commits a fiendish murder, but before he succumbs to temptation and savagery, there is a kind of antipodal probity in his courage and his helmsmanship, and a potential greatness that is lost when he surrenders his humanity to ambition.

What, where, and when is the precise point of engagement between your hero and heavy? Who initiates it?

Have you set up the possibility of a clash between opposing forces within the first few minutes of the fade-in?

Sometimes the conflict is immediate, as is that between husband Woody Allen and wife Helena Bonham Carter regarding the adoption of a child in *Mighty Aphrodite*. In *Bad Day at Black Rock*, the portent of mortal strife between protagonist and antagonist is established early, although the audience doesn't know at the time what is at stake. John Macreedy and Reno Smith are on a collision course even before they meet, but the reason why isn't revealed until the third act.

In *Destry Rides Again*, the peace-loving young protagonist, deep in the third act, commits himself to the battle by strapping on his six-irons. He has finally realized the heavy's unremitting capacity for malice, and concludes, however reluctantly, that he must do something about it.

The assault can be launched in many ways. In *Carrington*, script by Christopher Hampton, the attack is motivated by love, and early in the first act. Emma Thompson as Dora Carrington commits herself to lopping off the beard of Lytton Strachey, played by Jonathan Pryce. Her decision, at the last moment, not to shear him in his sleep is, it might be said, a commitment (in this case, to love) by negation.

In *Black Rock*, Smith, his goons and their bulldozing tactics to drive Macreedy out of town initiate the conflict. The stranger-protagonist fights back.

The moment of decision induces the first step in the catharsis, for what follows is rack and ruin that must be overcome. The determination of the hero to take charge of his own destiny and possibly the destiny of others (the tempest-tossed, the downtrodden) strikes an emotional chord in all of us. Moreover, an unconfined rapture accompanies the decision to act, to take a whack at the enemy, and no longer to watch and wait and play the passive game. "To drift is hell," said Bernard Shaw, "to steer is heaven," and that exhilaration is communicated to us, the audience.

Whatever the goal, it is never easy to attain. Doubts assail the hero and humanize him. The true post-Freudian protagonist is not an Olympian, nor is he an immature figment of knotty muscles and unqualified self-assurance, like Stallone or Wayne before him. And certainly the adult hero does not fit the mock-heroic mold of Professor Stragnell who, in his directorship of the Dead Sea Scrolls, admitted, "I have my faults, but being wrong is not one of them," although hubristic heroes have been known to exist, and to get their comeuppance.

Exposition is most effective when it is inverted or indirect. In contrast, your point of commitment, when your hero can no longer ignore the obstacles in his path, must be precise and explicit. Ambiguity at this juncture weakens the decision.

Does the discord in your screenplay emerge from a clash between protagonist and antagonist as two separate, distinct, and oppositional figures with conflicting ideologies, or does the contention and contrariety between them represent irreconcilable aspects of the internal self? Or both?

The outer depiction of inner experience seems better adapted to narrative literature, which can explore thoughts and passions in a stream of consciousness. Applying the technique to pictures, internal conceits and feelings are presented at times without clarity or logic—the seemingly random and obscure workings of the unconscious. As they surface, chaos never seems far away.

A problem thus arises in a screenplay, for the action demands a certain minimal rationality to keep the progression and the imagery relevant and recognizable to the audience. Many readers find Joyce's *Ulysses* (for example) as stimulating as it is profound. But it's infinitely more daunting on-stage or on-screen where the stream of consciousness comes off more like psychobabble, the self-contradictory effusions of a madman. If you're smitten with the idea of surrealism and the unconscious in a screenplay, practice it for your own amusement in the confines of a closet. Let it escape, and most audiences will not find it stimulating.

What is the major conflict, the core or focus of your story? Who are your combatants? Is your hero consciously trying to right a wrong as in *Spartacus* (screenplay by Dalton Trumbo, from the Howard Fast novel) or *Mutiny on the Bounty*?

Is he trying to avoid a fight until he can no longer ignore it, as in *Destry Rides Again*?

Is he seeking to avenge a loved one? (*Hamlet*.)

Who triggers the conflict? The protagonist? (*The Godfather, A Streetcar Named Desire.*)

The antagonist? (*High Noon, Shane.*)

A peripheral figure? (The superior officer who assigns Lawrence to the Arabian desert. The general who assigns Lee Marvin to *The Dirty Dozen*. The newspaper editor who assigns Gregory Peck to investigate a *Gentleman's Agreement.*)

What is at risk for your protagonist? To win what? To lose what? What is at stake? Victory or defeat? Prize or forfeiture? Life or death? Where is the battlefield?

The conflict can be internal, involving a decision to be made and an action to be taken, as with Hamlet wrestling with the dilemma of taking arms against a sea of troubles, or Destry in an agony about the inevitable consequences of a showdown. However, a few emergent filmmakers here and abroad seem to be searching for a viable departure from the awful violence that has accompanied conflict in the past and has led to the barbaric destruction of on-screen life that has burgeoned recently.

Two highly popular and critically acclaimed pictures of 1995 exemplify what might constitute an exciting and a more civilized trend. Both films have a solid foundation of conflict. In *Apollo 13* the clash is between Man and Nature: Three astronauts are fighting the unknown in deep space and are ravaged by it. Quintessentially, the theme of the film can be reduced to a single phrase: the power and the glory of cooperation. To wit: Hundreds of extraordinarily bright and dedicated people at the Houston Space Center, coupled with the courage and ingenuity of the three explorers in an ocean of galactic immensity, manage to guide the module home despite a total loss of instrumentation, the unbearable cold, a ruptured sunshield that probably cannot withstand exterior temperatures of 4,000 degrees Fahrenheit induced by the frictional assault of re-entry, and an impending typhoon at the point of splashdown.

In *Babe* (screenplay by George Miller and Chris Noonan, based on the book by Dick King-Smith), it is a kind and gentle pig that brings to the grange a revolutionary approach to sheep-herding, one that features courtesy, civility, and cooperation rather than fear and threats of violence. It would be merciful to dismiss the sequel, the second pig movie, as dull and with enough violence to more than make up for the first one, but it houses a literary bromide that dates back to the Greek pastoral poets, with a side order of Rousseau and Wordsworth: the evils and ugliness of the city vs. the goodness and beauty of the countryside. To which is added a salvo of maudlin preachment on tolerance, the homeless, and animal rights—fine subjects for a movie, but in this case the mixture (at least to me) come off as pretentious and arch.

Two highly popular and critically acclaimed pictures of the '90s—vanguard pictures that could generate an innovative and more complex structure to story-telling on the screen—contained the dual thematic fixtures of love and death. Love as depicted in *The English Patient* (screenplay by Anthony Minghella, based on the novel by Michael Ondaatje), verges on obsession, while *Lone Star* (screenplay by John Sayles) contains the powerful additive of greed.

Both films have the kind of splendid sinuosity usually reserved for the novel form. Each is broad in scope, deep in substance, many-leveled. Instead of reducing their principals within a tight and constrained microcosm to do their star turns, both pictures refuse to isolate their leads from the turmoil of their encroaching worlds. They interact with many people (more than fifty in *Lone Star*), just as we do off the screen. They constitute a tangible, interactive, and unexclusive sector of society, and their geographical range is wide. *Lone Star* slips over the Texas border into Mexico time and again, covering a period of four decades. *The English Patient* unfolds on two continents from the late 1930s in the North African desert to the final throes of WWII in Italy in 1944.

Both stories have a fine disregard for chronology. In each, the sequential passage of time is dismantled as scene after involuted scene ignores the clock and the calendar and builds emotionally to the climax.

In yet another departure from classical convention, each film has two pairs of lovers. *English Patient* has two plots; *Lone Star* has three. In *Patient* the conflict is triggered by the arrival of a British aerial photographer and his ravishing blonde wife at an archeological encampment in the Libyan desert. In *Star* the conflict is sparked by the discovery of a human skeleton, half-buried in the wasteland of an abandoned rifle range in south Texas.

In every film the conflict must be triggered by somebody or something: a birth in *The Lion King* (screenplay by Irene Mecchi, Jonathan Roberts, Linda Woolverton); a death in *Citizen Kane* (screenplay by Herman Mankiewicz); a bet and a challenge in *Pygmalion* (play by George Bernard Shaw, screenplay by Ian Dalrymple, Cecil Lewis, and W.F. Lipscomb); the trashing of an N.Y.P.D. patrol car in *The Usual Suspects*; the rise of a gifted but disturbed boxer in *Raging Bull*; the rise of a gifted but disturbed politician in *Nixon*.

Other examples: the arrival of Chilean poet Pablo Neruda at a slumbrous Italian village in *Il Postino* (screenplay by Anna Pavignano, Michael Radford, Furio Scarpelli, Giacomo Scarpelli, and Massimo Troisi, adapted from *Burning Patience* by Antonio Skarmeta); the arrival at Las Vegas of the exhausted alcoholic Nicolas Cage in *Leaving Las Vegas*; the arrival of Ingrid Bergman in *Casablanca*; mechano-electronic difficulties in the spacecraft *Apollo 13*: "Houston, we have a problem." A problem also erupts in a Soviet atomic submarine in American waters in *The Hunt for Red October* (screenplay by Larry Ferguson and Donald Stewart, from the novel by Tom Clancy); in Durrenmatt's *The Visit*, Claire Zachanassian (played by Lynn Fontanne on Broadway and Ingrid Bergman in Ben Barzman's screen adaptation), possibly the world's richest woman and certainly the most imperious of philanthropists, introduces another kind of conflict when she returns to the crumbling village of her adolescence and offers a billion marks to the townspeople on one condition: that the man who seduced and abandoned her to whoredom be killed.

The match that ignites the fire can be struck by anybody from the protagonist in *Deliverance* (the hero seeking adventure) to the antagonist in the second *Godfather* film (the Black Hand capo demanding pay for protection through intimidation and violence).

When the hot wire is provided by a secondary character, he is quite often a superior in a hierarchy: the big-juice gangster who appoints Cheech (Chazz Palminteri) to ride protective herd on Olive Neal (Jennifer Tilly), his lubricious girlfriend in *Bullets Over Broadway*, the frightful rack-

eteer and fight-fixer who chooses Vincent Vega (John Travolta) to entertain his wife Mia (Uma Thurman) with an innocuous night on the town
in *Pulp Fiction.*

If anyone or anything can initiate the strife, why is it important to determine the moment of blast-off or who/what depressed the
plunger that discharged the dynamite?

Because we have to know where to start chronologically, once
we know where we want to go. Or, as happens less frequently, we have
to know where to start in order to know where we're going, and in
order to determine what your hero has at stake, and in order for your
heavy to oppose him/her adroitly. Therefore, we ask: What is in jeopardy for hero and heavy? What is at risk? For whom? To win or accomplish what? To lose what?

In post-Arthurian literature, with the introduction and development of
a code that extolled chivalry, honor, the veneration of women, and
other excrescences of romanticism, love and death became the two
main ingredients of Western drama. Protagonists are vulnerable to
either, usually both, which form or motivate the main characters of
more pictures (and novels and plays and poems) than you could cata-
log in a set of metropolitan phone books.

When your hero faces death, it's a good idea to build a time
bomb under him to intensify the action. Suspense is invariably heightened when an inexorable clock is ticking away, threatening your
hero's death unless your problem is solved, unless the murderer or the
psychopath or the terrorist is apprehended before he strikes or strikes
again. Examples: Agatha Christie's *The Mousetrap* and Carl Foreman's
High Noon.

For your further consideration, will the doomsday machine
destroy the world before James Bond defuses it? Will a great man be
killed before Rambo can snare him from the jaws of death? Will
Benjamin Braddock (Dustin Hoffman) rescue his true love from a bad
marriage by sprinting to the church before the nuptials are finalized
(*The Graduate,* screenplay by Buck Henry and Calder Willingham,
based on Charles Webb's novel)?

In the development of your screenplay, have you locked in your rooting interest? Have you communicated it early and unequivocally to the audience?, i.e., are they unconditionally aware of the character they should root for?

There is a convention in the musical theater called the Girl's First Song—the initial number in which the heroine establishes her identity and what she wants, at the same time recognizing the dangers that might befall her if she follows the course she considers pursuing. Examples:

Mary Martin as nurse Nellie Forbush belting out "Cockeyed Optimist" in *South Pacific* (Rodgers and Hammerstein).

Julie Andrews as Eliza Doolittle yearning wistfully for shelter and a bit of chocolate as she sings "Wouldn't It Be Loverly?" in *My Fair Lady* (Lerner and Loewe).

In like manner, dramatize your hero's motivation in the first few minutes after the fade-in.

Building empathic passion in an audience is umbilically tied to the catharsis no well-made tragedy is without. The purgation of pity and fear that the audience feels for your hero and his worsening condition is built into a bond that is deeply personal, a feeling of uplift and purification that resembles a religious experience. It is the transference of emotion that does it, as the audience becomes a congregation in the grip of an epiphany. So Arthur Laurents challenged his students at N.Y.U. when he said, "Make me cry." He wasn't being the least bit soppy.

Empathy raises certain questions about your principals. Recognizing that the protagonist is the vortical figure in a vehicle, and that other characters turn to him/her for leadership and direction:

Can you define your hero? Can you identify what she wants? In like manner, who is your heavy, and what does she want?

In a tenable screenplay both hero and heavy are "right," i.e., each has what she considers a valid reason for pursuing her goal.

What is their justification? Why do they take oppositional action?

In some pictures the hero provides the drive and the heavy supplies the obstacle, as in *Black Rock*. In *Leaving Las Vegas* the heavy is

198

alcoholism. With James Bond and Rambo, the hero provides the obstacle that keeps malevolence from taking over the world or blasting it out of the solar system. There are situations when hero and heavy obstruct each other, as in Michael Mann's *Heat*.

Obstacles erected to keep the hero from achieving her goal are not always evil. The heavy in *Sleepless in Seattle* is situational, circumstantial. The machinery of life makes for the difficulties, but not one character sneers and flexes his thews in the whole picture.

Obstacles are the meat and muscle of conflict. The threat they pose and the barriers themselves evoke fear, and fear is the gut-wrenching implosion of empathy, just as in other infinitely more personal and shattering circumstances, physical fear can be stimulating, the chemical that spurs the best and the worst in us to fight or to flight.

Motivation is tied to an individual's roots; explaining it can be a big bore. At times exposition is unnecessary. Some heroes, like Alan Ladd in *Shane*, are wrapped in mystery. A figure of romantic intensity and silences, unless he has something to say, the man comes out of Nowhere and disappears back into Neverland at the squeeze.

Shane is powerful and protective, but too many movie heroes are frightening and destructive. To empathize with them, as we the audience are encouraged to do, is to applaud the defeat of reason by malice, to celebrate mindlessness as long as it is kinetic, to root for the advocates of stick-and-slash aggression with just one more kick in the plums for the jolly old hell of it.

As has been noted, the perpetrators of all this criminality, and the screenwriters who chronicle their mayhem, do it under the guise of righteousness, and they've done it on-stage and in books long before Hollywood made public its love affair with turpitude.

In *Jules et Jim*, by Henri Pierre Roché, the novelist talks about a playwright, never named, who "revels in vice to teach virtue." Pictures like *Natural Born Killers* and *Pulp Fiction* piously condemn violence while showing it in bloody Technicolor and vomitous profusion. In like manner, Rambo and all the Rambo manqués have this in common: They profess pacifism. To keep the peace, a sort of "Pax Ramborem," they litter the landscape with corpses.

Many students of American culture, professional and amateur, concur in the worrisome belief that there exists a correlation between the rash of sex and violence which has dominated the big screen for the past half-century, and the blacklist inquisition of the late forties and fifties when progressive thought in films expired and, except for a few pallbearers, nobody came to the funeral. The void left by the abandonment of humanism was filled by an uncomplicated physicality because many writers feared a recurrence of the bad old days and a revival of the un-American activities committees that had poisoned the federal and the California state governments and had persecuted so many artists and intellectuals. It would be curious indeed if today's emphasis on fearless athleticism, both in bed and on the battlefield, should be traced to the fear that still keeps screenwriters from exploring the vast and challenging country of ideas.

But let's break free from Bond and Rambo for just one paragraph: There have been over the years a few noteworthy pictures—which, unfortunately, have yet to establish a trend—the kind of screenplay that rejects the allurement of frontal nudity and the Sturm und Drang of optical illusions to explore our lives and times the way most of us live them. The pictures written by Stewart Stern, particularly *Rebel Without a Cause,* and those involving Joanne Woodward, such as *Rachel, Rachel,* are sensitive explorations into American normalcy. And, more recently, the novelist and screenwriter Peter Hedges has taken the same path with *What's Eating Gilbert Grape?* May pictures like these prosper, and may the tribe of Stern and Hedges increase.

16

THE PARABOLA OF CHANGE
The Three C's

Does your hero change? If so, what is the difference, before and after, in character or attitude? How does the transformation come about? Why? Is it rapid or gradual? Is it for better or for worse? How does it affect others?

Examples:

In *Il Postino,* Troisi, playing the lead, Mario Ruoppolo, overcomes his shyness and lackadaise with the help of the great poet Neruda and the power of poetry, and in the process achieves a vigorous and outgoing maturity, and wins the love of a good, bartending woman.

A change for the worse: In *Quiz Show* (screenplay by Paul Attanasio), an appealing young academic without sin and above reproach succumbs to the lure of money and celebrity and takes a dive into corruption.

Change in a secondary character: Forrest Gump's platoon leader, embittered and in a rage of withdrawal, having lost both legs in Vietnam, finally embraces life and an Asian fiancée.

There is no law handed down from Sinai or Aristotle that mandates change in a protagonist. In *Get Shorty*, Chili Palmer (John Travolta) never changes but his vocation does, and that's the joke. A brash and adept soldier in the Miami mob, he applies the same outrageous, unconscionable ebullience to Hollywood and prospers as a movie producer.

In *Heat* neither Vincent Hanna (Pacino) nor Neil McCauley (De Niro) changes but both of them are gonzo to begin with: a well-matched pair of obsessive/compulsive sociopaths.

In *Leaving Las Vegas*, Ben Sanderson (Nicolas Cage) is a mess and a hopeless alcoholic from fade-in to fade-out. But he does change. Once he finds love—Sera (Elizabeth Shue), another of those heart-of-gold, vulnerable hookers—his audacious intrusiveness, his irksome aggression go soft and sweet. Or maybe he's just so pickled he lacks the strength to venture beyond passivity.

The durable chestnut of fiction about supportive whores with hearts of gold once reminded director Bill Wellman of a friend who married a hooker.

"And do you know," he said, "she made him the best wife he ever had?"

A handy little gadget used by screenwriters to indicate a change in time or place, or to define a character or a plot point, is the montage, a series of short interwoven shots, with or without dialogue, in sharp or blurred focus as desired, the sum of their synthesis adding up to more qualitatively than the simple aggregation of their individual parts. Montages are used in *Nixon* to make more comprehensible the bleak personality of the protagonist, just as slow-motion is used at times to stress the importance of an action. Slo-mo, as well as the montage, began with the Soviet filmmaker Sergei Eisenstein in *Battleship Potemkin*, in 1925.

Montages are also used to convey subliminal impressions, usually the dark emotional disturbances and mortifications locked in the unconscious, such as the torments besieging the alcoholic Ray Milland in *The Lost Weekend*. They can also be effective in recording the passage of time, as a lobsterscope is used on-stage, or calendar leaves exfoliating, or with a series of newspaper headlines flashed and tilted across the screen, or to record the ebb and flow of war as in *Gone With the Wind* (novel by Margaret Mitchell, screenplay by Sidney Howard), or *Jules et Jim* (novel by Henri Pierre Roché, screenplay by François Truffaut and Jean Gruault).

And now let's hear it for the three C's of rising action.

Crisis is the point in a screenplay where suspense is heightened and the conflict is intensified. A viable script develops a series of crises; as each of them is resolved, a new obstructive force is brought into play which twists and deepens the struggle by inducing a reversal of fortune, by opening a fresh can of worms, and by exerting additional pressure on the object of your empathy. Each crisis in the progression should be more severe and more significant than the preceding one. Crises crest into the *climax*, the decisive moment that is of maximum intensity, the major turning point of the plot where the struggle culminates in favor of either the hero or the heavy until it is eclipsed by the next eruption. Each consecutive consummation hits a new peak in the story's progression. The result of all the interconnected conflicts that can lead to the final event of the plot's conclusion, the *catastrophe*. Catastrophe does not prescribe a sad ending but rather the termination of the conflict, the disengagement of the combatants.

The three C's crop up in every vehicle that is seriously considered for production. Examples therefore are without end; your supply is as copious and as germane as anybody's; nevertheless, here are a few wide-ranging and disparate specimens:

In *The Fugitive*, climax succeeds climax in a series of *crises* with each face-off between Dr. Kimble and his unshakable foe.

In *Babe* the *climax* comes with the piglet confronting and defeating the sheepdog in the herding championship.

In *Oedipus Rex* the *catastrophe* comes after all the pieces of the plot have been hammered into place, when the protagonist appears blind and bloody, having gouged out his own eyes with his wife/mother's golden breast pin.

203

In building to the three C's, and generally in the construction of a screenplay, it's worth keeping in mind that the audience, in identifying with the protagonist, yearns to be her/him, or sees her/him as the shining epitome of desire, and burns with an escalating passion to jump her/his bones.

It is fortuitous that the routine of real life seldom coughs up one crisis after another. And it is equally evident by now that a screenplay should never leave your computer without them. While the shooting of any film is certainly one aspect, however minimal, of real life, it more closely parallels the explosive shenanigans of the fictive plot than it does the less volatile conditions of off-screen dailiness. Although every element, every step in the picture-making process is planned down to the last gasp on the soundtrack, a terrible randomness all too often envelops the entire procedure, along with an awareness that chaos lurks in every dark corner of the stage, ready to pounce and disrupt, to crank out havoc with an unending series of crises until the whole damned enterprise is finally, mercifully captured in a can. A set seldom rings with love and laughter; there are times when you'll want nothing more than an escape route across the ice floes.

Not only do writers and other participants in picture-making get carried away when chaos takes charge, there are times when they lose all sense of proportion. This sort of excess even extends to people simply observing the making of a movie.

Hedda Hopper, the Hollywood columnist, once reported the following in the *Philadelphia Bulletin*, which was reprinted in *The New Yorker* under the head, "Perish the Thought Dept.":

> Stephen Ames had a hair-raising experience. He watched the overturning of a boat containing one of his actors, Kurt Kasznar in *Vaquero*. Kurt went up and down and up again. Had he stayed down the whole picture would have had to be reshot as Kurt has one of the important parts in the film.

Francisque Sarcey, a stuffy, stout, and ultra-conservative theater critic, made a considerable contribution to dramatic theory three years after he died with the posthumous publication of his *Quarante*

Ans de Theatre in 1902, wherein he formulated the principle called the scène à faire, a.k.a. the obligatory scene in English-speaking venues.

In the writing of a play or a picture, the obligatory scene fills an otherwise gaping void. It satisfies the audience's need to witness what it has been eagerly awaiting and without which it feels disappointed, betrayed, and depressed, a shapeless letdown of hopes dashed from which it recoils with collective frustration and an individuated resistance that ranges from a frown of pique to a yawp of outrage.

It is a scene that, once the writer has led the audience to expect, he is obliged to stage. It derives from a plant or a series of plants with a promissory note attached. The focus of the audience has been directed towards the confrontation, it has been channeled into a state of anticipation for a collision between antagonists.

Unlike the delicious shock of recognition that comes with a surprise duly and indirectly planted and when the results are unforeseen, the scène à faire is one that the audience anticipates and deeply desires. The viewers want to observe up close and directly the effect of the encounter on the principals, eyeball-to-eyeball. It might be said that the audience has poured a significant investment into the outcome of the script and the scène à faire constitutes a reward the audience deserves for its attention and empathy. It takes no great dramaturgical acumen to recognize that the obligatory scene invariably carries a heavy emotional charge and a great deal of combustion. But it is not always adversarial—obligatory scenes come in all shapes and sizes—particularly in those days when pictures of the '20s and '30s battened on a compost of syrup and sentimentality. The product was bittersweet, rooted in the What-She-Didn't-Know genre, offering a lachrymose progression that ran something like this: The cosseted heroine, a bit of a snob and a smarty-pants, is disdainful toward a piss-poor relative or a doting servant, discovers in the obligatory scene that the moldy old dogsbody has saved and sacrificed to put her through Miss Phoebe Swank's Finishing School for the Rich and Rotten, and showered her with silks and satins and is indeed her mother.

Or the child least appreciated by a parent proves to be the most loving, as in *Lear* or Steinbeck's *East of Eden* (screenplay by Paul Osborn).

In *Big*, we the audience, want to see Josh Baskin (Tom Hanks) shrink physically back into the childhood he has earlier forsaken.

In *Get Shorty* we are led to expect the final, death-dealing rumble between Chili Palmer (Travolta) and the brutal kingpin of Miami's underworld, and we are not disappointed.

In *Leaving Las Vegas* we've been promised the death of Nicolas Cage early on and finally we are witness to it.

In *Wuthering Heights* Catherine and Heathcliff are ultimately reunited in death in a scène à faire that provides us with a fine, tremorous pang and a tingling frisson of fulfillment.

A splendid scène à faire is the court scene exacting the pound of human flesh in *The Merchant of Venice*. Without it, the audience would feel cheated.

Hamlet's audience anticipates the obligatory scene between the prince and his mother, an accusatory confrontation in which he indicts her as an accomplice in the murder of the king, his father, her husband.

In *Babe* we learn of the overachieving piglet's ambition to become a sheepdog. The audience is satisfied only when the obligatory scene shows Babe herding the flock with unerring expertise, thanks to the intricate machinery of special effects.

In *Heat* we want to see the one-on-one encounter between law enforcer Hanna and lawbreaker McCauley to confirm what we have been led to expect: that an intuitive bond exists between them.

In *Jane Eyre*, the young governess at Thornwood, the mysterious house of Rochester, must come face to face with the madwoman who holds its secret.

In Jane Austen's *Sense and Sensibility*, Elinor Dashwood and Edward Ferrars share a scène à faire in which she learns why he had so unceremoniously abandoned her and why he has come back to renew the courtship. Her sister Marianne, rejected by John Willoughby, shares an obligatory scene with that charming cad and is cured of her infatuation.

We know that the pyrotechnics between each pair of principals is no longer avoidable. We'd feel violated if the scene hadn't been played out before our eyes and ears.

In *The Usual Suspects* we wait for the inevitable showdown, the close encounter between persistent drug dick David Kujan (played by Chazz Palminteri) and the elusive archcriminal Keyser Soze. It is done so adroitly and with such wit by screenwriter McQuarrie that we, the audience, are not aware that the confrontation has taken place until it's over.

An example of an otherwise fine picture diminished by the lack of a scène à faire is *A Family Thing* (screenplay by Billy Bob Thornton and Tom Epperson). Robert Duvall and James Earl Jones are half-brothers despite the fact that Duvall, by all external appearances, is white and Jones is black. Each overcomes his knee-jerk racial prejudices, and at the fade head back to Arkansas to meet Duvall's branch of the family. That confrontation never happens, but it holds all the constituents of one hell of an obligatory scene, and the picture suffers from its omission.

There are times when the obligatory scene is easily confused with the climax. The subject of contrasts and comparisons between the two can be dissected and analyzed as an academic exercise, but it isn't terribly important. Calling a scene by any other name has little value. What counts is what you put into it.

Nevertheless, and to play the pedagogic game for an indulgent but meaningless moment or so, consider that the scène à faire relates to the foreseen and therefore predictable and anticipated collision between antagonists, while the climax answers to the unforeseen final conflict that will determine triumph or tragedy, victor or vanquished.

Another difference: The obligatory scene contains what we have been encouraged to expect, without surprises. Climax is the result of a series of crises which have been building up to crescendo, resulting in a final action of the highest tension and pressure, which is not what we expected but possibly should have, had we interpreted correctly all the plot points peaking to it. We become aware of them diagnostically only after we have weathered the surprise. The climax comes at the zenith of the rising action.

Now flip backwards to the obligatory scenes chronicled a bit earlier. The obligatory scene and the climax overlap in time and place with the unreeling of *Get Shorty*, *Leaving Las Vegas*, *Babe*, *The Usual Suspects*.

As with crises, it hardly needs pointing out that obligatory scenes are rather rare in what we call, for want of a more precise term, real life.

If the climax is the final struggle in the mounting inconsonance between hero and heavy, the denouement is the final outcome of the struggle. It resolves the strife and tension and unties the knots— not an anticlimax but a postclimax that is played out between the climax and the squeeze.

In some stories the denouement with its resolution introduces another, even more disturbing impasse or an extension of the problem we the audience, thought was decisively put to rest.

In *The Usual Suspects*, we realize too late that Kujan, the F.D.A. bulldog, has Keyser Soze, the super-dreadful badass, in custody, only to release him to perpetrate more and nastier mischief.

In *Snake* (a novel by John Gadey,which aspired to become a film but never made it) a black mamba, eleven feet of lethal poison, is roaming Central Park, and New York's finest can do nothing to capture it. As the police and the herpetologists close in, the serpent gives birth to thirteen eggs. With the fade-out we realize that the peril and the death toll of the citizenry can only multiply.

The denouement closes down the battlefield and, as in Kipling's *Recessional*, "The tumult and the shouting dies; the Captains and the Kings depart." In a well-honed picture it can be compressed in less than a minute of screen time. Hit your climax, accentuate your resolution, and get off.

208

PLANTS AND PAYOFFS
Progressing Backwards

A good play thrives on surprises and switches of characterization as it progresses. How then does the writer blend the consistency of a character with his ability to change?

You plant.

Planting is the insertion of a line or lines of dialogue or a brief action subordinate to the mainstream progression, introducing an idea or a theme that will pay off later. By planting, you startle the audience, not with a scalding blowtorch or a bombshell that bursts out of nowhere, and not with a detour that leads down an irrelevant road. What we have here is another paradox, one that is as important in script construction as it is contradictory:

You must surprise your audience with what it should expect

but doesn't. A few wide-ranging examples:

Sleepless in Seattle: Early in the screenplay Sam Baldwin (Tom Hanks), mourning his dead wife, moves west from Chicago because the city holds too many poignant memories of her. His sorrow is so deep that he and we, the audience, feel he'll never remarry. Symbolic of his love and loss is a plant, a lovely line of dialogue, as early in the first act, he describes his reaching down to help her out of a car. When their hands touched, he knew she was the only woman for him. Then she dies.

He is lost until late in the third act when he reaches out and his hand closes over Annie Reed's (Meg Ryan's). Camera comes into a tight insert of their two hands touching, and the audience, including a clutch of brave and hairy men, sobs noisily, recognizing through the reactivated image that she is the new and only girl on his block forever and ever. The writers, Ephron, Ward, and Arch, have reprised a brief but moving episode to give it greater dramatic significance.

Bull Durham by Ron Shelton is a fine, funny picture about a journeyman ballplayer in the minors, a man with brains coping in an arena in which intelligence is detrimental ("Don't think, just hit the fuckin' ball") and knee-jerk physicality—what the play-by-play mavens call "athleticism"—is everything.

In an early scene of drunken rancor, contemptuous of his own acuity, he confronts a remarkably gifted and excessively dumb pitcher on his way to the majors. "I got brains," Kevin Costner, as Crash Davis, says, "but you've got talent."

At the squeeze, the plant and the values are inverted when he is offered work managing a bush-league team, but with the implicit proviso he will in the not-too-distant future be rewarded because of his smarts with a job running a club in the Bigs.

In *Bullets Over Broadway* a boss racketeer is charmed and captivated by his bimbo, who has an unfortunate drive to become an actress—unfortunate because she is totally untainted by any trace of talent. He bankrolls a play and puts her in it, assigning a sullen thug in his employ to guard her body (i.e., to attend all rehearsals as her chaperone, for she is generally known to have the moral fiber of a nanny goat).

The gunsel's boredom and disgust with the play is planted in the first act to establish in the minds of the audience that his contemptuous criticism stems from his loutishness and his insensibility to the theater arts. In the second act the writers reinterpret their plant for us: Now we are surprised and intrigued to learn that his churlish attitude sprouts from his aesthetic awareness that the play is abominable.

Moreover, the killer-savant knows how to fix it. Interested, energized, he then becomes the major contributor to the rewrite of the play-within-the-screenplay. His involvement is at first aggressive, then possessive, and finally obsessive. He concludes that much of the problem is determined by the outrageous performance of his boss' mistress. To preserve his play's integrity, he murders her.

In Robert Pirosh's *Battleground*, the hero, an infantry grunt in WWII, is increasingly irritated by the presence of his tag-along buddy. His annoyance, as his stress in combat mounts, focuses on the country boy's response to just about any development. "That's fer sure," the hick says. "That's fer danged sure."

Then the kid is killed. The hero finds to his astonishment that he misses him. His feeling of loss deepens; now, in answer to practically everything, he says, "That's fer sure. That's fer danged sure."

Another inversion of values occurs in the progression of *Big* by Gary Ross and Anne Spielberg.

Here the mystical, mechanical wishing machine in a scruffy amusement park is the "McGuffin." And this is as good a time as any to mention that a McGuffin was, to shaggy-eared veterans of the screenwriting wars—a goal, a target, an object that must be acquired by the forces of grace and goodness to progress the plot or to solve the problem—the Maltese Falcon and its secret, the Purloined Letter and its detection, the Lost Ark of the Covenant and its recovery, the Guns of Navarone and their destruction. The term was coined by Charles Bennett when working on a script with Alfred Hitchcock.

The coin-activated McGuffin of *Big* creates a time warp for the child-hero who, weary of the indignities to which all kids are heir, fervently wishes to grow up fast. The wish is granted and our boy-in-a-man's-body learns what many a seer has observed: Beware of your wishes; they might be intercepted by some meddlesome peri who has nothing better to do at the moment than make them come true.

Now with the sorrows and confusions of young manhood upon

him, he searches for the instrument that kick-started the youngster's descent into pernicious maturity. The damned thing has disappeared from the park. He finally locates it, reverses his wish, and more or less happily returns to the dubious joys of childhood.

In *The Maltese Falcon,* as in so many of the great impactive mysteries, the audience (or reader) is presented with all the facts of the crime and all the clues about the killer. Yet by misdirection and misemphasis we are led down a garden path paved with false conclusions which we are subtly encouraged to jump at. It is only after Sam Spade, with his superior powers of ratiocination, rearranges the facts for us that we are able to perceive what we should have expected.

A precise and persistent factor in *Falcon's* logic of misdirection begins with the opening sequence. Miles Archer, Spade's partner, is hired by the ravishing Miss Wonderly, née Brigid O'Shaughnessy, to shadow an armed and dangerous adventurer she feels will kill her. In the line of duty Miles is shot dead at the terminus of a blind alley on a foggy San Francisco night. We, the audience, know what the police tell Spade, that Archer was gunned down at point-blank range with a Webley revolver. We also know from Spade that his partner was a highly professional detective. But it was Wonderly/O'Shaughnessy herself who killed Miles. As Spade explains to her in the denouement,

> [Archer] had too many years as a detective to be caught like that by the man he was shadowing. Up a blind alley with his gun tucked away on his hip and his overcoat buttoned?. . . . But he'd've gone up there with you, angel. He'd've looked you up and down and licked his lips and gone grinning from ear to ear—and then you could've stood as close to him as you liked in the dark and put a hole through him.

Another dramatic technique is utilized in *Falcon.* Time-tested and enthralling, it is the progression that points to the hero as the killer—the double-jeopardy gambit. Sam Spade is suspect for good reason: He and Archer's wife are deep in a tawdry affair. Therefore, as the cops come after him, he must find Archer's killer to get himself off a sharp and nasty hook.

The hero-investigator can be the target of yet another stratagem: The heavies are trying to do him in (to close the case, to escape detection themselves, to pin the rap on him) while the police, thinking he's the malefactor, move in. He must, therefore, bring in the real culprit to prove his innocence.

"Life goes not backward," Kahlil Gibran decided in *The Prophet*, but writers do. That's how they harvest the desired yield of inversions, reversals, plants. The payoff comes, not with smoke and mirrors, but by weaving the fabric backwards.

Once you decide (vaguely) how your screenplay should end, you must go back and build your progression to realize that goal, peppering your scenes with the zigzaggery that makes for surprises.

With this in mind, let's reexamine *Sleepless in Seattle*. The writers chart the couple's romance to a finale with Annie Reed and Sam Baldwin finding true and durable love together. They concoct that hand-in-hand symbol of affinity for the couple and insert it in the third-act climax when his fingers find hers and hold them as if they were a trove of fragile and precious jewels.

213

The shot by itself holds a certain pseudo-poetic sentimentality that would induce snoring if the writers hadn't thereupon reversed their field, gone back to act one where, as noted, the hands belong to Hanks and his beloved wife, whose early death had so deeply damaged him.

It is the plant that maximizes the decisive, highly charged emotional moment in the third act. Designed as a metaphor of abiding love, it goes well beyond atmospherics because of its associated meaning once the two isolates are symbiotically combined.

The same procedure of what might be called reversion progression is followed in *Bull Durham*. The catharsis—the relief of emotional tension—experienced by the audience at the squeeze is induced when it is made apparent that Crash Davis' (Costner's) brains will finally do him some good: It gets him a managerial job more suitable to his talents, and wins the love of Annie Savoy (Susan Sarandon). This is the point of Ron Shelton's picture; to sharpen it he progresses backwards to plant the opposite notion in the first act, that in Costner's bailiwick muscle is the cardinal virtue and thinking is considered a dreaded waste of energy, not to be indulged in because it could ruin your swing at the plate.

It has been said that the hero of a story is the character who changes. Woody Allen is a master of human metamorphosis. In *Bullets* the three principals undergo qualitative switchovers, none more hypnotically than Cheech, the sociopath whose subliminal love of the theater surfaces to provide the self-justification for offing the actress who has cocked up his rewrite.

After the screenwriters establish Cheech's sensitive concern for the play in the third act, he conforms to the practice of progressing backwards to the first act, planting the adverse, stressing his earlier philistine insensitivity and flinty disdain for the play and all the people involved in it.

When Bob Pirosh, in writing *Battleground,* wanted to drive home John Hodiak's sense of loss for his buddy killed in the Battle of the Bulge, he chose a literary cinematic device to accent the bond between these two vastly disparate characters. He took a memory that was lodged but unattended in Hodiak's mind, and wrenched it into consciousness to dramatize his sorrow.

Pirosh decided to do it with dialogue. In *Sleepless in Seattle* the linkage of plant and payoff was forged with a gesture: the hands reaching out, finding each other. In *Battleground,* a few words murmured here and there against the unremitting thunder of combat might possibly suffice, but what should be said? Some notion, an idea or secret they shared? A joke, a hometown, a love of poker, the apotheosis of Ava Gardner? A mutual and abiding hatred of ballpark organs? Pirosh did it with that huckdummy barbarism.

It could be an improbable, even preposterous, weld to support a greater point, as in Forrest Gump's quoting his mother on the relationship between a box of chocolates and the randomness of life: In either case you never know what you're getting. The candy box is planted early and reprised often to point up the chaos that rules the picture and rides unbridled through the world.

But instead of settling for a commonality between plant and payoff, Pirosh found a unifying disparity by putting words in Hodiak's mouth that serve to recall the boy who was killed, and at the same time pinpointing the vexation Hodiak had felt with him and his barnyard expression that had grated on the urban and relatively sophisticated Hodiak. Now, to backtrack, Pirosh returns to act one and gives the identical words to Hodiak's unwanted buddy. And so that irritating incantation, "That's fer sure, that's fer dang sure," was born, bred, reprised, and then planted. And by the time the reprise comes, and the words are echoed by Hodiak, they undergo a dramatic transmutation, looming up like a monument to a lost and cherished friend.

The contrivance of recapping an incident by reverting to the same subject or theme and, without changing a word, altering the meaning to produce a qualitative switch in the fortunes or the character of the principal, is not unlike the reprise of a key song in a musical that uses lyrics (as they should be used) to advance the plot or to redefine character.

In *Gypsy*, with its strong book by Arthur Laurents, the song titled "Let Me Entertain You," by Stephen Sondheim, is an excellent example. Its first rendition is performed with sweet, brassy innocence by a child doing a turn in vaudeville. In its reprise a luscious Gypsy Rose Lee strips to the identical lyrics, but now they take on a totally different meaning, a sly, sophisticated sensuality.

In writing lyrics or scenes in a play or a picture, no analogy exists between plants/payoffs (or payoffs/plants as they might more realistically be termed to account for the sequential order of their discovery) and the chicken/egg confusion (being the dilemma regarding which of two entities came first, or which is the cause and which the effect). As regards plants and payoffs, there is no dilemma; the plant is the initial element introduced to the audience, but to the writer, it blossoms from the reprise, the seed from which it grows.

Big makes excellent use of the payoff/plant syndrome, not with dialogue but with a kitschy figure sculpted in what could be gypsum, an ominous, wish-granting oracle never to be confused with the Apollonian shrine at Delphi or the Wizard's cloud-cuckoo-land pulpit in Oz. Here again the inversion technique is invoked. In the third act Josh concludes that living out his boyhood, for better or for worse, is preferable to the distress and disharmony of young manhood brought on by a kid in an adult's body.

The ending of the picture rides on his finding the oracle, now domiciled in another fun fair, and reversing his earlier wish to grow up fast. Again, the writer:

1) starts with the idea generated in the reprise, then

2) goes back to the first act and plants its opposite.

If you've been paying attention to *The Maltese Falcon*, you are shocked at the climax with the revelation that gorgeous Brigid O'Shaughnessy (Mary Astor), who had hired first Archer (Jerome Crown) and then Spade (Humphrey Bogart) to protect her from grievous bodily harm, and who had become Spade's bedmate, is indeed the cold-blooded killer of Miles Archer. Dashiell Hammett in his book, and John Huston, the writer-director of the movie, introduce O'Shaughnessy all dewy-eyes and vulnerable, the confused and artless quarry of a dangerous killer. It is only a moment or two before the final fade that we learn that she is the aggressor. The contrast between the extremes of her duality allows for the shock of recognition (surprising us with what we should have expected) that makes the book and the film so enthralling.

A variation on working backwards by formulating an inverse progression for your story is one that many fine screenwriters, among them John Sayles, prefer and pursue. They go about accumulating an inventory of all the scenes they feel are essential to the telling of their tale. Then they arrange them in the order they consider most effective for the unfolding narrative. This done, they consolidate, pare down, combine or blend, adding what might have been left out or overlooked. Only then do they begin the screenplay.

A wisp of a footnote regarding the plant/payoff configuration involves a trio of attempts to bridge the theatrical concept with 1) the ancient Chinese religio-philosophical imperative of yin and yang; with 2) the Hegelian principle of "the negation of the negation," and with the unity of opposites, a Marxist tenet usually applied to the class struggle. Stale and musty, they are only mentioned here as a kind of oddment that some writers have found helpful in the past. In the present some writers might find them mildly interesting and somewhat useful as phrases in the specialist vocabulary professionals employ for quick communication.

Yin and yang symbolize two radically different elements: sunshine and shadow, mountain and valley, water and fire, light and darkness. Each attains fruition as the other fizzles. Their interactions influence everybody and everything in the cosmos.

Thus it holds, albeit tenuously, when a plant like the early characterization of Cheech in *Bullets Over Broadway* morphs into its opposite in the payoff. His transformation from Neanderthal in the first act to his emergence as the gifted playwright of act three is the propellant that turns yin into yang, upsets everybody's apple cart and sweeps the action on to an unexpected and tempestuous conclusion.

Workable pictures, early on, or within the first few feet of film introduce some disruptive force to normalcy or ordinariness or to the expectations and desires or to the well-being of a principal or of the lead even when he's heavily involved in an action that's far from normal. Like a war.

In *Battleground,* Hodiak carries out his duties as a dogface until the entry of the rustic whose dependence on the rube clichés ("That's fer sure. That's fer danged sure.") so infuriates him.

Whether war is considered a "normal" activity of the human race is an issue that must be assigned for examination to a higher ethical authority than is wielded here, but Hodiak goes grunting along until the appearance of the country boy, at which point the boy destroys Hodiak's composure; he negates it. And later, in the third act, Hodiak resolves the antagonism by interjecting the boy's prattle. Making it his own, imprinting it to resolve his agitation and his grief, he has "negated the negation."

Normalcy for Sam Baldwin (Hanks) in *Sleepless in Seattle* is accepting without challenge what he considers the prima facie fact of his life, that with the death of his wife he'll never be happy again. All this changes when his pre-teen son tells an exploitative talk show hostess of his father's unhappiness, and the thrust of the story that follows opens the way for Annie Reed (Ryan) to enter his life. Hence the child's intervention begins the negation of Sam's self-imposed solitude; his attraction to Annie in the third-act climax negates the negation.

In *Big,* it is Hanks as a boy whose disaffection with boyhood sparks his wish to achieve instant maturity. His repudiation of childhood is the negation that is negated late in the film when, a bit wiser after having reaped the problematic harvest of young manhood, he once more seeks out the Mephistophelean machine that made his metamorphosis possible and manages to return to the boyhood he had previously loathed.

At the fade-in of *The Maltese Falcon,* it's business as usual (normalcy) in the prosaic office of Spade & Archer, private investigators. It lasts only a few seconds, until Brigid O'Shaughnessy comes along and churns up a riptide that sweeps normalcy overboard, beginning a cycle of lies and betrayals that burgeon into multiple deaths. Not until deep in the third act does the mayhem subside. Order is restored, the negation is finally negated.

A plant contains within itself the seeds of its own negation. It shares an underlying unity or identity of opposites with the payoff.

For example, within the frame of Cheech's sociopathic passivity, as evidenced in the first act of *Bullets Over Broadway,* is encapsulated the embryo of his terrible violence in the third act. While the two elements are seemingly antithetic, they are, as Marx's collaborator Friedrich Engels said in a geopolitical context, ". . . as inseparable from each other as they are opposed."

The venerable linkage of plant and payoff still works in formulaic pictures in our postmodern, global village, but it's more of a challenge than ever to find fresh and dynamic applications of the procedure.

Granted that every culture and each new departure from the past has its own inherent problems to bedevil writers and other primates, it has become increasingly difficult to surprise an audience with the catharsis of a well-processed reprise. Small wonder: After a half-century of TV in perpetual, around-the-clock motion, everybody's on overload, having been zapped by every nuance of zigging and zagging, of twists and hairpin turns. Through overexposure and force-feeding they've learned to recognize a plant when they see one, and anticipate the payoff before it comes. The best-laid stratagems of many a writer are pounced on rather gleefully by the audience. Once recognized, our artifice loses its ability to delight. If you think the raised sophistication of the mass audience would be welcomed as an incitement for the writer to work harder and dig deeper, think again. Most writers don't want to work harder or dig deeper, anymore than the rest of humanity does.

There was a time not too long ago when people would sit back in the pleasant gloaming of a theater and let the festivities on-screen wash over them like amniotic fluid, or so we've been told. True or not, it no longer applies. The response of moviegoers today more closely conforms to what Golda Meir noted with rue and humor about her constituency. "I am the prime minister," she noted, "in a country of a million prime ministers."

So it is with those who work in pictures, the difference being that the criticism encountered comes from many more mavens than comprise the entire population of Israel.

And it is no longer limited to plants and payoffs and other flash points of construction. The expertise of our constituency has broadened to include a deep awareness and a shallow understanding of Freudian and Jungian principles, with curious results that have changed the scene-by-scene progression of screenplays.

Before Freud and his academic descendants became household words, screenwriters embraced an eminently sensible rule of thumb: Every shift in plot or character, every action, interaction, and reaction must be made crisp and unequivocal, with algorithmic precision, or the audience in its uncertainty will walk out. Now in their newfound enlightenment and with their decades of TV conditioning, the audience can, on their own, supply what isn't locked into the screenplay. Moreover, we've learned that life, to which we're holding a mirror, lacks that sort of lucidity. No longer must every 'i' be dotted and every 't' be crossed by the writer. The audience does it for him.

It can be extremely uncomfortable for a screenwriter to realize that an audience is so far ahead of his story that it's hacking and yakking with languor when it should be deep in a trance of attention.

Disturbances of this sort do occur many times because the writer has committed the rash and snobbish sin of underestimating the comprehension of the audience. You don't have to slam them between the eyes with the obvious. You don't have to "get down on all fours and look at the script from the audience's point of view," to resurrect a cliché that, unhappily, was popular in the not too distant past. That kind of judgmentality is unwarranted now, and it probably was then.

Let's take a swift look at the way a major story point in the plot progression of *The Adventures of Priscilla, Queen of the Desert*, was handled so satisfactorily and so economically by the writer, Stephan Elliott.

No physical love scene is at all necessary for the audience to discern the growing and mutual attachment of Bob (Bill Hunter), the grizzled outback auto mechanic, and Bernadette (Terrence Stamp), the transsexual performer. A few spare innuendoes, astutely spaced, suffice. Their eyes lock for a few brief seconds here and there. Each has a deep interest and respect for the other's métier, and his/her proficiency at it. A certain tenderness and admiration flicker in a brief exchange of dialogue, and that's it—all we need is to be surprised at the squeeze by what we should have expected, that they'll walk hand in hand into the sunset of their lives together.

220

An essential aspect of the artistry that converts plant into payoff is reductive and minimalist. Overkill blows it by focusing attention on what should be seamless, casual, incidental, as if it held no more importance than a throwaway line.

In *Barcelona*, Fred is by turns charming and perfidious, a lying, petty-thieving, politically naive j.g. in the U.S. Navy. He tells us succinctly and precisely what he wants, never lingering on it, and when at the fade he gets it, we are surprised once again by what we should have expected.

Pictures are universally reductive and minimalist in another sense: All art oversimplifies. It should be noted that in reality the character of an individual is infinitely more complex, more self-contradictory and wide-ranging than that of any adult *ever* portrayed on stage or screen, not excluding *Hamlet*. "Heroes are two-dimensional," Dustin Hoffman has observed, "but people are three-dimensional." Which means that you and I and the folks next door are so complicated and so mercurial that we can't be boiled down into a concentrate of limited ingredients that sustain our fictional silhouettes on the other side of the camera. Indeed people are so inconsistent in their actions that as soon as you put a label on them, it's untrue. Color them chameleons.

Drama, in imitating life, can never achieve more than an approximation of reality. There are times on a sound stage, during the shooting of a picture, when the conscious pursuit of de facto–objective authenticity is unconsciously blunted by the grace and deftness of skilled actors or the refinements of a meticulous director. When it happens, and if you as the writer have any voice in what's going down, use whatever clout you can muster to kill the scene and shoot it again. Why? Because the stuff of life is imbued with awkwardness; awkwardness is a significant contributor to reality. A small imperfection here, a slight loss of dexterity there does much to humanize, for we are all bumblers. That's why Billy Wilder always printed the second-best take. In *Everyone Says I Love You*, Woody Allen has his dancers muck up a routine now and then not only because it's more human, but because their fallibility is funnier than perfection.

The above strategy does not apply to writing. If it's awkwardness you want, lock your very best effort into the script. Don't depend on anyone—director, producer, actor—to capture it for you.

There are times when even actors can't count on fine directors for guidance. In *Wuthering Heights*, William Wyler began shooting a dramatic two-scene with Heathcliff and Catherine at about 7:30 A.M. Twelve hours later they were still at it.

"Mr. Wyler," Lawrence Olivier said tiredly, "I've been trying to do this scene every which way I know how and you keep saying, 'Try it again.' Would you please tell me what you want?"

"What I want," Wyler told him, "is for you to do it better."

Whether it's blundering ineptitude (for example) or prick-me-dainty precocity that you aim to imprint on a character, don't clutter it up with additional and irrelevant modifiers. If the structure of your screenplay dictates the need to establish, say, a certain kind of cruise ship captain, don't drown him in a sea of quirks, megrims, and whimsies—a sweet tooth, a sour disposition, an obsession to run in the Boston Marathon—which never pay off. You'll only succeed in confusing, boring, and alienating anybody who might otherwise be tempted to bid on your story.

But suppose you manage to flesh out your dashing sea dog with what is needed and nothing more—a few apposite strokes of your word processor to let the rest of us know who he is and what he's up to. Suppose you paint him as a jaunty libertine, an inveterate liar and a peachy dancer—impeccable characterization for a free-wheeling wolf with a wife in every port and an anchor in none. And that's how the Alec Guinness part in *The Captain's Paradise* was whelped.

DIALOGUE AND PREACHMENT
What's Said

When writers think too little, their characters talk too much. Inversely, you can accomplish a lot by saying nothing. Much of Gary Cooper's success, as well as that of many a strong, silent hero, depended on muteness.

As regards your dialogue, is it in keeping with the character who mouths it, and with her actions? Does it reveal her distinctive features, mark her traits? Does it advance your plot?

Dialogue in Catholic philosophy means argument; when transplanted to drama it means conflict. Linguists usually concur that language is a shoddy and imprecise means of communication, but it remains the best we have.

Nevertheless, some writers do miraculous things with words,

making language alive and pulsating, shaping unforgettable images.

Dialogue in a screenplay, as in any written form, is successful when it captures the essence of conversation. It is all too often the mark of a novice when the words between characters rattle on as if the writer had directly transcribed a conversation captured by a recorder hidden behind the office water cooler.

There is no place in dialogue for confabulation, the process of filling a conversational gap with any phrase or random thought that ventures within reach. Also to be shunned is the kind of filler called phatic communication—sub-verbal expressions like "How do you do?" and "I'm fine." Many directors cannot tolerate silence. They like to fill the void engendered by simple movement, like getting an actor from one place to another, with confabulation. Therefore, you as a writer must fill the stillnesses in your screenplay with dialogue that's meaningful. Nobody else will.

It's generally a good idea to keep dialogue clear and clean, or you'll be routed by the forces of logorrhea. This is a lot to ask and devilishly hard to accomplish. Our ears may be fine-tuned and sensitive to the braying of other voices, but we are slaves to our very own constructs. Like the spouse of an adulterer, we, in our blindness and possibly our self-approval, are usually the last to know.

Many experts in the field of story construction concur that comedy is more difficult to master than drama. They have their reasons, preferences, possibly prejudices. Perhaps it is because the world is not a particularly happy place; it might therefore be easier to depict familiar and recognizable calamity than it is to evoke thoughtful or spontaneous laughter. As always, much depends on the talents and persuasions of the practitioner. Neil Simon is possibly drawn to comedy because he is so infernally good at it. Dudley Nichols, who wrote *The Informer*, was adept at drama. Billy Wilder (*Sunset Boulevard*, *The Apartment*), William Goldman (*Butch Cassidy and the Sundance Kid*, *Misery*), Woody Allen and a few others, did both amazingly well. Shakespeare was incomparable doing either.

To traffic in comedy does not mean that the writer takes it more lightly and is, therefore, more relaxed doing it than are the composers of tragedy. "Much seriousness is required to achieve the frivolous," Coco Chanel noted. Or, as Chaplin warned, "If you're doing something funny, don't be funny doing it."

Funny lines must have contextual meaning; there is no such thing as a funny line per se. It must come out of a web of incidents, a distillation, an essence of what has led up to it. The funny line is the keystone of the building blocks supporting it.

Woody Allen in *Mighty Aphrodite* searches for the natural mother of his adopted infant son whom he perceives as brilliant, and therefore the possessor of exceptional genes. He finds her, Mira Sorvino, a marvelously ditsy and lamebrained whore.

Neil Simon's characters are hilarious because they never laugh at their own jokes and deliver their goofiest lines as though they were tragic. What also helps is that every nuance in the plot pays off. *Plaza Suite* is a fine example of humor that develops from situations that no one in the cast sees as the least bit laughable.

When you make a joke—and even the weightiest tragedy can benefit, as does *Hamlet,* from some comic relief—make sure, to the best of your ability, that your actors play it straight. Always give your audience the first crack at laughter. Audiences resent actors who laugh at their own jokes (Dig how funny I am!).

Exception: If it is your intention to delineate a character as a dope or a dildo, then let him laugh first (usually to the annoyance or sufferance of other, more sensible types in the script). Felicitous laughter—in the right place at the right time—is a precious asset. TV is aggressively aware of its value, providing laugh tracks for sitcoms to encourage viewers to join in the premeditated fun, as though it were spontaneous. In jump-starting the howls and giggles, do TV producers actually believe the track transforms their, at times, dreadful material into funny? I don't know of any survey that proves that they do or they don't.

Interlocking action combines the delivery of dialogue with stage business—a movement or a gesture, major (action) or minor (shtick). Actors full of twitches and attendant whimsies, practiced in keeping all eyes focused on them, can with little effort go too far. A famous director once told a celebrated actress, "For God's sake, don't just do something. Stand there."

In any scriptwriting hornbook the list of "don'ts" is as numerous as crabgrass on an abandoned lawn, and just as hard to overcome.

Don't (i.e., try not to) be long-winded. All of us have at times been captives of people whose prolixity has driven us mad. Remember, you with your screenplay are just as capable of victimizing others.

Don't mouth punditries. Invariably they ring false.

Ask yourself: Is this line pompous? Artificial? Overflowing with self-pity? Sometimes, on an excessively bad day, you might encounter all these shortfalls at the same time. A Nelson Eddy–Eleanor Powell cornball classic opens with him at West Point, she at Vassar. What he doesn't know: She is a princess of an Arabian realm and rich beyond the dreams of Rockefeller. On a goodwill cruise with his cadet buddies when school is out for the summer, he bops onto her turf, realizes her exalted and (for him) unattainable station in life. With abject remorse he says, "I have come 8,000 miles to learn that you are a princess and I am a fool." A sad observation, to be sure, but the audience greeted it with delighted, unquenchable laughter. It didn't help that he delivered the line like a robotized vegetable.

Don't indulge in what academics call periphrasis—precocious, round-about language. It's a big irritant, as is disjunctive dialogue, the quality of not connecting with or listening to the other speaker, except in a situation where nobody listens, as in *Seinfeld*.

Of course, use disjunction (or artificiality or pomposity or self-pity or whatever) if you're building or defining that sort of character—when the usage is purposeful. Otherwise, silence is an improvement.

A disimprovement is the use of coprolalia—compulsive swearing and scatological locutions. Too many screenwriters tend to equate obscenity with freedom of expression. An overload of just about anything is an oppressive bore, and that includes fornication and nudity. Witness *Showgirls*.

Preachment, too, must be reined in. Curiously enough, the more you have to say qualitatively, the easier it is to keep it sharp, concise and relevant, although prolixity and prattle are always tempting.

226

"It is difficult to keep quiet," Schopenhauer observed, "when you have nothing to say."

Writers, it seems, always think they have something to say. Writing has always been used to promote sociopolitical change, or to prevent it, or to prolong the status quo. Great dramatists have always been pedagogues, purveyors of one social creed or another. "The purpose of drama," Bertolt Brecht told *The New Yorker* (September 12, 1959), "is to teach us how to survive."

It is not possible to write without making some kind of social comment any more than a screenplay can exist without a theme. It can't help but say something about our cultural past or present or future. It can be a passionate political treatise by Oliver Stone or a banana split by Disney; in either case it cannot be done without being pro or con something, even if what's at stake is an exercise in triviality. It might also be noted that a fence-straddler takes a position.

Art as provocation (agitation propaganda) seldom works except in the hands of a master like Maxim Gorki (*Mother*), but many fine writers practice it. Sean O'Casey said he'd know when he wrote a "successful" play because people leaving the theater would hit the bricks and revolt.

Preachment in a play or a picture has never changed the world. It might support a political trend, or an idea whose time has not yet come, but, generally, changing the world, regardless of the elucidative skills of writers who make a stab at it, has not been a vehicle for popular entertainment. People seldom go to the movies for an evening of social comment or political didactics. Therefore, refrain from being preachy; shun paper barricades. Ultra-timely scripts have a short shelf life; they never get close to being timeless. Nobody listens much, if at all, about anything, but almost everybody gets starchy and resentful when fed agit-prop.

The ideological angling for converts is deadly, unless the writer has the subtlety and the manipulative power of God. Indeed, that is precisely what Gustav Flaubert thought every writer should have, regardless of her motivation and her creed. "The author in his book must be like God in his universe," he wrote, "everywhere present and nowhere visible." When the appeal of expressing your personal poli-

227

tics is overwhelming, give it the quality of allegory or dress it in the raiment of camouflage. Thus, *On the Waterfront* was Budd Schulberg's metaphor on the alleged communist control of the stevedores' union on the East Coast; *High Noon* was Carl Foreman's attack on those who betrayed blacklisted friends and allies; *Gentleman's Agreement* was Laura Z. Hobson's examination of anti-Semitism in middle-class America; *Black Rock* condemned racial prejudice in the Golden West. Hundreds of films have eloquently expressed the antiwar credo of their writers—*Grand Illusion, All Quiet on the Western Front, The Red Badge of Courage,* to name just three of the more memorable. In contraposition is the vast number of films glorifying, glamorizing, romanticizing war and nationalism—*The Big Parade, Lilac Time, Journey's End* out of WWI, and the spate of patriotic pictures of WWII.

The most jarringly realistic picture on infantry combat came in 1998 with the release of *Saving Private Ryan,* written by Robert Rodat. Decisive and unrelenting, it depicts twentieth-century warfare as unrelieved torment, a journey through nightmarish hell.

There have even been comedies about war—there have been comedies about everything—and they're always hard to do, whether they're confined to a subspecies of meager significance, as the idle aristocracy of *Four Weddings and a Funeral,* or about Hitler, as was Chaplin's *The Great Dictator,* or an incident in the precarious life of a child with a dysfunctional immune system, incarcerated in a plastic bubble to stay alive, as in an unrestrained episode of *Seinfeld.*

The above list, although limited and brief, is sufficiently inclusive to support the concept that you can write about anything without constraints, and you can address any subject in any way you like, no holds barred. All hail the First Amendment.

THE ORCHESTRATION
OF URGENCY
Exaggeration and Excitement

Repetition is hardly the spice of life. Yet there are certain spices in a screenplay—exaggeration is one of them, excitement is another—that bear repeating because of their importance.

It has been highlighted throughout this text that pictures are fraught with paradox, so it shouldn't come as a disconcerting surprise to find that there are certain exceptions, even to the ban on unplanted panaceas. When human behavior, not always fastidious, is depicted on stage or screen with prodigious skill, we willingly ignore the kind of coincidence that in less nimble hands we might be quick to condemn. Helpers and paracletes and guardian spirits do come out of nowhere—intercessors in all sizes and shapes—like the maladroit angel of *It's a Wonderful Life*, the seven dwarfs of *Snow White*, Alec

Guinness as the sage and teacher Ben Obi-Wan Kenobi in *Star Wars*.

At this point we might recap what was said in another context, about that rumpled, erratic attendant-stranger who appears in *The Front Page*. Moments before the final curtain, Hildy Johnson and Walter Burns—two of the most charming and unconscionable rogue-crusaders in the history of journalism and the American theater—are about to be overwhelmed by the twin forces of political corruption, personified by the mayor of Chicago and the sheriff of Cook County. Suddenly and inexplicably appears one Irving Pincus with enough ammo to shoot down the political grafters who had tried to railroad and to hang a pathetic simpleton they claimed was a Red or an anarchist or whatever aspersion they could pin on him to corner the law-and-order vote in the impending elections. The scene is so masterfully crafted and so hilarious that it merits applause rather than brickbats. We lose ourselves in the joy of the moment.

This technique for unsnarling the otherwise inextricable complexities of a plot was invented by the ancient Greeks, and they had a word for it—three words to be exact: theos ek mechanes, or deus ex machina in Latin, a god from the machine. Unexpectedly, the god was lowered on-stage by a crane-like contraption to resolve the problems of the protagonist and to ensure a happy conclusion.

Irving Pincus is a soused and scruffy deus ex machina, as is the cavalry racing to the rescue, the life-sustaining serum, and every other facile contrivance that constitutes substantive help and total victory when all seems lost.

The device was often used in Athens and Rome, perhaps most famously by Euripides. Aristotle railed against it, insisting that the conclusion of a play should emerge from the internal action leading up to it. Yet he maintained that a "likely impossibility is always preferable to an unconvincing possibility." *The Fugitive, The Front Page, Bullets Over Broadway*, etc., etc., all invoke "likely impossibilities."

The invention of "likely impossibilities" requires passion and hyperbolic intensity in the development of characters to make them larger than life, and in the creation of scenes that swerve off the beaten path.

J.D. Salinger's "willingness to risk excess on behalf of [his] obsessions," noted John Updike, "is what distinguishes the artist from the entertainer, and what makes some artists adventurers on behalf of us all." It's what relieves us from the commonplace—"the horror of the familiar," a reference by W.H. Auden to those mystery-detective stories whose terror arises from the banality of their surroundings.

In shaping a screenplay of some worth and magnitude, i.e., the depiction of an event to which "attention must be paid," as Arthur Miller put it in *Death of a Salesman*, a felicitous fusion of plot and character is requisite. The unswerving singleness of the plot, regardless of how many twists and turns it weathers as it beats to a conclusion, is what Aristotle termed "Unity of Action." Without it, chaos reigns. Nonetheless, the principle has at times required clarification to avoid the stuffiness and intractability of a too-literal or too-limited interpretation. Wide latitude, like the use of exaggeration in characterizing your players, can bear juicy fruit. Behavior that is aberrant, twisted, or eccentric can enrichen, and can indeed be integral to the main story, illustrating some aspect of the world the writer is trying to address in microcosm. As in:

Repo Man, screenplay by Alex Cox, shoots off on erratic tangents propelled by just about everybody surrounding the protagonist. He is a mild, sane outsider in a strange land of truculent zanies who repossess cars and who are at best idiosyncratic.

Dog Day Afternoon, by Frank Pierson. The thrust of the action is repeatedly arrested to hold on one member or another of the supporting cast. Their peculiarities are highly theatrical and add a fine burnish to the outrageousness of the mainstream story.

Deliverance, by James Dickey, from his book. The young idiot-savant of the backwoods and his banjo virtuosity might at first seem unrelated to the main story, but he symbolizes, with grotesque clarity, the dark, warped wilderness the hero and his companions are so jauntily about to enter.

The Perez Family, by Robin Swicord, based on the novel by Christine Bell. Among the best-remembered sequences are those featuring an old bare-assed joskin who climbs palm trees in Miami the better to see his native Cuba 200 miles away.

Excitement comprises many elements. In chronological order

231

of their appearance in a screenplay, they awaken the audience's interest in the action, arouse curiosity, provoke anxiety, heighten suspense, stimulate the uncertainty of the outcome, foment some emotional response, whether it be love or lust or anger or whatever, stir up hope or animosity.

In your screenplay, have you set up a brace of exciting expectations? And then, with your progression of scenes, fulfilled them?

The greater the magnitude of your plot evoking pity and fear, and the humanity of the characters with whom you empathize, the better your chance of holding your audience. Don't try to build a mountain out of a molehill. With a minimum of ninety minutes at your disposal, there is no way of turning an anecdote into an epic.

Elongation, protraction, diffusion, and reiteration are anathema to any approximation of a work of art because they drain it of energy. Their vapidity raises troubling analogies and distressing metaphors about life, its listless discontents and the cold, abrasive world outside the rococo playhouse. A wad of moviegoers, according to the statisticians who explore such subjects, don't like to be reminded of them. Approbation is most often accorded to scripts that deliver a happy or possibly a bittersweet ending. Better for business.

Regardless of endings, it is heightened excitement, and not chronological time or linear structure, that determines the sequence of scenes in many postmodern pictures. Examples: *The Usual Suspects, Pulp Fiction, The English Patient.*

The suspense of many adventure and detective stories is intensified when the writer includes a metaphorical time bomb in her story. The killer-antagonist has to be taken by the hero and handed over to the police before they, in their poor judgment and believing the hero's the culprit, close in on him, as in *The Maltese Falcon,* and many, many other applications of the formula. Or the killer, in a note that somehow finds its way into the heroine's hands, informs her that unless she complies with his wishes *tout de suite,* he's going to kill the hell out of her at midnight, just an hour or so away (*The Cat and the Canary*). And as the action evolves, the clock or the bomb ticks on as in *High Noon* and *The Clock.*

In *Fiddler on the Roof* (screenplay by Joseph Stein, from his book of the musical, with music by Sheldon Harnick and Jerry Bock; all out of *Tevye's Daughters*, a novel by Sholem Aleichem), Topol (Zero Mostel on Broadway) sings a song whose refrain, ". . . but on the other hand . . . ," imbues every thought with a complexity of contrasts and comparisons. Before the finality of any decision, he considers a wild variety of alternatives, including the opposite of whatever he started with.

It's a splendid yardstick for improving creative work generally. If you're willing to accept the fact that your preliminary draft, or any that follows, isn't carved in stone, it might then cross your mind that it can be improved. The first step in that direction would be asking yourself a question based on the doubts that assail Tevye, to wit, "On the other hand, suppose . . .?" And/or its corollary: "What would happen if . . .?"

Which is to say, don't move too fast, don't settle too quickly on what you have. Clichés and banalities can derive from not asking questions whose answers require some heavy thought, which is always painful and frequently resisted. But heavy thinking and exploration that departs from an earlier draft might contribute more originality, greater depth and an augmented exuberance to your story.

233

20

A MISCELLANY OF BASICS
Examined at the Risk
of Belaboring the Obvious

Whether you write your screenplay on a computer with the rapidity of a Browning automatic rifle or whether you stumble and sweat over each word, whether you plow forward or backwards or sideways (as in "Meanwhile back at the ranch . . ."), it's never a piece of cake; although some of the powers and glories of the business, none of whom ever wrote anything more complicated than an inter-office memo, thought it was a snap. Irving Thalberg, a disciplined decision-maker, was ambivalent about it. There were times when he felt dependent on writers, and there were periods when his disdain for them was evident. "You writers," he once told Frances Marion, "make such a big thing out of writing. All it is is putting one word after another."

"No, Mr. Thalberg," she answered, "it's putting one right word after another."

The attitude of people like Thalberg toward writers is off-putting. When Sid Zelinka and Howard Harris, veterans of many TV sit-coms, sold a story to Joe Pasternak at M-G-M and were hired to write the screenplay, Sid phoned his good friend and skilled old campaigner of the studio wars, the songwriter Harry Ruby, and told him about it. For a long moment the phone was silent and then, instead of tendering his congratulations, Ruby said, "Don't show up."

"What!" Sid was shocked, disbelieving what he had heard. Like many toilers in TV, he desperately wanted to do a feature film. "Why not show up?" he asked.

"Because," Ruby said, "once you show up they know they got you."

There is an axiom insisting that a good novel makes a bad picture, possibly because it is too internal. Examples: *Heart of Darkness, War and Peace*. Not always the case. Examples: *Pride and Prejudice, Anna Karenina, Wuthering Heights*.

In transposing a book to the screen, whether it's great or not so great, the secret (if there is one), might lay in Vincent van Gogh's self-direction in painting. "Exaggerate the essential," he said, "and leave the obvious vague." Whatever your approach, "There is no way of writing well," Anthony Trollope said in *Barchester Towers*, "and also of writing easily." One thing about writing, however, that isn't too difficult to determine: Every hero wants to achieve his goal. The reasons run a wide gamut from *Mr. Blandings Builds His Dream House* to the drive to become the honcho of honchos: *Macbeth*.

Yet *Forrest Gump* hasn't a focused, definable goal. Forrest dribbles the narrative ball from his park bench through a series of flashbacks before finally returning to the frame. The picture lacks a heavy. There is no unstoppable clock to pressurize the mild-mannered, sweet-tempered hero to do anything, nor is a bomb about to burst in his friendly face.

There was a time in the past when the studio insisted on a treatment—a synopsis of your story in the present tense—before you went to screenplay. There were a couple of reasons for this: 1) to acquaint a producer with what you had in mind; producers heartily approve of your surprising an audience, but they themselves don't like to be blindsided by the unexpected, and 2) to save time and money in case your story was rejected. The procedure didn't work for a couple of reasons: 1) the story and the treatment changed ideologically and sub-jectively, taking on an independent existence as it lengthened physi-cally, and so the value of the treatment was substantively diminished; and 2) it is impossible for a writer to incorporate the values he hopes to get in a 120-page script and reduce them to a relatively few words. When Paramount wanted a treatment from Scott Fitzgerald, he wrote a rough draft of the screenplay over the weekend and from it attempt-ed to siphon off a treatment.

A treatment is a closet story which never appears on film; yet it is not illogical for a producer to want one. If nothing else, it tells him, however imprecisely, where a writer intends to take his protagonist, how the character might get there, and the conclusion to be reached.

In a detective or suspense mystery, the protagonist at the squeeze may or may not expose the knave. However, not only the producer but the audience must be able to identify him, as in *The Usual Suspects*.

There is mystery and suspense in every story (how will it end?, for example). It is legitimate to keep both hero and audience unin-formed as to exactly what happened. Sometimes the audience is told: the meaning of "Rosebud" at the squeeze of *Citizen Kane*. Sometimes it works if the audience never knows what motivated the protagonist: Colonel Nichols' (Guinness') last desperate act of destruction in *The Bridge on the River Kwai*—was it a valiant commitment to patriotism or a physical collapse from his wounds? In the same way, the audience is abandoned to ignorance in the outcome of *Shirley Valentine*. Will the heroine go back to her husband and to England, or will she remain in Greece; if so, will he stay with her?

Another element of suspense that crops up in screenplays: Do you stay with the character who is about to be surprised or the char-acter who does the surprising?

Example: A woman and her lover are bouncing around a bed unaware that her unsuspecting husband is climbing the stairs to her room, and in a matter of seconds will discover the frolickers. To achieve the greatest effect, on whom do you direct the camera? All you

237

can do is think about it; there's no absolute, unqualified answer to cover all cases, but there does exist a rule of thumb, and it has little to do with story construction: You might intercut, but focus on the actor who makes the most money.

A not dissimilar issue: Do you identify the murderer early, or do you delay the shock of discovery until the end? As has been said, Hitchcock, the master of the genre, preferred coughing it up early.

Try to keep your script within the parameters of your own personal experience, which isn't always possible, particularly in adapting another writer's work to the screen, or when you consider all the savagery and mayhem committed to cellulose nitrate. Very few murderers are called upon to write *Crime and Punishment* or *Double Indemnity*, and to carry the notion to the limit of absurdity, it is well to remember that *Black Beauty* wasn't written by a horse. Nevertheless, "If your feet aren't in the mud of a place, you'd better watch where your mouth is," so Grace Paley was quoted in *The New Yorker*, May 16, 1994.

Nonetheless, the ranks of writers would be considerably diminished if their observations were limited to writing about only what they lived through. So writers superimpose imagination—possibly the greatest literary gift of all, "the prime agent of all human perception," Coleridge called it—on experience or the lack of it. Another bonanza is mined (unwittingly, of course) from the unconscious, sometimes down a most bizarre and unexpected path. The persona of the cartoon character Mr. Magoo, which I originated with the late great animation director John Hubley, derived from (I realized later) an unconscious conflict with a favorite uncle. Magoo's nephew was depicted in the first fable as a genuine, irreversible dork. (And who do you suppose that nephew of my uncle Magoo was?)

There is a certain, highly personal input in all writing, as well as a varying degree of agit-prop, because nobody lives in a vacuum. Writers invariably will use the power of pictures to propagandize, if they're in a position to do so, to impose their views—political, philosophical, dietary, whatever—on their audience. It is done consciously or unconsciously, subtly or with the impulsion of a full-throttled locomotive, aware that film does more to disseminate ideas, good and bad, than any invention since and including the stylus.

Here is an example of the power of pictures that was for me as personal as it was unforgettable:

After we of the Third Marine Division helped liberate Guam in WWII, I was transferred to the Sixth Marine Division, and we were sent back to Guadalcanal for—would you believe?—rest and recreation, and to prepare for what turned out to be the invasion of Okinawa. We had come up in the world since we last saw the Solomon Islands. Each night we had movies projected on a sheet spread between two palm trees. We had cigarettes that were only slightly mildewed. We officers had a limited supply of green booze that stank of a backwoods chemical lab, and which many of us shared with our men.

A PFC I'll call Isaac Hawkins began hanging out with us every evening after he had completed his chores as a steward in the Officers Mess (the only service sanctioned for a black Marine in the war against fascism). Somebody taught him to play chess; he couldn't get enough of the game. He told me that he dreamed about chess moves.

Then suddenly he disappeared, and it was two weeks before he came back.

"Where've you been?" I asked him.

"To a movie."

"A movie?"

"Following it around the island."

"Must be a hell of a movie."

He thought for a moment. Finally, "Can you get a jeep?" he asked, "Want to see for yourself?" He took from a pocket the monthly mimeographed schedule of picture showings for the entire island.

The following night, with my bars in my kick, Ike and I shared a bench in the enlisted men's section of a makeshift outdoor theater on the far side of Henderson Field, twelve miles away. The picture started, giving little promise of what could possibly fascinate anybody. Then, about one-third of the way through, Hawkins leaned forward on the bench as Dr. Kildare entered a hospital washroom in a scrub suit, a mask depending from his neck. He goes to a sink, begins washing his hands. Beside him is another surgeon in an identical scrub suit and dangling mask. He is black, and he too is washing up. For a moment the only sound is water spewing from the faucets. Then Dr. Kildare says, "Fine job, doctor," and the black man says, "Thank you, doctor," and Ike said to me, "That's it. Let's go."

We drove back in silence.

Pictures, that pearl of professions, have been brave in their promotion of popular causes, waging relentless war against cancer, communism, narcotics. To make a point or to sell a product, they have fictionalized history and distorted diverse realities to the point of what has been called "a schizophrenic impertinence." Many obvious examples can be cited, D.W. Griffith's *Birth of a Nation* through DeMille's *Crusades* to Disney's *Pocahontas*.

Comedy plots contain the same ingredients as those of drama: relationships that involve conflict, suspense, surprise, and twists to keep the progression in the kind of turmoil that emphasizes humor—jests, pleasantries, banter—brought to a happy conclusion; in brief, when adults act like children and children act like adults. An exception is what used to be called "drawing room" and "screwball" comedies, which dealt with the foibles and manners ascribed to the upper-middle class. They seemed to conform with Lewis Carroll's definition of adults as "refined animals." In both cases the antics onstage or screen allow the audience to feel deliciously superior to the rich bastards involved in them.

Modern-day pictures like *Pretty Woman*, by J.K. Lawton, seem to have inherited the screwball mantle. In *Pretty Woman*, the hooker-heroine is made palatable because those who cross her are totally repulsive, including an arrogant, sexist rogue in silk designer threads. Despite the unavoidable fact that our gutter-nymph conducts business with all comers in the back alleys off Hollywood Boulevard and on the rear seats of briefly parked cars, she doesn't cotton to the villain with his occupational sneer and his prurient aggressiveness.

One of the most pleasurable kinds of film made between the late twenties and the early '40s, with the outbreak of WWII, was the screwball comedy. It usually featured an adorable but ditsy and borderline certifiable young woman—a winsome, whimsical, somewhat helpless eccentric, portrayed by marvelously gifted comediennes like

Jean Arthur and Carole Lombard. There was an innocent, virginal aura about them which audiences found both charming and irresistible. Men particularly were enthralled by the rescue fantasies they invoked.

But when women joined the armed services, flew planes across the Atlantic to bases in Britain, and mastered heavy machinery in armaments factories, the helplessness of even the most endearing gamine became ridiculous. Moreover, the advance of assertive feminism interpreted the dingbat depictions as unappealing, demeaning, condescending, and not in the least funny.

Nevertheless, the genre had been too profitable and too promising to be dumped. It took on cultural characteristics—a sexy, experienced sagacity in place of sweet innocence, an aggressive self-reliance instead of helplessness.

Injecting a bit of comedy into a drama relieves tension or intensifies dramatic action, keeping it in suspension for a time. Inversely, a dollop of drama dropped into a comedy endows it with a presentiment of seriousness, possibly pain, so the audience doesn't lose the thread that stitches it to reality.

Nonetheless, it's easy to confuse and exasperate an audience by pouring too many genres into the same soup.

Example: In *Joe Versus the Volcano*, John Patrick Shanley starts out with a dramatic situation that threatens to become tragic. Instead it segues into comedy, veers like a defective firecracker into farce, and then shifts incongruously into fantasy. Unable to pin a humanly possible ending on the tale, it finally succumbs in a swamp of absurdity as big as the Pacific Ocean that its two leads, Tom Hanks and Meg Ryan, can't seem to get out of.

This sort of unfettered, incautious metaphor-mixing has been the terrain of many superb writer-explorers who seem to be searching for a new departure from orthodox dramatic structures. Or maybe they're just fooling around, for laughs or the hell of it.

Truman Capote applied the technique, if such it can be called, in *Beat the Devil*, which a vast number of moviegoers avoided as if it carried some deadly contagion. If either screenplay, Shanley's or Capote's, had been written by an unknown, it would have been precipitately deep-sixed by a studio reader, but Shanley and Capote are

241

names that resonate from Broadway to Malibu, and rightly so. Unfortunately, nobody's infallible.

There are more good pictures made for mature people today than ever before. Nevertheless, there are far too many ventures into triviality, or fertilized with obscenities, vocal and visual, that contribute not to character but to cheap shock. Pictures depicting heroes as acrobatic wrecking balls committing a rash of disasters turn the world into a meat market draped with bushels of bloody corpses, providing an amplitude of raunch and violence, sexual and otherwise. They illustrate what Oscar Wilde termed "the survival of the vulgarest," when he applied the phrase to the yellow journalism of his day. They stink things up for a while but generally and deservedly live a short shelf life.

Suddenness is perhaps the most attractive and exciting element about violence. Perhaps the most unattractive and disturbing is the cynicism of action-aggression pictures: The protagonist professes pacifism and abhors cruelty but is forced to use it to wipe out his beastly enemies. Writers, directors, and producers piously condemn violence while drowning their hero-killers in a sea of Technicolor blood, as in *Natural Born Killers*. Is this how Hollywood demonstrates what it sees as its mission to combat the ethical and moral morass at the fin de siècle? Jean Baudrillard, the leading philosopher of chaos theory, has observed that "Responsibility is not dead, it has become violent." Both the product and the producers say a lot about the human condition at the dawn of the twenty-first century.

Fairy tales have said a lot about the human condition for centuries. They are as irresistible to adults as they are to children. Their appeal is universal. The archetypal hero is empathic to so many people of all ages because, as W.H. Auden noted, "At the beginning he (or she) is either socially obscure or despised as being stupid or untalented, lacking in the heroic virtues, but at the end he has surprised everyone by demonstrating his heroism and winning fame, riches, and love."

George Lucas has created a mythos for postmoderns with his *Star Wars* cycle. Recognizing severe defects in twentieth-century American culture, he has, through a synthesis of intuition and research, structured his work to embrace the ancient and honorable values of goodness and valor, of grail-questing and the search for identity, and their ultimate triumph over aggression and evil. Putting a new twist on fairy tales, contributing to the literature of archetypal heroes, he has nonetheless advanced and encouraged the proliferation of filmic violence. The *Star Wars* saga is constructed like the cliffhanging serials of Saturday matinees of the distant past. Only moreso. In Lucas' canon, a violent, confrontational climax explodes about every six to eight minutes. The intervening time is devoted to the buildup for the next outburst of hostilities.

The *Star Wars* tempo was a Lucas innovation adopted universally for the genre. Today no action-adventure epic is without it, and audiences of all ages, possibly because of the constant accelerated locomotion of our warp-speed society, eat it all up.

Action in a movie, regardless of its velocity, is in itself not enough. It must be coherent and must involve characters we care about. No matter how adept the stunt people are, unless the action is an integral part of the story, it's a bore. Example: In *Rodeo*, the hero and his buddy are swilling a couple of brews in a bar. Enter two nameless cowboys hell-bent on destroying each other. Their fistfight is choreographed as well as any disturbance ever recorded on film—*Tol'able David* or *The Quiet Man*, to name just a pair of bare-knuckle wars—but nobody cares. The audience isn't interested because we don't know what they're fighting about—we don't even know who they are. Matter of fact, the fracas doesn't qualify as action because the audience has no rooting interest in either of the warriors. Without empathy, all the ass-kicking adds up to no more than frantic movement, a *pas de deux* or *trois* or *mille* of irrelevant ciphers.

243

In the early days of Hollywood it was said that "God must have loved Westerns because he made so many of them." But now they've lost their appeal. Unless a big bankable star like Clint Eastwood wants to do it, you can't give a Western away in today's market.

Oaters used to help people get away from the perplexities and complexities of modern life and back to the tranquilizing absolutes of a less complicated age. But values have changed. People are too occupied with the present and immediate future. Men and horses are no longer esteemed for their snorting and ramping—that sort of machismo is rather frowned upon. Women are no longer admired and pedestalized for their passivity and compliance. Today it is hard to believe that a William S. Hart Western, *The Narrow Trail,* was once advertised with a still of the star caressing his Appaloosa over the caption "Better a Painted Pony Than a Painted Woman."

If a picture makes money, expect more in the same vein. If it does not, the door is slammed on any offending genre that bombs at the box office. Said Jack Warner, on an anti-costume kick: "No more pictures where they write with feathers." And Sam Goldwyn, who too had had enough of historical epics: "No more pictures about wet rocks," by which he meant, in his picturesque argot, that castle walls, misty and luminous in the gloom, were not big at the box office. And L.B. Mayer, whose post-Depression slate of releases did not include realism: "No more cats crawling in garbage cans."

Pictures change; fads and foibles are unending. They seem, for a while at least, to follow some immutable law of nature until the next trend sizzles in, only to give way to the succeeding sizzler. Trendiness and a fervor to embrace whatever lures and appeals on or off the screen seems irresistible to most Hollywood commanders. Pictures haven't changed in one aspect: The quantity of performers in them is often confused with the quality of the product ("with a cast of thousands" or "at a cost of zillions," as though sheer numbers gave it greatness). This sort of non-cognitive thinking seems in some cases to invade the very reality of existence.

Eddie Small was a producer with space at the Goldwyn Studio. When I went to work for him he assigned me to an office with a lush, walled-in patio. I arrived one morning to find it packed and overflowing, like a turbulent and untamed river, with dogs. Big dogs, little dogs, dogs that barked and growled and wailed and howled, fighting and sniffing and pissing all over the place and each other. Forty obnoxious canines. Forty.

I jogged to Small's office to make a few inquiries; our picture had nothing to do with dogs.

Eddie enlightened me. It seemed he lived in Palm Springs with a dog. Business required his presence in town five days a week. His dog missed him terribly, so he decided to get the beast a companion. The menagerie in my courtyard, supplied by a local pet store, held one lucky animal which Eddie, when his study was completed, would drive to Palm Springs. Until he decided which dog, there, about ten feet from my typewriter, they would remain.

Five days later, after much soul searching, Small reached a decision. He chose one of the least smelly beasts and took it home with him that weekend.

The dog was back in town Monday. Eddie's hound in Palm Springs wouldn't let it in the house.

I don't know that anyone reading this book will take anything in it to heart. "Writers only pretend to listen to advice," Joyce Carol Oates told members of the faculty at a Silliman College, Yale University, master's tea. "I always had the feeling I'd do what I wanted to do."

Oates' independence is masterful. Unfortunately, there are few members of the human race, and that includes writers, who share her self-reliance and autonomy. Most of us, despite staunch protestations, are full of doubts about our work and indeed about ourselves. We want to be loved or at least appreciated by most everybody. Something to do with insecurity. But there is, happily, an obverse side of the coin. You don't have to be loved to sell a script. All you need is just one taker. All kinds of people in Hollywood and elsewhere buy all kinds of scripts including *The Return of the Cheerleader Nurses*. So you never know who'll turn up and latch on to something you've written. "What's a goose for one," Archie Moore said, "may be a gander for another."

A supplemental note to Oates' observation: Some writers don't want to probe how they do it, fearing that in some arcane, not-to-be-explored manner, they'll lose their inspiration or their ability. They seem to regard talent as a mystery best left unexamined, a wondrous gift horse not to be looked in the mouth. And there are writers who use all the elements of composition without an awareness of them, like the Molière character who admits, with some astonishment, that "For more than forty years I have been speaking prose without knowing it."

Seventy-six million people lived in the U.S. in 1900 when Georges Mèliès first used a story line, in a motion picture called *Cinderella*. Three years later Edwin S. Porter wrote the continuity for

245

The Great Train Robbery. Since then, it seems (stats are not available) that at least seventy-six million screenplays have been knocked out. The overwhelming preponderance of them never reached the screen. Of those that made it, only a few might qualify as brilliant, in the true sense of a much-overused term. Those that come immediately to mind include *Citizen Kane, The Wild Bunch, Grand Illusion, The Blue Angel, Open City.* Perhaps these, perhaps others shape your list.

There is no such thing as a perfect screenplay. All of them are flawed to some degree, if only by the imposition of external and restrictive forces—limited time, money, etc. And also because they were written by human beings—members, like it or not, of a flawed race and not by daemons or angels.

Yet I suppose each of us, within the parameters of practicality, strives, if not for perfection, at least for betterment. We try to invest our writing with some sort of Dionysian passion and frenzy combined with an application of Apollonian order and restraint.

Easier said than done. As Sherlock Holmes told his constant companion, "It's one thing to diagnose a problem, Watson, but another to resolve it."

Factors that discourage resolution are not limited to the writing of a screenplay. People with executive duties are themselves quite often blunted and enfeebled in getting things done by the excesses of nepotism.

Certainly any paterfamilias who accepts a responsibility for the welfare and preservation of his descendants, including the people they marry, wants to find a niche for them in his workplace, but the procedure and the results have been known to go too far.

M-G-M had on the payroll a relative whose job nobody could figure out. He was known as the "Iceberg Watcher"—the sentinel who would sound the alarm if ever the Arctic icecap approached Culver City.

The minor producer who married the daughter of the owner and operator of a major studio was given his very own unit and imprint, and guaranteed distribution through the parent company. He made a picture.

"How was it?" a writer asked Julie Epstein, who had attended the preview.

"Let's just say," Julie told him, "that it set the son-in-law business back twenty years."

At M-G-M, a facility not unlike the outmoded B-picture division (which TV decommissioned) was set up, with an enrollment of second-generation beneficiaries. Immediately the unit was dubbed "The Sons of the Pioneers." It did not prosper.

Charlie Lederer was a nephew of Marion Davies, one of Metro's most luminous stars. She got him a job interview with executive Eddie Mannix. Charlie got the idea that Mannix was trying to guide him towards a bright career as a company spy.

"Take a look around," he told the young man. "Then come back and tell me what you find."

Two weeks later Charlie reappeared in Mannix's office. "I found a bottleneck," he told his patron.

"Who?" Mannix asked.

"You," Charlie said, and was forthwith fired before his career began.

247

One of the problems of a studio is the manner in which the patriarch in charge of production is hired—not unlike the election of the Pope by the College of Cardinals, without, however, the burning of dry straw that signals the emergence of His Holiness to the populace.

A studio's overlord is chosen by a board of directors, the committee responsible for the company's financial and artistic despair at the time of the election.

Sol Segal, offered the job, was hooked on the horns of an age-old dilemma. "To be successful," he confided to a friend, "I'd have to fire all the people who put me in office. I can't do that."

But he did take the job, and the extent of his loyalty was such that he fired nobody, with the result that the studio continued to crumble.

The theories of Occam and Ortega y Gasset as to the trimming of scenes and the filing of fat off screenplays, were often enthusiastically adapted by studio executives—even those who had never heard of Occam and Ortega y Gasset—in their untiring pursuit to bag more product with the expenditure of less money.

Understandably so, for pictures remain the most wasteful business since the advent of the industrial revolution. Executives have always been conscious of it and concerned with it, and, from time to time, have made a stab at doing something about it. Most of their forays into efficiency have proven absurdly inadequate.

Harry Cohn wandered through the offices at Columbia on his way home, flipping off light switches.

Augie Spadafore, the monitor of office supplies at Metro, simply would not part with a new typewriter, regardless of how badly it was needed. I pestered him for six months before he agreed to grant me a new machine, and then only after my old one had so many impediments that it was beyond surgery.

I followed Augie into the subcellar of the Iron Lung, into a storage area protected by a double thickness of heavy chicken wire. He unlocked the door and there, arranged like soldiers on parade, were eighteen (I counted) brand-new typewriters, all of them frozen with rust and irreparable.

In the war against waste, Metro even went so far as to bring in an efficiency expert. He spoke to executives and middle management. Quite naturally they began by trimming the secretarial budget where there was, arguably, less waste and more cost-effectiveness than anywhere else in the shop.

The expert then lectured producers. What sterling advice he gave them was never disclosed to writers who, possibly because of their exclusion, made up jokes about what transpired. One writer claimed the expert called in a trio of secretaries to make a point. He asked the first, "How much is two and two?"

She said, "Four."

He dismissed her. The second secretary, expecting chicanery said, "Twenty-two."

The third guinea pig said, "Well, it could be four or it could be twenty-two."

When she had left, the expert turned to the assemblage, "Here," he explained, "we have an interesting situation. The first woman answered literally, the second showed some imagination while the third showed both. Which," he asked Nicky Nayfack, "would you choose?"

Nicky said, "I'll take the one with the big tits."

21

END GAME
The Road to Fade-out

We're down to the short strokes. Perhaps a few summational generalities are in order. But first a personal note and a true confession:

I fear that generously sprinkled among the preceding pages is an abundance of testimony that has brought me exceedingly close to contradicting myself, not once but many times. There's some consolation in the fact that the finest people do it.

"Do I contradict myself?" Walt Whitman asks in "Song of Myself." "Very well then, I contradict myself."

Now about those generalities:

Don't write anything soothing.

A screenplay should be disturbing; i.e., it should excite by disquieting, and so it can, without resorting to a profusion of bellicosity. Indeed, it wasn't until 1740 that a Western European poet and playwright depicted an onstage murder. With the production of Jean Baptiste Louis Gresset's *Edouard III*, the destruction of a human being before an audience was considered by critics, authors, and academics as rude, crude, and indecent—a notion first propounded in the *Ars Poetica* of Horace in the first century B.C. A short, wry commentary on M. Gresset: He had taken orders in the Society of Jesus at seventeen but grew excessively anti-clerical with the years, and was finally expelled by the Jesuit fathers on charges of licentiousness, possibly because of the ridicule with which he assailed the entire sisterhood of nuns in his poetic canon.

A far cry from *Edouard III*, *Babe*, with all its cutesy warmth and huggable innocence, begins with a murder (mercifully performed off-screen), further intensified by a powerful and harrowing note of abandonment. Abandonment is the blast-off for many a classic: *Tom Jones*, *Silas Marner* by George Eliot (born Mary Ann Evans).

250

Babe has formidable enemies. He overcomes them, along with other impossible odds. At the film's epicenter is a cold, calculating atavism of primordial fear and universal anguish—the psychomotor dread of desertion, particularly of a child (with deliciously distressing parallels to Snow White, Hansel and Gretel, Romulus and Remus, the infant Oedipus). In this rendition the valiant hero is a cuddly little piglet whose mother is not only taken from him but is turned into pork.

When a seemingly innocuous story becomes a hit, look into the subconscious machinery that makes it go and you're likely to find a folk tale that appeals to all times and all nations—the despised and inferior foundling—outcast, The Ugly Duckling who triumphs.

Try to be graphic, writing for the eye rather than the ear. The primacy of the optic image is not limited to pictures or plays. Thomas Hardy, Dickens, and Jane Austen, as well as Kurosawa, Fellini, and Woody Allen write visually. Think of your favorite authors. Can you think of one who didn't? Readers are only conscious of seeing words on a page when the narrative is so boring or so confused that you can't picture it.

Many movies today are cartooned and undertextured. Arthur

Miller found the same lack of humanity in modern plays, which, in the *London Times* of June 3, 1990, he characterized as "unstructured effusions." The tendency toward animated, computerized reductionism of characters possibly in some degree derives from the technical magic of special effects. Anything is physically possible on a modern screen, including miraculous feats of dexterity and the doings of imaginary monsters in live-action which until recently only cartoon characters could perform. Free from all restraint, the laws governing the movements of human beings and other creatures no longer apply. Visual wizardry affords an almost irresistible temptation to fiddle with this superficial world of wonders rather than explore the complexities of the human heart and brain. When Shakespeare wrote in Act III, Scene iii of *A Winter's Tale* (1610–11) of Antigonus' *"Exit, pursued by a bear,"* the stage direction might have given the company manager fits, or at least presented him with something of a problem, but it could be done on-screen today with no sweat whatsoever.

Much has been broadcast about the screenwriter's unenviable and much deplored position as the lowliest, rear-rank grunt in the Hollywood army of creative contributors. It is equally lamentable to cite the lesser-known truth that some writers themselves adopt a posture of superiority toward just about everybody—internationally esteemed colleagues in the producing, directing, and acting trade as well as the unknown and silent majority who make up the audience and without whose perennial attention pixbiz wouldn't even exist. Writers have at times been insolent, arrogant, contemptuous, seeing themselves as *narodniki*, the Russian intellectuals who went out into the fields and worked with the peasants.

Many operators in Hollywood have showered derision on those anonymous civilians they try so desperately to please. To a distinguished producer, the symbol of the great American audience was an imaginary fan he called Sadie Fuckface. An executive referred to her as Sarah Coozbine.

There have been otherwise astute and sincere people in show business who felt that audiences were a detriment to the production of first-rate theater. "If it weren't for the audiences," Robert Benchley said semi-facetiously, "the drama would be miles ahead of where it is now."

Almost any amateur psychotherapist could tell you that expressions castigating people who accept, at times graciously, what you offer them indicate on your part an unconscious self-hatred—along the contours of Groucho Marx's self-contempt in his unwillingness to join any country club that would have him as a member.

Why raise so distasteful an issue? Because writers have been known to funnel precious passion that should be directed toward work into displaced hostility. Before you rage and rant toward a total and irreversible meltdown, stop for a moment to consider what possible gain could come out of biting the hand that buys the booze.

Some writers concentrate their dislike and assign their bedevilment, unfairly or not, to directors or producers. The writer's pervasive attitude toward the producer's contribution to a screenplay is best expressed in a joke that's been making the rounds for at least fifty years:

A producer and a writer are hopelessly lost in the Sahara, dying of thirst. After days of torturous wandering, the writer stubs his toe on something half-buried in the hot sand—an ice-cold quart of fresh orange juice. As he raises the thermos to his lips, the producer says, "Wait a minute. Let's piss in it first."

I'm sure the story has been told by producers, but with the roles reversed.

It could be no more than a prejudice, but it seems to many writers that producers pick on petty things—worrying about a sip of water while poisoning the well, imposing changes in the script that bungle it beyond recognition. Producers, on the other hand, characterize writers as irresponsible, disdainful of practical considerations in getting the picture done. They accuse writers of using artsy, overblown devices and procedures that imperil cost-effectiveness. The director wants from the writer guidelines and signposts, lean but sufficiently developed to avoid confusion on the set and along the road, but nothing that would seriously challenge his primacy or disqualify him as the auteur or the creator and major contributor to the movie. Of the disaffection shared mutually among writers, directors, and producers, I can only speak as a writer, tentatively and with an awareness that I'm indulging in another generality, always a dangerous enterprise. Nevertheless, what exists is a power struggle. At this time, the hegemony is invested in the TV producer and in the director of feature films. In either case, the figure holding the highest rank in the endeavor is loathe to surrender it. Conversely, the alpha male seems for the most part to enjoy flexing muscles and kicking ass—exercising clout at the painful expense of those beneath him in the food chain. There's nothing mysterious about the application of control by the Kaiser. Everybody wants things done his own way and, given the opportunity, would probably insist on it.

Writers, directors, and producers don't concentrate all their ire on each other. A favorite target is actors; those who savage them include many of the great and near-great. When Shelley Winters didn't show up one day on the set of *A Place in the Sun,* director George Stevens managed to reach her by phone. "Don't bother coming in tomorrow," he told her. "We got a replacement for you—an ape in a fright wig."

Bernard Shaw treated actors like props; in his eyes he was indubitably the star of the production. "I do not want actors and actresses to understand my plays," he made clear. "That is not necessary. If they will only pronounce the correct sounds, I can guarantee the results."

253

Surprisingly, some of our finest actors agreed with Shaw.

"You do what the script tells you," said Katharine Hepburn in *Time* magazine (November, 1981). "Deliver the goods without comment. Live it—do it—or shut up. After all, the writer is what's important."

There are no generalizations that hold about writers, but there are a few characteristics that bear mentioning. Most of us would sooner be flayed than ignored. We all have some kind of Icarus complex: an inclination to take chances, a willingness to stand naked under a microscope and take the shots of strangers—a perhaps masochistic impulse to reveal all. You might say that actors do the same and more, and it's true, but most performers are handsome, graceful, and carry a heavy wattage of charisma, while most of us are not and do not. We, all of us, are willing—the more hermitic of us are eager—to spend long, uninterrupted periods of time alone in a room that has no distractions. And most of us who qualify as successful enjoy a remarkably precarious tenure of eminence.

All of us are subject to the weird, unexpected skews that direct much of our writing; the work itself is full of surprises. When you sit down in the morning or whenever you sit down and begin to write, you may have a vague notion or a wild hair about how to start and where to go. Or you might have a calculated outline or synopsis on paper or in your head. But what comes out is usually quite different and unexpected from the anticipatory blueprint or the developed paradigm you started with.

The act itself is clothed in phrenic mystery. I don't believe it's ever quite clear, even to those who practice it. "All good writing," said Scott Fitzgerald, "is swimming under water and holding your breath."

And it looks so damned easy, just as a .300 hitter with his sweet swing makes it look effortless. Good word work looks like a piece of cake; just about every producer thinks he can do it. But those who know, through struggle and experience see it differently. "Writing is easy," Red Smith admitted. "You put a piece of paper in a typewriter and bleed."

254

I hope you'll find something in these pages to stanch the flow of blood.

FADE OUT

Index

257

Photo Credits and Permissions

Publisher's Acknowledgments

Many talented and dedicated people contributed to the publication of this book. First and foremost, we are honored to have worked so closely with Millard Kaufman, who brought exceptional wit, insight, and experience to this project— and made the publishing process a great deal of fun, too. Thanks also to Dorris Halsey, who helped us to acquire the book.

We truly appreciate the great attitudes and quality work of Frank Culbertson and Buck Winston, who worked under intense deadline pressure to make this book as accurate and comprehensive as any published work can be. Many thanks also go to Larry Underhill for shooting our author.

A really big thanks to the smart people at the Margaret Herrick Library at the Academy of Motion Picture Arts and Sciences for their willingness to research and fact check the many difficult questions thrown their way. They really do have all the answers.

265